T5-BPY-628

THE BODY IN MYSTERY

The Political Theology of the
Corpus Mysticum *in the Literature*
of Reformation England

~

JENNIFER R. RUST

NORTHWESTERN UNIVERSITY PRESS
EVANSTON, ILLINOIS

PR
428
.R46
R87
2014

Northwestern University Press
www.nupress.northwestern.edu

Copyright © 2014 by Northwestern University Press. Published 2014.
All rights reserved.

A portion of chapter 1 was published in the collection *Political Theology and Early Modernity* (ed. Julia Lupton and Graham Hamill; University of Chicago Press, 2012). A substantially shorter version of chapter 2 appears under a slightly different title in *ELH: English Literary History* 80 (Johns Hopkins University Press) in the fall 2013 issue: 627–59.

Printed in the United States of America

10 9 8 7 6 5 4 3 2 1

Library of Congress Cataloging-in-Publication Data

Rust, Jennifer R.
    The body in mystery : the political theology of the corpus mysticum in the literature of Reformation England / Jennifer R. Rust.
        p. cm.—(Rethinking the Early Modern)
    Includes bibliographical references and index.
    ISBN-13: 978-0-8101-2963-4 (cloth : alk. paper)
    ISBN-10: 0-8101-2963-9 (cloth : alk. paper)
    ISBN-13: 978-0-8101-2931-3 (pbk. : alk. paper)
    ISBN-10: 0-8101-2931-0 (pbk. : alk. paper)
    1. English literature—Early modern, 1500–1700—History and criticism. 2. Jesus Christ—Mystical body—In literature. 3. Christianity and literature—Great Britain—History—16th century. 4. Christianity and literature—Great Britain—History—17th century. 5. Kings and rulers—Religious aspects—Christianity. 6. Church and state in literature. I. Title. II. Series: Rethinking the Early Modern.
    PR428.R46R87 2013
    820.382617—dc23

                                                                2013015576

♾ The paper used in this publication meets the minimum requirements of the American National Standard for Information Sciences—Permanence of Paper for Printed Library Materials, ANSI Z39.48-1992.

THE BODY IN MYSTERY

Rethinking the Early Modern

Series Editors
Marcus Keller, University of Illinois, Urbana-Champaign
Ellen McClure, University of Illinois, Chicago

CONTENTS

ILLUSTRATIONS

ACKNOWLEDGMENTS

This study of medieval and early modern ideas of community could not have been written without its own special diverse and wide-ranging community, for which I am deeply grateful. Portions of this book (particularly chapters 4 and 5) were originally drafted in a much different form as part of my doctoral dissertation at the University of California, Irvine. I was fortunate to have the guidance of an excellent dissertation committee at UC Irvine, beginning with the chair, Julia Reinhard Lupton; I could not have hoped for a more generous and inspiring (intellectually and otherwise) director and friend than Julia. Lowell Gallagher, who first keyed me into the significance of de Lubac's work, was willing to work with me across UC lines. Vicky Silver initiated me into the mysteries of Milton and Hobbes, and Jane Newman inspired me to hold to a comparatist tradition, which I believe informs particularly chapter 1 of the final project. I was also fortunate to have a fabulous cohort of graduate student colleagues, with whom I have maintained ties over the year. Nichole Miller was particularly supportive during my last year at UCI, and she has remained a close friend and generous reader of multiple drafts of many of these chapters in the years since. I have also valued my conversations with Melissa Sanchez, Catherine Winiarski, and Matt Ancell about early modern cultures, religious or otherwise, during my time at UCI and beyond. I was able to complete my dissertation with the support of the Strauss Endowed Dissertation Year Fellowship.

At Saint Louis University, I have been extremely fortunate to be a member of a uniquely collegial and supportive English Department. I have benefitted from the support of two excellent department chairs—Sara Van Den Berg and Jonathan Sawday—who are also fine scholars of early modern literature and excellent mentors. Toby Benis, Tony Hasler and Don Stump were also exemplary mentors: wonderfully encouraging and helpfully pragmatic at every stage of this project. Ruth Evans also offered tremendous sympathy and encouragement for this project in its later stages. I have deeply appreciated the camaraderie of many other colleagues in the department over the years. The English Department Library Liaison, Jamie Emery, provided fantastic support for my research needs. Beyond the English Department, I have had productive interdisciplinary exchange with colleagues in Theological Studies and

History, most notably, Grant Kaplan, Bill O'Brien, S.J., and Hal Parker. I have always felt at home in the College of Arts and Sciences at Saint Louis University; I particularly appreciate the support of my current Dean, Michael Barber, S.J. The writing and research for several chapters of this book (notably chapters 1 and 2) were supported by several Mellon Faculty Development Grants from the College of Arts and Sciences. I received support for the final stages of this book project from a Summer Research Award from Saint Louis University.

In the wider community of St. Louis, I have been fortunate to participate in the Early Modern Reading Group at Washington University in St. Louis. Early drafts of several sections of this book (particularly chapters 2 and 3 and the epilogue) were circulated among this group, and I benefitted enormously from the insightful scrutiny of its members, including Steve Zwicker, Derek Hirst, Daniel Bornstein, Musa Gurnis, Kurt Schreyer, Matt Augustine, Jenny Westrick, Meredith Beales, Megan Allen, Amy Sattler and others.

In the larger academic community, I would like to thank Kathy Biddick and Graham Hammill for their immense support during the time I developed this project. My thinking and research for this project has also been enriched by conversation and exchange—at conferences, symposia, workshops or elsewhere—with the following scholars: Gary Kuchar, Chad Pecknold, Susannah Monta, Gin Strain, Ineke Murakami, Kir Kuiken, James Kuzner, Chris Pye, Bruce Brasington, David Gay, Matt Milner, Laura Sangha, Susan Cogan Bulthuis, Brodie Waddell, Peter Marshall, Regina Schwartz, Travis DeCook, Will West, Victoria Kahn, Margreta de Grazia, Brian Cummings, John Parker, C.J. Gordon, and Lea Frost.

I would like to thank the staff of the Folger Shakespeare Library in Washington D.C., particularly Rebecca Oviedo; Mark Greengrass, John Foxe Project Director; Michael Pidd, Digital Manager of the Humanities Research Institute at the University of Sheffield, UK; Chris Sutherns, British Museum Images; and Jennifer J. Lowe, Rare Books Librarian at Saint Louis University for their assistance with archival resources and queries related to chapters 2 and 5. The editorial staff, particularly Henry Carrigan, at Northwestern University Press, have been outstanding at every stage in the process of producing this book.

I would like to thank my parents for their constant support of my intellectual pursuits over the years. Finally, this book would not have been possible without the endless patience, care and support (both editorial and emotional) of Vince Sherry.

INTRODUCTION

The *corpus mysticum* or "mystical body" is one of the earliest figures for
a specific ideal of Christian community. It conveys the notion that all of
the faithful are incorporated into a single body of Christ by participation
in the sacraments. The "mystical body" is first articulated in some of the
earliest Christian texts—the epistles of Paul—and from its roots in the
fledgling messianic community in the first century, it came to encompass
imaginatively the whole world of Western Christendom in the Middle
Ages. This book traces the vicissitudes of this medieval concept of the
corpus mysticum in political, theological, and literary discourses in Reformation England. My argument connects the social and sacramental
corpus mysticum of the medieval church[1] to the early modern development of a politicized mystical body of the commonwealth. This argument
identifies an innovative reimagining of the ancient Christian tradition of
martyrdom in Reformation terms in sixteenth-century England as crucial
to this volatile process, which does not necessarily correspond to a linear
pattern of secularization. The locus of the mystical body may pass from
the Mass to the martyr in Reformation England, but this passage, it will
be shown, does not entail eliminating its sacramental or mystical character, even if the passage appears, at times, to be encouraged for purely
political purposes. The *corpus mysticum* resists complete colonization by
the emergent absolutist politics of early modern England, even in the displaced form in which it lingers in the Reformation era. In fact, the figure
of the mystical body more often than not signifies the *misalignment* of
theological and political orders, the point at which underlying theological forms of life turn projections of political power awry.

To trace this development conceptually, I have revisited and interpreted anew several classic twentieth-century accounts of early modern
political and religious culture, accounts whose insight and value, I believe,
have not been exhausted for scholars in the twenty-first century. On the
broadest level, my argument is an extended, critical engagement with
Ernst Kantorowicz's landmark volume, *The King's Two Bodies: A Study
in Mediaeval Political Theology* (1957).[2] I am interested in an element
that is crucial to Kantorowicz's argument, but often overlooked by critics who have engaged with his work: the genealogy of the king's second
body—his *mystical body,* the body that gradually comes to be identified

also as the *body politic,* a body perpetually in excess of the king's *natural* body. For Kantorowicz, identifying the sacramental and liturgical origins of this mystical second body is a key moment in narrating the long history of "political theology" as a matter of legal, constitutional *corporate* institutions (as opposed to Carl Schmitt's account of political theology as an exceptionalist and personalist concept). The corporate, sacramental *corpus mysticum* that Kantorowicz identifies in the fifth chapter of his book is, I argue, crucial not just for understanding premodern legal and political entities, but also (to go beyond the scope of his claims) essential for grasping more broadly the fundamental forms of pre-secular social and religious experience. The significance of the *corpus mysticum* as a sacramental condition of possibility for pre- and early modern European social and political phenomena has not yet been fully appreciated in areas of Renaissance literary history and theory otherwise so profoundly impacted by Kantorowicz's work. My book argues that we must develop a deeper understanding of the *corpus mysticum* as a primary premodern category of social belonging to grasp the complex nature of the crises that roiled early modern Europe in the wake of the Reformation.

In making this argument, I also engage in a recovery and reevaluation of one of Kantorowicz's crucial source texts: *Corpus Mysticum: The Eucharist and the Church in the Middle Ages* (first edition, 1944) by Henri de Lubac, a text that has been influential among medievalists and theologians, but whose implications have yet to be widely received in early modern literary studies.[3] A Jesuit historian of theology and philosophy, later an influential cardinal during the Vatican II Council, de Lubac persistently searched for paths for renewal by reaching back into the traditions of the early church (*ressourcement*). In this way, de Lubac unsettles secular assumptions about progressive enlightenment: his account suggests the possibility of a past more dynamic than the present, of "traditional" relations between the social and the sacramental that may take unexpected forms. Chapter 1 of the present volume explores how Kantorowicz appropriates (and misappropriates) de Lubac's excavation of the social-sacramental *corpus mysticum* in *The King's Two Bodies,* and argues that we should take more careful account of aspects of de Lubac's work of recovery that Kantorowicz glosses over too hastily in assembling his own narrative of progress toward secularization. These aspects are: first, a notion of sacramental ritual, liturgy, as potentially constitutive of social relations in premodern Christian culture, and second, the notion that the "sacrifice" at the heart of the liturgy is something better understood in terms of a performative action encompassing clergy and laity (who become in the "mysterious" action, the body of

Christ) rather than the miraculous transubstantive event, the production of the Real Presence of Christ as an objective thing, divorced from any necessary connection to a social or communal context.

While my argument accepts de Lubac's implicit claims for the centrality of a more dynamic concept of Eucharistic celebration to social forms of life in the early church and the Middle Ages (and its persistence even in the face of an increasingly dogmatic insistence on the doctrine of transubstantiation in the late Middle Ages), it ultimately pushes beyond both de Lubac and Kantorowicz to consider what new forms the performative, liturgical mystical body takes after the Reformation—beyond the notion of a ruler's second, mystical body—in the peculiar circumstances of a partially reformed, newly nationalized and politicized church in England. This question leads in a direction (developed in chapter 2) anticipated in neither de Lubac's nor Kantorowicz's prior work, toward an evaluation of the increasingly central figure of the Protestant martyr in English political and religious discourse after the Reformation. In turn, this development leads me to reconsider the thesis of yet another classic (and controversial) historiographical account of the era: William Haller's *The Elect Nation: The Meaning and Relevance of Foxe's "Book of Martyrs"* (1963).[4] In chapter 2, I argue that in reading the articulation of Protestant martyrdom in John Foxe's magnum opus *Actes and Monuments* (first edition 1563) as central to the development of English national identity, Haller was intuitively correct, although not for reasons he may have anticipated. It is my contention in this chapter that the sacramental socially cohesive experience formerly located in the Catholic Mass (the essence of the *corpus mysticum*) is conspicuously relocated by Foxe into the experience of the Protestant martyr—with profound effects for the subsequent political and religious development of England in the sixteenth and seventeenth centuries, culminating finally in the outbreak of the Civil War in the 1640s (as is most fully demonstrated in chapter 5, which engages with the legacy of Foxe in the work of Milton and his Royalist rivals). Understanding the full social significance of the Mass paradoxically enables us to understand more fully the significance of those martyrs who most vehemently contested it—and who were the heirs to its social meaning.

Although this book makes ambitious claims in the realm of social and intellectual history, it remains fundamentally grounded in literary studies throughout. It is my belief that the techniques of figurative analysis cultivated in the study of literature actually enable this study to substantiate its broader historical claims. This is particularly true when addressing works such as Foxe's *Actes and Monuments* or the purported royal spiritual autobiography *Eikon Basilike* that blur modern generic boundaries. *Actes and Monuments* is acknowledged to be a significant work by both literary critics and historians, and rightly so, as it is neither pure history nor literature, but a curious hybrid genre: in its narrative and dramatic character, it is literary, but, in its documentary quality, it is equally a written history—in both broader and narrower senses of the term. It is broadly historical in its ambition to reinterpret the scope of sacred history (and England's place in it) in apocalyptic terms, as a struggle between visible and invisible, true and false churches. It is more narrowly historical in its concern with documenting local narratives of recent martyrs, who each play a significant, if repetitive, role in the broader apocalyptic drama. Foxe's historiographical impulses are profoundly shaped by his literary techniques, and the task of discerning the liturgical dimension of these local martyr narratives, in particular, requires the reading practices of literary criticism.

Shakespearean drama occupies the central section of this book, which I believe is appropriate for a study concerned with the fate of liturgical performance in the wake of profound religious change. My argument is anticipated in some ways by the New Historicist interest in dramatic appropriations of desacramentalized religious ritual, what Stephen Greenblatt has referred to as Shakespeare's habit of adapting "weakened or damaged institutional structures" in his theatrical art.[5] However, the *corpus mysticum* is not exactly an "institution" but the performative, sacramental condition of possibility for socially meaningful institutions in the premodern Christian world. The mystical body may be initially actualized in the institution of the Mass, but it proves capable of becoming manifest in other institutions—in kingship, as Kantorowicz has shown, in martyrdom, as I show. Without a doubt, this passage occurs in the early modern period precisely because of the disruptive effects of the Reformation on traditional ritual life, the same disruptive effects that allow Shakespeare to "take over" for his theater beliefs and practices such as purgatory and exorcism, as Greenblatt has so ably recounted. However, the incessant return of an ideal of communitarian sacramental life (cast in corporate terms deriving ultimately from the Pauline figure of the body of Christ) in both traditional and Reformed discourses throughout the period suggests that the concept of the mystical body is more than the sum of its parts, so to speak. It suggests that this communitarian paradigm is the very medium in and through which early modern people conceive of social and political order.

My emphasis on the paradigmatic status of the mystical body suggests that the extent to which *theatrical* figures of the *corpus mysticum* may be considered "secularizations" (in the modern sense of the term) of religious material must be put into question. This is particularly the case given the long English tradition of sacred theater prior to the Reformation: the medieval mystery cycles and morality plays which clearly influenced Shakespeare's drama and which were also "paraliturgical" institutions through and in which the mystical body came to coalesce.[6] Rather than a process of secularizing what was formerly sacramental, Shakespeare's Reformation-era drama may be conceived more dialogically, as a working through of the traumas, a staging of the crises attendant upon the gradual shifting of the *corpus mysticum* paradigm, but not necessarily a departure from this paradigm: if such a departure was not possible for Shakespeare's culture overall, we certainly should not expect to find it in his individual works of fiction.

My arguments dwell on the religious ambiguities of a Shakespeare who is attuned to both the rhythms of traditional religion and the more disruptive tempo of an emergent modernity. The more "radical" Shakespeare in these readings is often, startlingly to the modern reader, the more medieval Shakespeare; in this regard, my readings are in sympathy with the impulses of recent work by Sarah Beckwith and others.[7] This medievalist Shakespeare is more often than not skeptical about new migrations of the mystical body, even as he also obsessively stages them in performances that summon forth a collective recognition that is not yet the gaze of a critical, secular public. Shakespeare's ambiguity and skepticism toward these Reformation migrations may be related to personal affiliations with traditional Catholicism, as myriad critics have suggested, but I believe it is more interesting to understand them as part of a broader cultural response to tectonic shifts in the ways and means of making manifest the mystical body in the period, a response shared across religious boundaries that were often more fluid than we currently credit.

I do not revisit *Richard II*, despite this book's debt to Kantorowicz, but seek to find the imprint of the mystical body in less expected dramatic venues. The two middle chapters address two generically distinct works by Shakespeare which, at first glance, might appear to have little in common: *Titus Andronicus* and *Measure for Measure*. Yet I argue that each play, in its own way, is preoccupied with the fate of the *corpus mysticum* in Reformation England. The early tragedy, *Titus* (the focus of chapter 3), in some ways adapts Foxe's prose martyr narratives for the stage, as other critics have observed. I argue that the play's peculiar horror resides not simply in the rawness of its violence, but also in the way that this violence discloses a larger spiritual trauma. The repetitive performance of travestied sacramental rituals structures the play, which begins with a human sacrifice and ends with a cannibalistic banquet, with myriad episodes of rape, mutilation, and murder interspersed between. These travestied ritual performances are framed by the tragedy's setting in a "headless Rome," the first of many distortions of the commonplace early modern metaphors of the body politic and the mystical body scattered throughout the play. These dislocated metaphors link the play's travestied sacrifices to the more pervasive crisis of making the mystical body manifest during the Reformation. Most notably, the play stages figures of martyrdom and Eucharistic sacrifice in ways that cast a critical perspective on their conflation by Foxe. Ritual confusion is insistently shown to disintegrate (rather than knit together) the corporate body of Rome.

In *Measure for Measure* (the topic of chapter 4), Shakespeare shifts the terms of his exploration of the Reformation "mystical body": the crisis of the *corpus mysticum* now takes shape in the sphere of the urban erotic economy of Vienna, where an emergent money economy appears in tension with an older, medieval conception of the link between the divine and the human as an economic relation continuous with the sacramental sociality of the *corpus mysticum*. The play turns on a crisis provoked by a situation in which the sacrament of marriage, a traditional metaphor for the relationship between Christ and his church in the mystical body, is transformed (and deformed) by new economic and political pressures. This deformation of sacramental marriage in turn sets the stage for debates between the Catholic novice Isabella and the Puritan magistrate Angelo that rehearse a fundamental conflict between a sacramental conception of the mystical body and a body politic constituted as an incipient system of legal and economic bonds. The play illuminates how, for the early modern imagination, economic language continues to convey powerful traditional ideas about the integrity of the social world as a *corpus mysticum*, a sacramentally constituted form of life, even as this "fiscal theology" becomes increasingly conflated with social bonds measured in more strictly monetary and contractual terms.

The final chapter returns to the concerns of the opening chapters as it examines the legacy of Foxe's sacramentalized martyrdom as a manifestation of the mystical body in the English Civil Wars of the mid-seventeenth century. It examines how the concept of the *corpus mysticum*, as articulated via martyrological tropes, remained a powerful imaginative resource in both Royalist and Parliamentarian discourses during this conflict and in its aftermath. The chapter traces an antimonarchical reception of Foxe in Milton's polemical prose and poetry (notably Milton's sonnet on the Piemontese massacres), where martyrological language is used to articulate a vision of a militantly reformed English nation. Milton's "republican" notion of the martyrological mystical body is effectively countered by the Royalist martyrology *Eikon Basilike,* a purported spiritual autobiography of Charles I disseminated in the immediate wake of the regicide. *Eikon Basilike* also powerfully draws upon and augments the legacy of Foxe: it resanctifies the executed monarch by casting the king not only as a martyr but also as a defender of the prohibited liturgy of the English Book of Common Prayer. *Eikon Basilike* reinforces this argument by inviting readers to treat the text itself as a prayer book, a script for reconstituting the mystical body through collective devotional practice. Both Milton and his Royalist antagonists appropriate Foxean martyrological motifs. These appropriations demonstrate how the medieval, corporate tradition of the mystical body persisted through the early modern period, a persistence that culminated in its absorption into a more recognizably modern concept of national political identity.

The story of the mystical body appears from the perspective of the final chapter as the prehistory of modern nationalism. It is beyond the scope of this study to explore the extent to which this "mystical" prehistory continues to subsist—in further displaced or repressed forms—even into the era of the secular state.[8] This argument, however, does invite scholars to consider the possible forms the communitarian tradition of the mystical body might take in later periods. Deformed, negative variations of the *corpus mysticum* tradition may be discerned in the mass totalitarian movements of the twentieth century—or more recently, in globalized forms of consumerism.[9] On the other hand, recovering more affirmative articulations of the tradition of the *corpus mysticum* in modernity can constitute a counterpoint to the hegemony of subjective individualism in classic liberalism. This book offers a genealogy for a concept that should not be considered wholly obsolete or archaic—indeed, it may speak to us with ever more urgency in the current moment of political and economic crisis.

In its focus on liturgy as a socially generative performance that brings the political and the theological into close proximity (if not absolute identity), this project ventures into some of the same territory recently explored powerfully in Giorgio Agamben's *The Kingdom and the Glory* (first published in English translation in 2011).[10] I regret that I did not have the opportunity to engage with Agamben's study until this project was nearly complete. Despite some distinct differences in emphasis, I believe that the arguments that I develop here are ultimately complementary to Agamben's rich analyses of economic theology and liturgical acclamations. We are, I believe, looking at a similar problem from different angles. Agamben approaches the liturgical acclamation in the Christian tradition as part of a larger effort to provide a theological genealogy for Foucault's concept of "governmentality." This genealogical effort leads Agamben from inquiries into the originarily "economic" character of Trinitarian doctrine to an analysis of the political, "governmental" stakes of liturgical acclamations that ultimately blur the distinction between the political and the theological (this later analysis is deeply indebted to the debate between Carl Schmitt and Erik Peterson). In crucial ways, our inquiries converge. For example, like Agamben, I seek to emphasize the "performative" character of liturgy, its complex of gestures and words in which "meaning coincides with a reality that it produces."[11] I emphasize as well its "constitutive" capacity to generate collective forms of life, which is most visible in Agamben's provocative linking—via Schmitt—of popular acclamations, public consensus, and the modern liberal "society of the spectacle" embodied in the media and theories of "communicative rationality."[12] While Agamben tends to read the acclamative power of liturgy as political, as a zone where the political and theological merge and reinforce each other precisely as forms of power, I would like to emphasize that there is embedded as well in Christian liturgy a resistance to pure political power relations, in the liturgy of the Eucharist specifically, which Agamben only elliptically addresses. These resistant elements of liturgy maintain the imaginative potential of the "messianic life" that Agamben envisions as escaping the theological-political apparatus of the "providential machine."[13] Here, I can only suggest the possibility that the tradition of the mystical body always incorporates something of the Pauline vision of the "messianic community" as the body of Christ, which is most evident when the mystical body performatively produced in the liturgy of the Eucharist is understood in its deepest relational and eschatological complexity. Put another way, I argue that we must recognize how a communitarian, perhaps utopian, dynamic persists in Christian liturgy in tension with the "glorious" acclamations that establish hierarchies and mix theology and politics.

My argument does ultimately challenge Agamben's assertion that "no body" exists under the perpetual exchange of "the garment of glory" between theology and politics.[14] I argue that we need to consider more carefully how the sacramental figure of the mystical body can simultaneously provoke and resist political appropriation. The idea of the mystical body, like Agamben's notion of "glory," is intimately linked to a liturgical performativity and a dynamic economy of immanence and transcendence: both produce a form of consensus, a collective body. However, the eschatological aspect of the mystical body, its multiple temporalities as it enacts a sacrifice, past, present, and to come, might bring it closer to the messianic temporality Agamben discovers in Paul and associates with "inoperativity."[15] Is the mystical body an "inoperative community"?[16] It is not possible to answer in this context, but it is my desire to distinguish provisionally between the "mystery" associated originally with the canon of the Mass (from which the adjective "mystical" derives) and "glory" with its more overtly political implications. A more complete genealogy of "mystery" and "mystical" (which de Lubac initiates) and a corresponding genealogy of "charity" or *caritas* would seem to be in order, along the lines developed so admirably by Agamben for concepts (or rather, "signatures") such as "glory."

While I cannot fully develop these inquiries here, I believe that it is possible to discern a desire for the "messianic life" of Agamben's account inscribed in the life of the mystical body. The liturgical dynamic of the mystical body produces an aspirational version of the messianic community within the profane sphere of the social. The messianic aspirations of the mystical body are linked to its imagining of social order as a body of Christ, to social bonds that coalesce in terms other than those of political hierarchy. It is nonetheless true that the mystical body in the fullest sense often remains an aspiration rather than an actuality, precisely because it becomes enmeshed with the political-theological liturgies of glory. The value of Agamben's work is that it makes visible this legacy of political theology and demonstrates its pertinence to the modern era. While my study is more circumscribed in its inquiry, and gives more attention to some areas that remain unaddressed in Agamben's account (such as the Reformation), I believe it complements Agamben's work and hopefully furthers the analysis in new ways.

Agamben's most recent work might be put into productive dialogue with the theological movement known as "Radical Orthodoxy," a label associated with a largely Anglo-Catholic group of theologians (most prominently, John Milbank) who similarly seek to develop an engagement between an "orthodox" Christian tradition and recent Continental philosophy. Their purpose is to critique the crises of secular modernity. Although Milbank's most important work shares Agamben's concern with the "theological construction of secular politics,"[17] addresses some of the same cruces (for example, Trinitarian theology, providence, and political economy), and similarly owes a deep debt to Foucault's analysis of power, a direct dialogue has yet to occur between the two.[18] The potential proximity and difference between these approaches perhaps only truly comes into view with Agamben's *Kingdom and Glory* and merits more extended study, as both schools represent serious efforts to address the theological legacy within secularism and to think about this legacy in ways that differ dramatically from the habits developed in liberal political discourse. The present context does not allow for a full appraisal; I can only note in passing that Milbank and company are decidedly more optimistic than Agamben about the capacity of orthodox Christian theology to chart an alternative to the power dynamics of the liberal political state. Radical orthodox theologians have championed de Lubac's theological work as crucial to the "Catholic" social alternative that they seek to delineate.[19] As is evident in my first chapter, my argument sometimes runs parallel with Milbank's account of how "the secular as a domain had to be instituted and imagined, both in theory and practice" from within a Christian theological tradition that originally defined the social world in quite different terms, as a "single community of Christendom."[20] However, in tracing the fate of the liturgical mystical body in Reformation England, I seek to offer a more fine-grained historical and literary account of the way in which this "institution" of the secular gradually emerges. I focus on one contingent moment of a larger historical shift (although given England's contributions to the development of liberal philosophy, a quite important one) that eventually makes possible the distinctions between secular and religious, political and theological, public and private spheres essential to the liberal state that both Agamben and "Radical Orthodoxy" seek to critique in their own ways.

In looking at this transformation from the perspective of literary history, I emphasize particularly the role of "imagination" alongside "institution" in this process. Early modern imaginative literature contributes significantly to the transformation of older understandings of the mystical body and martyrology. This literature also provides occasions for resistance to these transformations insofar as it suggests alternatives to the teleological advance of secularism often too easily assumed by modern critics.

THE BODY IN MYSTERY

CHAPTER ONE

Political Theologies of the
Corpus Mysticum

More than fifty years after its publication, Ernst Kantorowicz's *The King's Two Bodies*[1] has generated a flurry of renewed interest. In a 2009 issue of the journal *Representations,* Kantorowicz's volume garners careful attention from a range of notable early modernists, including Stephen Greenblatt, Victoria Kahn, and Lorna Hutson.[2] Kantorowicz's classic volume holds interest for these critics not so much, as in an earlier generation, as a New Historicist work avant la lettre, but now rather for the extent to which it responds to, and critiques sub rosa, Carl Schmitt's work on political theology, itself recently revived as an object of critical attention by Giorgio Agamben and others.[3] These essays emphasize Kantorowicz's strategy of countering the troubling authoritarian tendencies of Schmitt's thought with an alternative account of premodern political theology, one which stresses the role of fictiveness in transmuting theological concepts into political abstractions.[4] The consensus of the *Representations* writers is that the ultimate value of Kantorowicz's "political theology" lies in its willingness to demonstrate how politics and theology share certain fundamental fictions.

Certainly, Kantorowicz's emphasis on the fictiveness at play in both realms accounts to some extent for the strong appeal of his work in the field of early modern literary studies, where his interpretation of the two bodies doctrine as a structuring principle of Shakespeare's *Richard II* has long had considerable influence. My argument begins in a similar spirit by seeking to reevaluate Kantorowicz's work in light of its potential critical response to Schmitt, but I will pursue this goal through a different trajectory: I will show how, via Roman Catholic sources, Kantorowicz develops a concept of the *corpus mysticum* as a mode of communal organization that implicitly counters the authoritarian tendencies of Schmittian decisionism. In turn, this trajectory will suggest a different context for the role of fiction in Kantorowicz's larger claims about pre-modern developments in political theology.

The year 2007 marked not only the fiftieth anniversary of the publication of Kantorowicz's volume but also the first publication in the United States of the translation of a crucial source for this volume: *Corpus Mysticum: The Eucharist and the Church in the Middle Ages,* by Henri de Lubac, S.J., a work of historical theology, first published in 1944, whose effect on modern Catholicism and contemporary theological discourse cannot be overestimated.[5] The influence of this study inside and outside Catholic circles is perhaps comparable to the continuing power of Kantorowicz's monograph within the disciplines of literature and history. Despite great differences in their intellectual commitments, Kantorowicz and de Lubac share some methodological similarities. Both assemble a wide range of primary sources from late antiquity through early modernity in an effort to reveal previously unconsidered dimensions of political or religious tradition. Both excavate the deep history of tradition to achieve a new, even radical (in both senses of this term) perspective on familiar institutions, although the primary sphere of their concerns is distinctly different: Western secular political institutions versus Roman Catholic ecclesiastical and Eucharistic theology. Despite these affinities, and despite their enormous impact on numerous fields of study, the fascinating intersection of these two works has so far been noted only in passing and has yet to be subject to significant critical scrutiny.[6]

The current argument will show how Kantorowicz uses de Lubac's meticulous study of the concept of the *corpus mysticum* in the early church and the Middle Ages to carry out a critique of Schmitt's notions of "political theology." This anti-Schmittian agenda is not, however, the only factor that draws Kantorowicz to de Lubac's work. The *corpus mysticum* proves to be a compelling figure for Kantorowicz, one that he weaves throughout the main argument of *The King's Two Bodies.* The key role of this concept is perhaps clearest as Kantorowicz recapitulates the steps of his argument in his concluding paragraph:

> The tenet . . . of the Tudor jurists definitely hangs upon the Pauline language and its later development: the change from the Pauline *corpus Christi* to the mediaeval *corpus ecclesiae mysticum,* thence to the *corpus reipublicae mysticum* which was equated with the *corpus morale et politicum* of the commonwealth, until finally (though confused by the notion of *Dignitas*) the slogan emerged saying that every abbot was a "mystical body" or a "body politic," and that accordingly the king, too, was, or had, a body politic which "never died." (506)

This statement illustrates the considerable extent to which Kantoro-wicz's genealogy of the legal doctrine of the ruler's two bodies rests on the discovery of an earlier doctrine of a "mystical body" that designates a corporation bound together by a theologism enabling it to transcend the limits of concrete time and space. In constructing this genealogy of the mystical body, Kantorowicz is deeply indebted to de Lubac's earlier work. To the extent that Kantorowicz constructs a political theological alternative to Schmitt's personalist and decisionist model of sovereignty, he finds in de Lubac an interpretation of Catholic tradition that is not so easily collapsed into authoritarianism. Kantorowicz's adaptation of the *corpus mysticum* demonstrates that the seemingly disinterested histori-ography of *The King's Two Bodies* is in fact interwoven with a polemical agenda: to defend the enabling fictions of the liberal constitutional state against the "idols of modern political religions."[7]

However, it is also necessary to question how Kantorowicz himself strategically misapprehends crucial elements of de Lubac's account as he argues that the mystical steadily turns into the fictional in medieval polit-ical theology. For de Lubac, as a Jesuit theologian, is emphatically not guided by an impulse to reveal the fictiveness of the *corpus mysticum,* at least in any conventional, secular sense. Indeed, for de Lubac, it is precisely the becoming-fictive of the *corpus mysticum* that represents the signal disaster of collective spiritual life in the Middle Ages. De Lubac seeks to counteract this transformation of the *corpus mysticum* into a political fiction by recovering a more traditional mystical body not so easily translatable into purely fictional or abstract terms. Engaging with a tradition in which "mystical" and "mystery" coalesce as "secret and dynamic" forms of signification (*Corpus Mysticum,* 63; trans. 52), de Lubac discloses dimensions of the *corpus mysticum* that resist sublima-tion into sheer *corpus politicum.* De Lubac's interpretation of the *corpus mysticum* as a dynamic paradox—simultaneously transcendent and immanent—offers a theological perspective that elucidates the potential inadequacy of both the vertical orientation of Schmitt's account of sov-ereignty (as personal and transcendent) and Kantorowicz's emphasis on horizontal bureaucracy as a mysticized "body politic."

Henri de Lubac and the *Corpus Mysticum*

In this context, it is only possible to indicate briefly the significant impact of de Lubac's work on twentieth-century Catholic theology and, indeed, on the very form and liturgy of the Catholic Church itself after

Vatican II.[8] De Lubac's early and midlife experience, like that of Kanto-rowicz and Schmitt, was marked by the wrenching experience of total war and the destructive rise and fall of fascism in Europe. *Corpus Mysticum* itself was written during the difficult circumstances of wartime France, where Lubac was allied with the Resistance to the Vichy regime in distinct opposition to the "Catholic Rightists . . . collaborating with the occupying Germans."[9] Indeed, John Milbank emphasizes that de Lubac's "*political* opponents" were also "*theological* opponents."[10] This personal detail hints at how far the Catholicism manifest in de Lubac's study of the *corpus mysticum* will depart from Schmitt's brand of politi-cal Catholicism, which notoriously accommodated itself to the rise of fascism in Germany.

De Lubac's postwar work, most notably the *Surnaturel* of 1946, became controversial, and for a time he was banned from teaching and publishing by the Catholic Church.[11] After some years in the wilder-ness, he was restored to good standing in the late 1950s and played an influential role in the Vatican II Council in the 1960s. The groundwork for this role, however, was laid by de Lubac's work of the late 1930s and 1940s, most notably in this context, *Corpus Mysticum*. De Lubac's theological influence played a part in enabling a revitalization of the church by introducing a new way of conceiving of its own tradition that encouraged an effort to overcome the phenomena of an overemphasis on the Real Presence in the Eucharist as a miraculous fact, excessively individualistic piety, and a misunderstanding of church hierarchy as an authoritarian structure. As Hans Boersma argues, de Lubac believed that all of these problems, as well as the earlier political tragedy of a tradi-tional Catholicism that had too readily accommodated itself to fascism in the Second World War, were symptomatic of a general "extrinsicism" which posited "grace as something that came strictly from the outside and had no intrinsic connection with human nature,"[12] and which a neo-Thomistic separation of natural and supernatural had nurtured. Such a doctrine had eroded an earlier tradition in which the church was con-ceived as simultaneously sacramental and social; it was this spirit that Vatican II, in its best moments, sought to restore.

De Lubac's work from the 1930s and '40s, including *Corpus Mys-ticum*, thus laid out a blueprint for reforming the Catholic Church by returning to its earliest traditions. One of the most influential imperatives that the Vatican II Council derived from de Lubac is succinctly stated in the conclusion to *Corpus Mysticum*, where de Lubac urges a "return to the sacramental origins of the 'mystical body' in order to steep ourselves in it . . . a return to the mystical sources of the Church. The Church and the Eucharist are formed [*se font*] by one another day by day: the idea of the Church and the idea of the Eucharist must promote one another mutually and each be rendered more profound by the other" (*Corpus Mysticum*, 292–93; trans. 260). In this claim, de Lubac urges that both the sacrament and the church be understood in dynamic rather than static terms. This dynamism brings the concept of the "mystical body" into being as the simultaneous mutual relation and interpenetration of the church and the sacrament. In its most originary sense, it contains "an implicit and indirect reference to the action, whatever it is, in which this 'body' is engaged" (62; trans. 51). The Eucharist is thus not an objective Real Presence produced by the intervention of an extrinsic miracle, nor is the church simply a hierarchy channeling this intervention. If we apply the terminology of speech-act theory, we could say that de Lubac is arguing for a *performative* rather than constative understanding of "mystical." In this performative sense, then, "mystical" refers not simply to one entity over against another (church vs. sacrament), but rather evokes a state of affairs in which the relation between these two figures is ceaselessly dynamic—they make each other in an ongoing process. This dynamism is underscored at the beginning of *Corpus Mysticum* as de Lubac emphasizes the derivation of "mystical" from "mystery": "A mystery, in the old sense of the word, is more of an action than a thing" (60; trans. 49).

This dynamic sense of "mystical" also includes a social or communal dimension insofar as the church is encompassed within the sacramental action. De Lubac stresses that, as a term associated with the community of the church, "mystical" stems from the earliest Christian texts. It is evident in St. Paul's First Letter to the Corinthians (1 Cor. 10:17–18), a passage which de Lubac glosses: "The 'communion of the body of Christ' of which St. Paul spoke to the faithful of Corinth was their mysterious union with the community, by virtue of the sacrament: it was the mystery of one Body formed by all those who shared in the 'one Bread'" (279; trans. 248). De Lubac finds his thesis about the intrinsic link between the Eucharist and the church confirmed not only in the Pauline text but also in the writings of the earliest church fathers, especially Augustine. For de Lubac, this performative sacramental and social sense of "mystical" is far removed from the more modern notion of the term "as a watering down of 'real' or of 'true'" (280; trans. 249) as a synonym, that is, for something immaterial or even imaginary.

The long story of the "degeneration of the *mystical body*" (130; trans. 115) is a major concern of de Lubac's volume, however, and, as we will see, it is the part of this work that most interests Kantorowicz. According to de Lubac, the dynamic, social, and also deeply symbolic traditional logic behind the original sense of the *corpus mysticum* was gradually effaced by a growing rationalism and politicization of the church in the late Middle Ages. For de Lubac, it is actually the political metaphor that comes to inhabit the theological concept, rather than the other way around. Ironically, this shift ultimately "dissolve[s] the social edifice of Christendom" and culminates in the disaster of the Reformation in the sixteenth century, contributing to the "breaking up of the Church itself" (131–32; trans. 116). The degenerative process that de Lubac describes is complex: thus, at the early stage of this process, in the ninth century,

> *mystical body* is in some sense a technical expression that serves, inadequately at times, to distinguish the Eucharist from the "body born of the Virgin," or from the *"body of the Church,"* while *at the same time placing it in relation with both one and the other.* By what curious cross-country route [*curieux chassé-croisé*] the "body of the Church" came in its turn, *and precisely in opposition to* the Eucharistic body, to take the name of *mystical body,* is what we will see . . . (88; trans. 73–74, my emphasis)

The "curious cross-country route" at issue here is the emergence of a substantial new opposition between two terms (Eucharist, church) that *mysticum* had effectively linked, even in their distinctness. To make distinctions is not the same thing as to oppose, however, particularly in the paradoxical logic that de Lubac pursues in his argument. In fact, the reason why the transference could take place at all was because of the earlier nuanced relation between the two terms. Indeed, it is this traditional relation that enables the work of tracing the "mystical body" back to its Eucharistic roots.

De Lubac's account of this inversion of the "mystical body," particularly the divorce of "mystical" from its sacramental roots, has resonated beyond Catholic circles, and this dispersal is due in part to the influential interpretation of his fellow Jesuit, the psychoanalytic theorist Michel de Certeau. Certeau's interpretation recasts the main import of de Lubac's *Corpus Mysticum* in post-structuralist terms in his own study of mysticism in the sixteenth and seventeenth centuries, *The Mystic Fable.* Certeau reads de Lubac's book as a narrative of how the "caesura" structuring the "threefold" body of Christ (historical, sacramental, and scriptural), as conceived in the early church, shifted in the twelfth century.[13] After the shift that de Lubac documents, according to Certeau, the mystical loses its "mediating" force, as sacramental and historical bodies are "split off from the Church."[14] This split is the condition of possibility for the Reformation: Reformers privilege the "scriptural" body as the proper "historical" body, while Counter-Reformation Catholics stress the "sacramental" body "recast in the philosophical formality of the sign."[15] Meanwhile, the "mystical body," stripped of its communal mediatory capacity, becomes "other in relation to visible realities," inspiring the growth of early modern "mysticism."[16]

Certeau's synthesis of de Lubac's work is very lucid, but it may be accused of imposing a schematic structure on *Corpus Mysticum* that limits the actual complexity of the work.[17] Nonetheless, Certeau's interpretation of de Lubac, and, more generally, a certain reading of de Lubac's entire life's work, has proven very influential in recent theological discourses.[18] Despite de Lubac's prominence in these circles, however, Kantorowicz's early engagement with his work still remains to be fully scrutinized. Before turning directly to Kantorowicz's appropriation of de Lubac in *The King's Two Bodies,* however, it is necessary to explore Schmitt's own approximations of a *corpus mysticum,* as articulated in his early efforts to define Catholicism as "political form," efforts intimately intertwined with his elaboration of a theory of "political theology" in the early 1920s. This exposition will clarify how sharply Kantorowicz diverges from Schmitt in placing the figure of the *corpus mysticum* at the heart of his own account of "mediaeval political theology."

Schmitt: *Corpus Mysticum* as the Negation of the "Visible Church"

Carl Schmitt's brief, dismissive reference to the concept of the *corpus mysticum* occurs in an early tract, "The Visibility of the Church" (1917), which is included as an appendix to the English translation of *Roman Catholicism and Political Form* (1923), the companion piece to the more celebrated *Political Theology.*[19] A brief sketch of Schmitt's overarching argument in *Roman Catholicism* will reveal the significance of this reference. In this essay, Schmitt seeks to posit the Catholic Church as a public, visible institution that may counteract the dominance of a sphere of modern economic rationalism that Schmitt associates with Protestant private, interiorized religiosity. Schmitt's project is thus in dialogue with Max Weber's *Protestant Work Ethic and the Spirit of Capitalism* throughout.[20] Schmitt agrees with Weber that the Protestant "inner-worldly" ethic in principle opens the way for the reign of economic rationalism, but he seeks to oppose the hegemony of this sphere in modernity by developing the "political" potential of the Catholic Church as a counterweight. Schmitt begins by seeking to understand Catholicism initially through the converse phenomenon of anti-Catholicism: "There is an anti-Roman temper that has nourished the struggle against popery, Jesuitism and clericalism with a host of religious and political forces, that has impelled European history for centuries" (Schmitt, *Roman Catholicism*, 3). He casts this "anti-Roman temper" as a reaction to a "political idea" of the Catholic Church that lies beyond the simple historical fact that the Roman church is frequently understood as a continuation of the "universalism" of the Roman Empire (6–7). Instead, for Schmitt, the "political idea" that provokes such sustained hostility is rooted in two essential characteristics: the Catholic Church as *complexio oppositorum* (7) and its form of "representation" as the realization of divine authority in the "concrete" person (the pope being the most obvious embodiment—in this, Schmitt follows de Maistre) (18–19). In developing these characteristics of the church, a tension arises in Schmitt's argument. On one hand, he makes statements that imply that he assumes a further underlying opposition between the pure materialism of the "economic" and the inherent need for a transcendent "idea" in the "political." The complex character of "representation" in the church results in its status, in Schmitt's view, as the bastion of the "political" in a thoroughly economic world: "the Church requires a political form" (25). On the other hand, Schmitt's development of the *complexio oppositorum* as an inherent characteristic suggests a potentially less oppositional and also less hierarchically authoritative vision of the church: "There appears to be no antithesis it does not embrace," whether in terms of its governmental structure, its political alliances, or its theology—"this *complexio oppositorum* also holds sway over everything theological: the Old and New Testament alike are scriptural canon, the Marcionitic either-or is answered with an as-well-as" (7). In the *complexio oppositorum*, we could see a concept akin to the paradoxical, dynamic character of de Lubac's *corpus mysticum*. Schmitt, however, tends to short-circuit the potential of the *complexio* in favor of reinforcing a vision of the church that emphasizes the singularity of hierarchical authority.

Schmitt's arguments for the simultaneously personal and political character of Roman Catholic representative authority are motivated, in part, as a polemical response to the Lutheran legal and theological historian Rudolf Sohm, who also deeply influenced Weber's theories of charismatic authority.[21] Sohm posited that the early church, and indeed, all true Christianity, was deeply and exclusively personalistic. Sohm cast the ideal Christian community as a "pneumatocracy" and, in classic

Protestant fashion, he saw the Catholic Church as a deep corruption of this original reign of the charismatic persona: "The leadership of the Ecclesia comes from *above,* through the medium of the *individual* who is personally endowed by God. The government of Christendom is from first to last authoritative, *monarchical.*"[22] The similarity of Sohm's claim here to many of Schmitt's formulations in *Roman Catholicism* is striking, and indeed, it is no accident that Schmitt directly refers to Sohm at several points in his argument. Schmitt argues against Sohm's dualistic view that the true church of Christ is purely invisible and spiritual in contrast to any worldly order of institutions and laws: "The great betrayal laid to the Catholic Church is that it . . . does not conceive Christianity as a private matter, something wholly and inwardly spiritual, but rather has given it form as a visible institution. Sohm believed the fall from grace could be perceived in the juridical sphere; others saw it in a more grandiose and profound way as the will to world power" (Schmitt, *Roman Catholicism,* 31–32). Contra Sohm, Schmitt embraces the essence of the church as "juridical form" (18), acknowledging that it does embody the contradiction of the *complexio* in its capacity for representation, but that it has a legitimate claim to connection with the person of Christ animating its authority.

Although "a high-minded Protestant like Rudolf Sohm could define the Catholic Church as something essentially juridical, while regarding Christian religiosity as essentially non-juridical" (Schmitt, *Roman Catholicism,* 29), this view does not adequately consider the true public nature of the authority of the church, which Schmitt validates by its deep association with "not only the idea of justice but also the person of Christ" (30). In its embodiment of an "idea" the juridical church is like "secular jurisprudence," but in the additional personalistic dimension bequeathed by its linkage to Christ, the church can claim an authority beyond the secular: "It can deliberate as an equal partner with the state, and thereby create new law, whereas jurisprudence is only a mediator of established law" (30). In this claim, we find Schmitt's eagerness to transfer a mode of personal authority, which is proper to the church, directly to the realm of political power. And although Schmitt adjusts the thrust of Sohm's argument in crucial ways, he essentially accepts Sohm's valuation of "personal" charisma. Schmitt insists on personalizing the representative "offices" of the church to counter Sohm's claim that the Catholic Church counterfeits the authority of Christ in its establishment of divine offices. This move is also likely intended to rebut Weber's version of Sohm's claim, which emphasizes a depersonalized "office charisma" in the church.[23] Thus, Schmitt defends the notion of the visible church and also positions this church as a reservoir of political power in the modern world.

This personalizing of "offices" may be an effective way to counter Sohm and Weber, but it leads Schmitt to neglect the "mystical body" as a figure for the social and sacramental organization of the church.[24] In 1917, Schmitt anticipates the arguments of the 1923 work insofar as he develops a critique of the overly spiritualized Protestantism that ultimately produces the modern economic state. Schmitt's dismissal of the "*corpus mysticum*" occurs in a passage that insists on the vitality of the visible institution of the church as essential to any properly Christian system of belief:

> One cannot believe God became man without believing there will also be a visible Church as long as the world exists. Every religious sect which has transposed the concept of the Church from the visible community of believing Christians into a *corpus mere mysticum* basically has doubts about the humanity of the Son of God. It has falsified the historical reality of the incarnation of Christ into a mystical and imaginary process.[25]

Schmitt's explicit reference is to a "*corpus mere mysticum*"—*mere,* in the Latin phrase, is a variant of *merus* (undiluted, unmixed, pure)— a purely mystical body. In qualifying the idea of the *corpus mysticum* in this way, he associates it with the denial of the visible church, and thus with Sohm's arguments, which, for Schmitt, actually culminate in a denial of any valid political authority. This understanding of the *corpus mysticum* as a spiritualized, seemingly Protestant concept is symptomatic of Schmitt's larger insistence on conceptualizing "authority," whether religious or political, in sheerly vertical terms. A few lines before this passage, Schmitt asserts: "An arrangement making the invisible visible must be rooted in the invisible and appear in the visible. The mediator descends because the mediation can only proceed from above, not from below."[26] The 1917 essay makes it clear that Schmitt develops his claims for the authority of the church from a notion of the "essence" of the church as "mediation,"[27] which is conceived in a particularly hierarchical way. This is consistent with Schmitt's arguments in the later essay on Roman Catholicism, where it is asserted that the church "has 'no representative institutions'" in the modern parliamentary sense because it does not derive its authority from the people, but rather "'from above'" (26). For Schmitt, it is this vertical, "transcendent" dimension—necessarily personified in the representative authority—that guarantees authentic political force (27). Modern parliamentary institutions, from this perspective, become depoliticized entities when they are understood in purely horizontal terms; their norms simply replicate the lower bonds of the economic sphere, since they are posited on an absolute separation between visible and invisible realms originally inspired by Protestant doctrine. This insistence on a vertical, transcendent authority is later reiterated in Schmitt's account of decisionist sovereignty in *Political Theology*, where it occurs at the expense of more lateral forms of organization, including those potentially implied by the *complexio oppositorum*.

Schmitt's characterization of the *corpus mysticum* as a concept at odds with any "incarnational" notion of Christianity—as something purely "invisible" and "imaginary"—is a profound misapprehension of this figure within the history of the church, as Kantorowicz and de Lubac demonstrate. The point of de Lubac's study, as we have seen, is to recover an earlier sense of "mystical" rooted precisely in the most vivid incarnational ritual in traditional Christianity, the celebration of the Eucharist. The sense in which Schmitt uses the term "mystical," as synonymous with "imaginary," is, from this perspective, a later "degeneration" in usage that stems from the transference of the phrase from the sacramental to the institutional realm (de Lubac, *Corpus Mysticum*, 130; trans. 115).

Kantorowicz: The *Corpus Mysticum*
in *The King's Two Bodies*

Kantorowicz's appropriation of de Lubac's *corpus mysticum* in *The King's Two Bodies* is motivated as a riposte to Schmitt on several different levels. For Schmitt, the quintessence of political theology resides in the instant or *punctum* of the decision: the exception that transcends the norm but also constitutes it. In *Political Theology*, Schmitt famously illustrates his claim that "all significant concepts of the modern theory of the state are secularized theological concepts" with the example of the "omnipotent God" who becomes the "omnipotent lawgiver" and a further structural correspondence: "The exception in jurisprudence is analogous to the miracle in theology."[28] The corollary to this claim in Schmitt's companion essay on Roman Catholicism is the definition of the political as inherently involved with an idea "from above" that transcends the hegemony of pure economic rationalism. The person of the sovereign with the power to decide the miraculous exception is clearly akin to the Roman Catholic representative who, as mediator, wields transcendent authority. In both cases, authority is concentrated in a singular person and is imagined as an intervention that descends from a metaphysical dimension higher than any normative economy.

In *The King's Two Bodies,* Kantorowicz will go to great lengths to reconstruct a political theology that contradicts Schmitt in crucial ways. Kantorowicz will be keen to show that the theological aspect of the political should actually be understood to reside in the perpetuity, the *longue durée,* of the institution rather than the miraculous instant of the decision. In other words, theology will turn out to belong to the sphere of the norm rather than the exception. In a recent essay, Richard Halpern shows how Kantorowicz's discussion of the origins of taxation in the "singular emergency" (*King's Two Bodies,* 285) of the *casus necessitatis* works as an "anti-Schmittian parable" that emphasizes "bureaucratic regularity and continuity" over the urgency of the exceptional decision:

> Here the narrative of *The King's Two Bodies* seems implicitly to invert Schmitt's vector of influence running from the theological to the political, since the increasing bureaucratization of both church and state in the Middle Ages demands a God who does not intervene via miracle but rather governs in more predictable fashion: a "chairman God" who acts only in consultation with his corporate board.[29]

Halpern's characterization of Kantorowicz's critique of Schmitt at such moments in *The King's Two Bodies* is apt, as is his contrast between the "theologies" invoked by each theorist. To extend this conceit further, Kantorowicz seems to find a theological figure for God's "corporate board" in the history of the *corpus mysticum* that he has derived from de Lubac's study. *Corpus Mysticum,* adapted to the coordinates of a markedly anti-Schmittian historiography, also allows Kantorowicz to highlight how theological tropes become increasingly attenuated into abstract fictions as they become assimilated to lateral, relatively static institutional bodies. Kantorowicz uses the narrative of the decline of the sacramental dimension of the *corpus mysticum* to produce an immanent, rather than extrinsicist, political theology.

The *corpus mysticum* is crucial to Kantorowicz's effort to redefine "political theology" in normative bureaucratic terms. As we have seen in the previous section, Schmitt himself appears to have an underdeveloped sense of this concept, leaving a void that Kantorowicz's magisterially researched volume seeks to fill. Kantorowicz is particularly concerned with tracing how the *corpus mysticum* as a figure for the institutional body of the church was transferred conceptually to figure the institutional body of the state. To this end, Lubac's 1949 edition of *Corpus Mysticum* is provided with footnotes that are particularly concentrated in the first section of chapter 5 ("*Corpus Ecclesiae mysticum*"), which develops a genealogy of "Polity-Centered Kingship."[30] In a footnote at the beginning of this section, Kantorowicz acknowledges his debt to de Lubac's "excellent evaluation" of the history of the concept: "in the following pages, I have merely ransacked the wealth of [de Lubac's] material (much of which was inaccessible to me) and his ideas" (*King's Two Bodies*, 194n4). At the same moment that Kantorowicz signals the importance of de Lubac's prior work for his own study, he also implies that his own argument will trespass on or violate in some way ("ransack") the earlier "history of ideas." Kantorowicz works perpetually with and against the tenor of de Lubac's argument throughout this section of the book. While, as we have seen, "*corpus mysticum*" for Schmitt represents a notion that belongs more to the realm of "inner-worldly" Protestantism, Kantorowicz adapts the term from de Lubac's study and restores "mystical" to the context of twelfth-century ecclesiastical and political debate. It now comes to mean something like "fictional, ideal, abstract," particularly insofar as it qualifies the model for corporate, collective associations that forms a transitional conceptual framework for the modern secular state.

It is important to stress the point that "mystical," the very term that Kantorowicz most avidly "ransack[s]" from de Lubac's work, originates in the ritual practice of Eucharistic celebration. At the end of a summary of de Lubac's account of a ninth-century Carolingian Eucharistic controversy, Kantorowicz highlights the importance of what otherwise might seem an obscure debate. Because the terminology and conceptual framing that Kantorowicz deploys in this passage are crucial for the subsequent argument, I quote at length:

> Here then, in the realm of dogma and liturgy, there originated that notion whose universal bearings and final effects cannot easily be overrated. *Corpus mysticum,* in the language of the Carolingian theologians, referred not at all to the body of the Church nor to the oneness and unity of Christian society, but to the consecrated host. This, with few exceptions, remained, for many centuries, the official meaning of the "mystical body," whereas the Church or Christian society continued to be known as the *corpus Christi* in agreement with the terminology of St. Paul. It was only in the course of a

strange and perplexing development—*un curieux chassé-croisé*—
that finally, around the middle of the twelfth century, those designations changed their meaning. . . . That is to say, the Pauline term
originally designating the Christian Church now began to designate
the consecrated host; contrariwise, the notion *corpus mysticum*,
hitherto used to describe the host, was gradually transferred—after
1150—to the Church as the organized body of Christian society
united in the Sacrament of the Altar. In short, the expression "mystical body," which originally had a liturgical or sacramental meaning, took on a connotation of sociological content. (*King's Two
Bodies*, 195–96)

On one level, Kantorowicz is faithful to the outline of de Lubac's claims
about the significant change in the idea of the "mystical body" that
occurred around the twelfth century—the *curieux chassé-croisé* that
transferred "mystical" from a sacramental to a primarily ecclesiastical sense. However, if we recall de Lubac's original text, it is also clear
that Kantorowicz flattens out what de Lubac presents as an originally
dynamic situation which involves a fluid relation between *ecclesia* and
Eucharist, to further his own idea of a genealogy of secular polity, one
in which theological structures are progressively taken over by political
secular forces as metaphors or fictions. For de Lubac, it is simply not
the case that in the early Middle Ages *corpus mysticum* "referred *not
at all* to the body of the Church *nor* to the oneness and unity of human
society" as Kantorowicz insists. Instead, it would be more accurate to
say that *Corpus Mysticum* seeks to demonstrate that the "liturgical or
sacramental" was always already "sociological" in the milieu of the
early church. Kantorowicz seeks to play down the claim about the earlier "sociological" aspect of the "sacramental" because it could interfere
with the progressively immanentizing thrust of his larger argument. As
theological tropes become sociological in *The King's Two Bodies*, they
tend also to be tamed into pliable fictional material for representing specific political, very human, interests, evacuated of all but the barest hint
of transcendent content.

Indeed, Kantorowicz directly associates the emergence of the "mystical"
designation with the "so-called secularization of the mediaeval Church"
(*King's Two Bodies*, 197). This move is most evident in Kantorowicz's analysis of Aquinas as the switching point for the definitive "'seculariz[ing]'
[of] the notion of 'mystical body'" (201). Kantorowicz again turns to de
Lubac for the documentary material to substantiate this claim. He cites a
passage footnoted in *Corpus Mysticum:* "That last link to the sphere of

the altar . . . was severed when Aquinas wrote: 'It may be said that head and limbs together are as though one mystical person' " (*King's Two Bodies*, 201–2).[31] Kantorowicz finds here a crucial turning point:

> Nothing could be more striking than this *bona fide* replacement of *corpus mysticum* by *persona mystica*. Here the mysterious materiality which the term *corpus mysticum*—whatever its connotations may have been—still harbored, has been abandoned: "The *corpus Christi* has been changed into a corporation of Christ." It has been exchanged for a juristic abstraction, the "mystical *person*," a notion reminiscent of, indeed synonymous with, the "fictitious person," the *persona repraesentata* or *ficta*, which the jurists had introduced into legal thought and which will be found at the bottom of so much of the political theorizing during the later Middle Ages. (*King's Two Bodies*, 202)

In Kantorowicz's footnote 24, de Lubac is cited as the reference for the Aquinas quotation. However, the source of the interpretation of the significance of this moment in Aquinas is not de Lubac at all. In de Lubac's account, while Aquinas may at times appear more modern insofar as he uses "mystical body" in a simple analogical sense "in contrast to '*natural body*,' " the theologian also emphasizes that Aquinas generally tends to stay consistent with the older tradition that identifies sacramental and ecclesiastical bodies.[32] Indeed, Aquinas ultimately illustrates for de Lubac how slowly the tradition actually changed. To substantiate the claim that at this moment Aquinas radically changes the character and interpretation of the *corpus mysticum*, Kantorowicz must turn away from de Lubac's text. Interestingly, the source of the sentence, " 'the *corpus Christi* has been changed into a corporation of Christ,' " is Rudolf Sohm—Schmitt's Lutheran nemesis in *Roman Catholicism*.[33] Although Kantorowicz inserts this direct quotation of Sohm as if it is a gloss on Aquinas's "mystical person," Sohm does not directly address Aquinas at this point in his text, nor does he explicitly refer to the concept of the *corpus mysticum*. Instead, he is summarizing the passing away of an original "sacramental" and "mysterious" (*geheimnisvolles*) Christian Church at the end of the twelfth century in favor of a church structured like any other earthly community.[34] Superficially, this language appears to have an affinity with de Lubac's project of recovering an earlier "sacramental" sense of *corpus mysticum;* like de Lubac, Sohm finds a crucial turning point in the twelfth century when a newer juridical, dialectical rationalism effaces an older sacramental tradition.[35] Nonetheless, Sohm's

overtly anti-Catholic Lutheran "pneumatology" is not ultimately conge-
nial with de Lubac's effort to reassess the tradition of the early church
from within an incarnational Catholic tradition that understands sacramental mystery as equally visible and spiritual, human and divine. Like
Schmitt, de Lubac would feel compelled to defend the spiritual integrity
of the visible church.[36]

Practically speaking, Kantorowicz cites Sohm to make Aquinas into
the key element in the transformation of the *corpus mysticum* into the
"juristic abstraction" of the "mystical person," a purely legal and ultimately "fictitious" entity. This swerve away from the letter and spirit of
de Lubac's account occurs here for at least three interrelated strategic
reasons. First of all, giving Aquinas a momentous role in the transformation of the *corpus mysticum* may simply stem from Kantorowicz's
desire to make the shift that he is describing seem even more dramatic
and authoritative, insofar as it derives from a virtual fiat of the "*Doctor angelicus*" (*King's Two Bodies,* 201), the "doctor" who, of course,
was also distantly related to the subject of Kantorowicz's famous early
biography, Friedrich II.[37] Furthermore, Kantorowicz's citation of Sohm,
a controversial figure whom Schmitt sharply critiques at length in several important works in the 1920s, strongly reinforces the notion that
in this section of *The King's Two Bodies,* as in other places, Kantorowicz is engaged in a subterranean riposte to Schmitt's account of political
theology. While Kantorowicz relies more heavily on a newer, Catholic
source unknown to the Schmitt of the 1920s to develop his own account
of "mediaeval political theology," the reference to Sohm, a figure vehemently opposed in several ways to Schmitt, reminds us that Schmitt is a
long-term target of this account. Kantorowicz is not simply presenting
a disinterested history in invoking the name of Sohm, for Sohm enables
Kantorowicz to further dissolve Schmitt's claims for the personalistic
authority of the church into a matter of mere fictions.

Finally, Sohm may also subtly function as a way for Kantorowicz to
ignore de Lubac's more nuanced formulations about Aquinas, a move
symptomatic of his resistance to the larger implications of de Lubac's full
argument about the original sense of the *corpus mysticum* in the early
church. For Sohm, whatever his superficial affinities with de Lubac's claims
about the shifting of the ecclesial and legal worlds of the high Middle Ages,
ultimately assumes a dualism between spirit and flesh that is antithetical
to de Lubac's project of recovering the mysterious unity between them.
It may be easier for Kantorowicz to make the *mysticum* into "fictitious"
matter if a certain disenchanting juridical interpretation is heightened,
beyond the perspective allowed or available in de Lubac's work. Indeed,

in the passage quoted, Kantorowicz strongly emphasizes the increasing abstractness of "*mysticum*" in the hands of Aquinas. "*Mysticum*" becomes a curious conceptual matter, the primordial stuff ("mysterious materiality") of secularism, malleable for new ideological purposes once the church has unleashed it from the liturgical sphere. Seemingly amorphous, but also residually charged with ritual religious associations, the *corpus mysticum* will prove the ideal medium for subliming transcendent theology into a substance to be manipulated by immanent politics.

Kantorowicz's claims for the ideological efficacy of the *mysticum* extend beyond the immediate section engaged with de Lubac's work. In the next section of this chapter, "*Corpus Republicae mysticum,*" we find the mirror image of the church's aspiration to the status of a "political and legal organism" (*King's Two Bodies,* 197) in developments on the secular political side of the equation. "The world of thought of statesmen, jurists, and scholars" more easily appropriated the idea of the *corpus mysticum* to the emergent nation-state because it was already "politicized and . . . secularized by the Church itself" (207). The burgeoning nation-state sought to sanctify itself in appropriating such "mystical" terms, but in the process, the "mystical" itself became more than ever a fictional property, a counter to be attached to the abstractions formulated in legal arguments:

> The jurists, thereby, arrived, like the theologians, at a distinction between *corpus verum*—the tangible body of an individual person—and *corpus fictum,* the corporate collective which was intangible and existed only as a fiction of jurisprudence. Hence, by analogy with theological usage as well as in contrast with natural persons, the jurists defined their fictitious persons not seldom as "mystical bodies." (209)[38]

Kantorowicz again replicates the structure of de Lubac's argument here in his discussion of secular legalisms. The analogy that he invokes also bears comparison to Schmitt's analogy between the sovereign and God in *Political Theology;* Kantorowicz's analogy is between collective bodies, not single sovereign deciders. Beyond this, Kantorowicz's analogy emphasizes how authentic theological value is depleted, demoted to the realm of the fictional or figural, when it is transferred to the political. Nevertheless, he also implies that something of a sacramental residue yet adheres to the *corpus mysticum,* enhancing its appeal to secular jurists. *Mystical* imports into the commonwealth "some of the super-natural and transcendental values normally owned by the Church" (208). While this "super-natural" aspect would seem severely attenuated in the legal-political developments that Kantorowicz meticulously describes, he still insists that "the designation *corpus mysticum* brought to the secular polity, as it were, a whiff of incense from another world" (210). It is thus not simply its conceptual malleability, its imaginative resources, or its abstractability that accounts for the continued appeal of thinking of political or legal associations as "mystical bodies." Kantorowicz appears to try to have it both ways as he intimates that final total secularization never fully or completely arrives. Even in the desiccated abstractions of the legal realm, the sense of "mystical" retains a trace of the "mysterious materiality" of the sacrament. Curiously, it is only when he turns to the ostensibly "secular" legal realm that Kantorowicz dimly echoes de Lubac's contention that despite the misapprehension of "mystical" in the late medieval and post-Tridentine church, it was never completely evacuated of its traditional sense and efficacy, which remain latent, to be recovered on an ongoing basis in modernity. Nonetheless, such suggestions remain only marginal for Kantorowicz; his emphasis falls on the various ways that the immanent secular sphere overwhelms the theological or "mystical" figures that it takes over from the church.

If Schmitt's "from above" ecclesial authority fatally short-circuits the paradoxical interplay of spiritual and human realms, Kantorowicz's flattening out of the *corpus mysticum* into mere metaphorical material to provide an underlying structure for the secular polity is, in its overemphasis on immanence, merely the flip side of Schmitt's authoritarianism. While Kantorowicz's emphasis on the "mystical body" as a horizontally organized collective body is a necessary corrective to Schmitt, Kantorowicz misses de Lubac's effort to go back behind the modern dualism of nature and spirit, fiction and reality, produced by the dialectics that became dominant in the twelfth and thirteenth centuries. Although Kantorowicz admits to some lingering ambiguities, his dominant understanding of mystical as fictional perpetuates a modern dualism and narrative of progress that de Lubac seeks to put into question. In his appropriation of de Lubac, Kantorowicz ironically rationalizes and substantializes the very tradition that de Lubac is striving to render more fluid and dynamic.

In a later reprise of the arguments of *Corpus Mysticum*, de Lubac provides a striking formula that gives access to his thinking about the relationship between "mystery" and "symbolism": de Lubac claims that the first theologians who had referred to the church as a *corpus mysticum* had meant "the *corpus in mysterio*, the body mystically signified and realized by the Eucharist—in other words, the unity of the Christian community that is made real by the 'holy mysteries' in an effective symbol (in the strict sense of the word 'effective')."[39] In de Lubac's terms, the "symbolic" or figural need not signal an evacuation of spiritual value or efficacy. If it is understood in a fully dynamic, "effective" (we might prefer "performative") sense, it becomes a paradoxical union of transcendence and immanence. It is only from a static, secular position that figuration or symbolism necessarily takes on the meaning of abstract or empty fiction.

The *Corpus Mysticum* and the English Reformation: From Medieval to Early Modern Political Theology

Despite the limitations of his interpretation of the *corpus mysticum,* Kantorowicz's work nonetheless stands as one of the most intensive studies of the premodern and early modern permutations of analogies between the living body and political and religious structures: the "body politic" and the church as the "body of Christ."[40] The period of the English Reformation, which will be the focus of the remainder of this volume, presents a particularly striking case of this mutation, one implicit in Kantorowicz's study, which begins the excavation that leads to de Lubac's work precisely in the Tudor era, with Plowden and *Richard II*. The religious turmoil that marked the Tudor dynasty—and its relation to the political theological dynamic that Kantorowicz is concerned to trace— is, however, rarely directly addressed in Kantorowicz's account. Indeed, at the outset of his volume, Kantorowicz explicitly sets aside the question of the Reformation as he develops the outline of his inquiry into the political theology of the king's two bodies:

> The religious strand within political theory was certainly strong during the age of the Reformation when the divine right of secular powers was most emphatically proclaimed and when the words of St. Paul "There is no power but God" achieved a previously quite unknown importance with regard to the subjection of the ecclesiastical sphere to the temporal. Despite all that, there is no need either to make the religiously excited sixteenth century responsible for the definition [of the king's two bodies] of the Tudor lawyers, or to recall the Act of Supremacy through which the king became "pope in his realm" . . . the jurists' custom of borrowing from ecclesiology and using ecclesiastical language for secular purposes had its own tradition of long standing. (*King's Two Bodies,* 19)

Kantorowicz downplays the novelty of the Reformation moment in favor of an emphasis on its continuity with a larger tradition of figural exchange between legal-political theory and ecclesiology. It is, of course, the great value of Kantorowicz's work that it establishes so many continuities in this era that might otherwise have been overlooked. However, this choice does entail certain costs: the perspective that favors continuity is always in danger of underestimating innovation and historical rupture. The "secular" itself is precisely the post-Reformation innovation that Kantorowicz underestimates, a term whose self-evidence and transhistorical value appear to be taken for granted in the passage cited.

In what sense were there "secular purposes" (as distinct from ecclesiastical or theological ones) in the long tradition prior to "the age of the Reformation"? The answer that has emerged in the fifty years since Kantorowicz's study—from scholarly work in social history, religious studies, and literary theory—is that the premodern sense of "secular purposes" differs significantly from how we understand "secular" or "secularism" today.[41] Following this trend, I suggest that we might read some of Kantorowicz's evidence somewhat differently if we adjust some of his foundational assumptions about the meaning and purpose of "the secular" in premodernity. The notion of the ruler's two bodies remains significant from this perspective, but it appears in a different light: as a symptom of a crisis (including, but not limited to, the Reformation) from which the "secular" and the "religious" as distinct spheres emerge, rather than as the culmination of a slowly developing tradition. What appears to be a secular "custom of borrowing" in the medieval era may instead be taken as a sign of the intimate interrelation of law, politics, and theology throughout the era. In other words, law or politics are articulated in theological terms because they are never clearly distinct from theology: one sphere of thought does not stand over against another as a discrete, comprehensive entity. In the understanding of the tradition that I am concerned to trace, both with and against Kantorowicz, the sacramental resonance of the *corpus mysticum* may persist meaningfully, even as its "political" status is heightened. Kantorowicz is aware of this persistence, but he tends to downplay it in the interest of empowering the figurative free play of secular politics.

We can assess how far Kantorowicz resists recalibrating his notion of the "secular" for a premodern context by looking more closely at a specific example of the mingling of political, social, and sacramental under the aegis of the *corpus mysticum*: an early fifteenth-century English conceit that likens the meeting of Parliament to a Mass. Kantorowicz describes this figure for an English Parliament in 1401 in the following terms:

> The Speaker compared the procedures of Parliament with the cel-
> ebration of a mass: the reading of the Epistle and the expounding of
> the Bible at the opening of Parliament resembled the initial prayers
> and ceremonies preceding the holy action; the king's promise to
> protect the Church and observe the laws compared with the sacri-
> fice of the mass; finally, the adjournment of Parliament had its anal-
> ogy in the *Ite, missa est,* the dismissal, and the *Deo gratias,* which
> concluded the holy action. (*King's Two Bodies,* 227)[42]

For Kantorowicz, this conceit illustrates how not only the royal person
but also the collective representative political body was dignified with
a "semi-theological mysticism" in the later Middle Ages (227). However, his emphasis falls on the conceptual or theoretical significance of
the allegory: it illustrates how "political thought in the 'high Gothic' age
gravitated towards mysticizing the body politic of the realm" (227). More
importantly for Kantorowicz's larger argument, it provides evidence for
a "composite" idea about authority—"the king jointly with lords and
commons formed the 'mystical body' of the realm" (228)—that stands
as a precursor to the full-blown notion of the ruler's two bodies. In this
reading, the political impulse is decidedly in control of the sacramental
metaphorics. Kantorowicz marginalizes the possibility that the relationship between socio-political and sacramental spheres might be more
reciprocal than, or even the reverse of, modern secular expectations. As
we have observed in earlier sections of this chapter, Kantorowicz treats
the action of "mysticizing" as a simple metaphorical gesture; in his view,
such "comparisons do not mean very much all by themselves" (227).

Another interpretation of this conceit is possible, however, one in
which the figure of the Mass is crucial insofar as it represents a complex of effects that negotiate social difference. In this reading, the social
effectiveness of the figure is not contingent on the emptying out of its
sacramental value; to the contrary, the vitality of this sacramental dimension is crucial to its significance as an emblem for community.[43] Indeed, in
this regard, it is not irrelevant that the fifteenth-century Parliament that
is likened to the Mass was explicitly concerned with passing legislation
to combat the Lollard heresy, a movement that anticipated Protestantism
in its attack on the value and efficacy of the Mass and other practices
of traditional religion.[44] This historical detail (unmentioned in Kantorowicz's account) makes it more likely that the analogy between the
Parliament and the Mass was ready at hand because the Parliament was
seen as continuous with the sacramental order of the church—the church
and the Parliament mutually reinforced each other as legitimate and

legitimating orders, rather than one borrowing the trappings of the other as a mere figure.

I want to develop this claim further by suggesting that we can read this curious fifteenth-century conceit through an Augustinian lens, as one late variation on a set of figures derived from Augustine's *City of God,* the foundational text for medieval thought on the intersection of political, social, and spiritual life,[45] and a text immersed in the older, sacramental notions of the *corpus mysticum* that de Lubac so carefully traces.[46] In particular, the reference to the "sacrifice of the mass" in the fifteenth-century conceit is illuminated by allusion to a crucial passage in *City of God.* According to Kantorowicz's source for the conceit, the full sense of the sacrifice comparison appears in these terms: "The king's repeated declaration that it was his will that the faith of Holy Church should be sustained and governed as it had been by his progenitors, and that the laws should be held and kept in all points, as well by rich as by poor, to the great pleasure of God and comfort of his subjects, seemed like the sacrifice in the Mass to be offered to God by all Christians."[47] This more extended version of the analogy makes it clear that the "sacrifice" is understood not only to entail a pledge to preserve the traditions of the church, but also to encompass a sphere of mutual obligations that knit together various classes, "rich" and "poor," as well as ruler and ruled. The king articulates an ideal of peace and charity that all "subjects" have a role in upholding, just as the priest in the Mass articulates a "sacrifice" that "all Christians" have a part in "offering to God." The individual actor is only the focal point for a dynamic action that is understood to have wide implications for the ecstatic relationship between the community and God.

It is the notion of "sacrifice" presupposed within this fifteenth-century text that Augustine's earlier work elucidates. In a crucial passage of *City of God* (book 10, chapter 6), Augustine elaborates on the nature of the "true sacrifices" of Christianity (as opposed to the "false" sacrifices of the pagan world):

> Since, therefore, true sacrifices are works of mercy shown to ourselves or to our neighbours, and done with reference to God; and since works of mercy have no object other than to set us free from misery and thereby make us blessed . . . it surely follows that the whole of the redeemed City—that is, the congregation and fellowship of the saints—is offered to God as a universal sacrifice for us through the great High Priest Who, in his Passion, offered even Himself for us in the form of a servant, so that we might be the

body of so great a Head . . . This is the sacrifice of Christians: "We, being many, are one body in Christ."[48] And this also, as the faithful know, is the sacrifice which the Church continually celebrates in the sacrament of the altar, by which she demonstrates that she herself is offered in the offering that she makes to God.[49]

Augustine develops an intricate figural logic of sacrifice as a necessarily collective offering (of the "fellowship" of the "whole redeemed City") in and through the original sacrifice of Christ, which is not so much mimetically repeated as entered into by the faithful in conjunction with each other in the ritual action of the Mass. In this passage, Augustine asserts a reciprocity between the mystery of the sacrament and the mystery of community, the fellowship between Christians that takes shape in the sacramental celebration: the sacramental mystery is, first and foremost, for Augustine, a "mystery of unity."[50] It is this "mystery" of communion and community, understood as the rites that bind Christian society together, that the fifteenth-century conception of the Parliament as a Mass attempts to convey when it compares promises to uphold mutual communal obligations to the church offering itself in sacrifice; in both cases, a mystical body coalesces through a performance of incarnated community. Understood in this light, its "mysticism" is not merely "semi-theological," nor are its sacramental analogies negligible. The conceit of the Parliament as Mass reveals a political system profoundly enmeshed with liturgical practice. Such practice established a community or society coalescing before and extending beyond the sphere of political power relations. Indeed, the figure suggests that the political only had meaning *within* a larger sphere of sacramental ritual, despite the slow decay of ecclesiastical-Eucharistic relations recorded by de Lubac and Kantorowicz. Eucharistic habits of thought constitute a repertoire of ideals about communal experience and social order that remained available to reinforce political agendas throughout the late medieval and early modern period, even after the Reformation, although the relative power of the political over the ecclesiastical steadily increased.[51] Such notions were powerful on an ideal and imaginative level, even if they did not translate perfectly into actual lived experience.

This example of the Parliament imagined in terms of the Mass helps us to appreciate how drastically, in spite of his surface traditionalism, Henry VIII broke with the deeper tradition of the *corpus mysticum* in his singular Schmittian decision to declare himself the head of the Church of England. It is ultimately the mode of "ecstatic collectivity"[52] enacted in Eucharistic celebration that is altered and absorbed by the absolutist state in the wake of Henry VIII's transformation of the *corpus mysticum* into a *corpus politicum* at the outset of the English Reformation. Despite his reservations about specifically addressing the particulars of the Reformation in his study, Kantorowicz cannot avoid commenting on the radical nature of Henry's gesture as he elaborates on the later fate of the *corpus mysticum* in chapter 5 of *The King's Two Bodies*. He cites Cardinal Pole protesting Henry's collapse of political and mystical "bodies": " 'Your whole reasoning comes the conclusion that you consider the Church a *corpus politicum* ... so great [is] the difference between this body of the Church, which is the body of Christ, and that, which is a body politic and merely human' " (*King's Two Bodies*, 229). Kantorowicz's commentary on this point is evocative of his earlier appraisal of the material derived from de Lubac's study:

> Here the fronts have been curiously reversed. Instead of treating the state as a *corpus mysticum* Henry treated the Church as a simple *corpus politicum* and therefore as part and parcel of the realm of England. Contrariwise, Cardinal Pole tried in vain to restore the supra-political character of the Church and to undo the process of secularization which the *corpus Ecclesiae mysticum* had succumbed to ever since the thirteenth century. (229–30)

The peculiar way the Reformation happened in England constitutes another "curious revers[al]," reminiscent of the *curieux chassé-croisé* identified by de Lubac in the earlier section on the twelfth century. As we have seen, in the older view, the mystical encompassed the political, rather than the other way around, at least in the sense that the king was as much a member of the body of Christ as his subjects, embedded in the same mystical bonds of "ecstatic collectivity," if at a higher level. It is this prior condition that Kantorowicz's "supra-political" gestures toward.[53] Kantorowicz emphasizes the desacramentalizing nature of Henry's action in terms reminiscent of de Lubac: the political realm becomes the privileged term for defining the mystical body, just as previously, in the twelfth century, the institutional body of the church had supplanted the Eucharist as the referent for the *corpus mysticum*. This earlier reversal laid the groundwork for the later one; the glancing reference to the "process of secularization" that had supposedly been ongoing since the "thirteenth century" confirms that Kantorowicz is conceptualizing this move according to the paradigm he has adapted from de Lubac. The English Reformation thus appears as one more step in secular progress. The *corpus Ecclesiae mysticum* is so weakened, so divorced from its liturgical moorings that it cannot fend off its appropriation by a vigorous political absolutism; indeed, this appropriation appears to be an inevitable outcome of the *curieux chassé-croisé* initiated in earlier centuries.

However, this "fusion" of bodies mystical and political is not only a matter of gaining a new set of metaphors to aggrandize the political. The sense of sacramental sociality still so pervasive up into the early sixteenth century—in spite of whatever degradation occurred in the late Middle Ages—is not simply or immediately transformed into a useful ideological fiction upon Henry's break with the Roman church.[54] The political does not quickly or easily replace the cohesive force of sacramental sociality. In ways perhaps unanticipated by Henry (well known for his personally conservative religious habits and liturgical tastes)—and also, I have been suggesting, underappreciated by Kantorowicz—this merging of *politicum* and *mysticum* exerts a mutating effect on the realm of the political. The political is mysticized in new and sometimes frightening ways as relations between the mystical body and the political body are reconfigured. The political doctrine of the king's two bodies is only one ideological effect of this new fusion between the *mysticum* and the *politicum,* and perhaps not the most significant one, a symptom rather than a resolution of this dynamic.

Although Kantorowicz does not address it in the English case (tracing the development instead through the example of France), far more consequential for the English polity was a virulent discourse of martyrdom, simultaneously charged with political and mystical value, that arose in this period.[55] The most famous martyrs were created by religious divisions within the dynasty itself, the sickening seesawing between various strains of Reformed and traditional doctrine and practice, depending on the particular proclivities of the ruler who now claimed the right to decide the religious allegiance of the realm. In the Henrician Reformation, the very doctrinal diversity of the martyrs produced by the regime—from the champion of traditional religion, Thomas More, to Anne Askew, the heroine of more forward Reformers—testifies to the violent and unstable merger of the political and mystical at the inception of the idea of England as a Protestant nation. With the relative stability of the reign of Elizabeth, however, a politically coordinated (if not entirely politically inspired) genre of Protestant martyrology arose to reformulate the meaning and form of a mystical body, without, however, entirely abandoning the liturgical repertoire reminiscent of older forms of sacramental community. In the Elizabethan era, the mystical nationalism embodied by the Protestant martyr emerges as the necessary corollary to the religio-political endeavor of the Tudors. To appreciate the nuances of this development, it is necessary to look carefully at the most celebrated and successful example of Elizabethan martyrology, John Foxe's magnum opus, *Actes and Monuments,* otherwise known as the *Book of Martyrs.*

CHAPTER TWO

From Mass to Martyr in John Foxe's
Actes and Monuments

The *Corpus Mysticum* After
the English Reformation

Beyond the doctrine of the King's Two Bodies, in what might the Reformation English *corpus mysticum* consist? In what other forms might it be imagined, once the sacramental sociality of the Mass has begun to be dismantled by Reformist critiques and political agendas? The figure of the martyr provides one answer, an answer that is supported by a voluminous body of literature in English from the period, although not one addressed by Kantorowicz. The most celebrated and officially sanctioned of these works is John Foxe's *Actes and Monuments,* issued in successive editions between 1563 and 1583 (and into the seventeenth century, up to the period of the Civil Wars, 1641). The history of the *corpus mysticum* traced in the previous chapter will be brought to bear on Foxe's work to illustrate two major points. First, Foxe's book testifies—albeit negatively—to the centrality of the Mass as the ordering principle of the pre-Reformation *corpus mysticum*. It is precisely this Mass that is the main object of dispute throughout the various martyrs' discourses (a dispute carried on even visually in the book's famous frontispiece). Second, in the process of this disputation, Foxe's martyrs effectively become an alternative *corpus mysticum* via their sacrificial deaths, which are narrated to accord with the expectations of medieval Christianity, frequently including transubstantive language and liturgical gestures that associate their bodies with the very sacramental systems which they appear overtly to abjure.

The paradoxical traditionalism of Foxe's martyrology has been noted before, although it has not previously been linked in any systematic way to the larger tradition of the *corpus mysticum*. In a study of the *Book of Martyrs* from the 1970s, Geraldine Thompson claims that Foxe is incapable of registering the "irony" of the "Eucharistic debate" that suffuses his text, specifically the irony that "we see the primary Christian sacrament of unity and community of the Church of 'mystical body of Christ' become the focal point of division."[1] While recognizing the importance of Thompson's emphasis on the Eucharistic subtext of Foxe's work, I claim that Foxe's text actually turns on this very irony: he repetitively and controversially evokes the "mystical body" formerly believed to coalesce in the Mass, only to recalibrate it to a unity founded in identification with the very martyrs who contest this Mass, a new unity that also coincides in significant ways with ideals authorized by the Tudor regime. Foxe strives to achieve a principle of collective mystical unity in a way that simultaneously builds upon and departs from medieval tradition.

Actes and Monuments thus represents a transitional work situated between late medieval sacramental sociality and an emergent modernity characterized by centralized state authority and a new sense of national identity cohering around Protestantism. The long-standing debate concerning the thesis of William Haller's influential 1963 book, *Foxe's Book of Martyrs and the Elect Nation,* is a symptom of the transitional status of Foxe's project.[2] While Haller seeks to read Foxe as laying the groundwork for the kind of apocalyptic nationalism that was to explode in mid-seventeenth-century England, and ultimately as the precursor to a modern notion of English national exceptionalism, other critics have insisted on an equally legible universalist (i.e., "catholic" with a small "c") ecclesiastical dimension in Foxe's work, which appears to contradict a more narrowly nationalistic agenda. According to my argument, both schools of thought have merit: Foxe's text is explicitly universalist in its ecclesiastical, evangelizing mission, but, as its political sponsorship and reception within England demonstrate, it is also amenable to being harnessed to a nationalist agenda.[3] Foxe's reconfiguration of the *corpus mysticum* tradition is key to understanding how his text manages the tension between these apparently conflicting impulses.

While Foxe does introduce an oppositional strain of martyrological identification into English national discourse (with all the tension between the godly community and temporal rulers that this implies), he also tracks a story that is close to one that Kantorowicz also follows: the resistance of political leaders to "the machinations of a newly militant papacy" in the late Middle Ages.[4] Warren Wooden characterizes Foxe's "grand scheme" as centering on a double agenda: the "twin themes of histories of martyrs and emperors opposing the papacy dominate."[5] When we place Foxe next to Kantorowicz, we can see the martyrological narrative as a logical corollary to the growing sanctity of political leaders that Kantorowicz records: both monarchs and martyrs in Foxe's account represent the "true Church" that is oppressed throughout the high Middle Ages. The martyr and the monarch become symbiotically linked in his text. While Elizabeth Tudor was imagined to merge two bodies according to Kantorowicz, she also merged two statuses according to Foxe: she was simultaneously an imperial ruler following the model of Constantine to promote a purified Christianity[6] and a persecuted Protestant—a virtual martyr—during the reign of her sister Mary, the era that Foxe's work most vividly documents.[7] Mary Tudor's stunted efforts to construct a Counter-Reformation English polity were answered by Foxe's book, which recounts the martyrdoms that these efforts produced.[8] Foxe was rewarded for this answer with a prebend at Shipton "procured for him on the Queen's instructions by William Cecil" after the initial publication of *Actes and Monuments* in 1563.[9] His book itself, meanwhile, was famously ordered by the Elizabethan government to be chained next to the Bible in all English cathedral churches of the period.[10] While the extent to which such orders were actually implemented remains in question, their very existence testifies to an ambition that deeply informs Foxe's book: it was designed to be disseminated as part of a wider effort to reconstruct the English polity according to an innovative interpretation of traditional religious protocols. This effort goes beyond simply recasting the monarch herself in martyrological terms, however; it aims to reshape the very character of collective Christian experience in England.

Foxe's volume strikingly juxtaposes martyrdoms suffused with medieval sacramental imagery with arguments that vehemently attack traditional conceptions of the sacraments themselves. Previous critics have observed that the sacramental motifs embedded in Foxe's martyr stories evoke older martyrological traditions, such as those preserved in that medieval best seller, *The Golden Legend*.[11] Nonetheless, it is important to keep in mind how radical Foxe's aspirations still remain: the miraculous Eucharistic motifs of the *Golden Legend* are not accompanied by extensive polemics against the Mass. I argue that the *corpus mysticum* tradition can help us to understand the paradox of Foxe's text more clearly: Foxe retains the Eucharistic overtones of medieval martyrologies to articulate the communitarian ideal embedded in the medieval Mass and to transition this ideal to a Protestant political establishment that will (in his view) more authentically realize it. As established in the previous chapter, for the earlier Christian tradition, the essential bonds of a community were understood to be sacramental. The community was imagined to coalesce around sacramental practices that made the transcendent available within the immanent, the eternal within the ordinary. Foxe's martyrs share the aspiration for this sacramental community with their Catholic opponents; what they deny is the ritual means of effecting this dynamic. The Protestant martyrs are supposed to be true sacrifices, replacing the false one of the Mass, yet they also mimic its liturgy just enough to appropriate to themselves the mystery of the ritual that they contest.

Thus, beyond abstract theological principles or purely semiotic claims about the relation between signifier and signified in the bread and wine, the social coherence of a politically and religiously transformed English polity is crucially at stake in the incessant Eucharistic polemics of Foxe's book. Foxe seeks to refashion the *corpus mysticum* of England for the new dispensation of an absolutist Elizabethan monarchy. This refashioning does not simply involve abandoning and opposing the mode of sacramental sociality into which Foxe's generation was born and which still had a great deal of purchase, particularly after its revival during the reign of Mary Tudor. Indeed, Foxe's text is an ironic testament to the degree to which the traditional sacramental sociality most directly embodied in the liturgy of the Mass still maintained a powerful hold on the popular imagination. The success of Foxe's work is partially attributable to the extent to which it succeeded in rechanneling this older ideal of mystical community into a Protestant martyrological discourse that also reinforced a growing sense of English national exceptionalism.

Iconographic Anticipations and Echoes of *Actes and Monuments: The Lambe Speaketh* (1555) and Bright's *Abridgement* (1589)

The legacy of the idea of the *corpus mysticum* in Foxe's book can be usefully approached through several related examples of Protestant iconography that vividly transfer the ideal of Christian sacrifice from the ritual of the Catholic Mass to the figure of the Protestant martyr. One, an image known as *The Lambe Speaketh,* 1555 (figure 1), is a precedent for Foxe's volume: a piece of Protestant propaganda, dating from the reign of Mary Tudor and almost certainly produced by exiles on the Continent.[12] The other, the title page to Timothy Bright's *An Abridgement of the Booke of Acts and Monumentes of the Church,* 1589 (figure 2), postdates the major editions of *Actes and Monuments* produced during Foxe's lifetime.[13] Both images help to contextualize the centrality of Eucharistic debate for Foxe in several ways. Each visually recapitulates Foxe's persistent rhetorical association of martyrs and lambs, an association with both scriptural and liturgical resonance. Furthermore, the images explicitly associate martyrdom and Eucharistic sacrifice, also a subtext for many martyrological narratives in Foxe's own volume. Finally, these illustrations—particularly *The Lambe Speaketh*—reveal the Mass to be the negative emblematic paradigm not only for Foxe's narratives, but also for the famous frontispiece of *Actes and Monuments*, analyzed in greater detail in the next section of this chapter.

The interweaving of religious and political polemics in *The Lambe Speaketh* is an illuminating Reformation counterpoint to the fifteenth-century conceit of the Parliament as a Mass addressed at the end of the previous chapter. This engraving with Latin inscriptions appears in some editions of William Turner's *Huntyng of the Romysh Wolf*, an English Protestant exile work printed in Germany in 1555; a contemporaneous version with English and Latin inscriptions also evidently circulated in England as a broadsheet (it is this broadsheet version, preserved at the British Museum, that is the focus of my discussion here).[14] The lamb and wolf motifs in the engraving update a long tradition of Christian pastoral allegory for a moment of Reformation crisis. Furthermore, the engraving is clearly influenced by a German Protestant tradition of graphic propaganda; it is thus also an artifact of the cosmopolitan experience of English Protestant exiles.[15] Nonetheless, Rowena Smith has argued that the immediate historical inspiration for the image is quite English and overtly political: the 1554 Marian Parliament that reinstated the heresy statues of the late Middle Ages (including those passed in the Parliament of 1401).[16] In the context of the current argument, the most pertinent feature of the engraving is its conflation of this Parliament with a perverse image of the Mass. In the *corpus mysticum* tradition, the Mass encompasses both laity and clergy in a dynamic sacramental and social relationship; however, in this grotesque parody, the sacramental dynamic is divisive rather than unifying, as the sacrifice traditionally located at the heart of the ritual is literalized as an act of murder.

The amalgamation of text and image in this engraving must be read both vertically and horizontally. Moving from left to right, we find a divided *corpus politicum* on the left, countered on the right by a monstrous *corpus mysticum* of corrupt, bloodthirsty prelates—dehumanized caricatures of the English Catholic bishops of Mary Tudor's reign as wolf-men clad in sheepskins. Both are oriented around a travestied

Figure 1. *The Lambe Speaketh* (Emden, 1555). British Museum, Department of Prints and Drawings. Reproduced by permission of the Trustees of the British Museum.

AN
ABRIDGEMENT
OF THE BOOKE OF ACTS
AND MONVMENTES OF
THE CHVRCH:

Written by that Reuerend Father , Mai-
ſter Iohn Fox : and now abridged by Timothe Bright,
Doctour of Phiſicke, for ſuch as either through
want of leyſure, or abilitie, haue not the
vſe of ſo neceſſary an hiſtory.   27 · E · 9 ·

All day long are we counted as sheepe for the ſlaughter. Pſal. 44.

Pſal. 44 Ver. 22

*For thy sake also
are we killed all the
day long : and are
counted as sheep
appointed to be slain*

How long Lord, holy and true? Apocal. Cap. 6, verſe 10.

Imprinted at London by *I. Windet,* at the aſſignment
of Maſter Tim. Bright, and are to be ſold at Pauls wharf,
at the ſigne of the Croſſe-keyes.   1 5 8 9.
Cum gratia, & Priuilegio Regiæ Maieſtatis

Figure 2. Title page of *An Abridgement of the Booke of Acts and Monumentes of the Church* (London, 1589). Reproduced by permission of the Folger Shakespeare Library.

Roman Catholic Mass at the center, celebrated by a wolfish prelate in sheep's clothing, identified as Bishop Gardiner, the chief villain of the Marian Counter-Reformation from a Protestant perspective.[17] As the chief wolf-bishop officiating this obscenely literalized ritual, he sinks his teeth into the neck of a "lamb of God" hanging from the top of the page, which the text encourages us to identify with Christ himself ("Why do you crucifie me agen"), while several waiting lamb-martyrs—identified with the names of the chief English Protestants persecuted and ultimately executed during Mary's reign (Cranmer, Ridley, Latimer, Hooper and others)—lie ready for sacrifice below his feet.

In the political world on the left side of the image, the various classes are divided by their reaction to the sacrificial act: the bearded men at the top attempt to restrain the wolf-bishop Gardiner, while the shaven men at the bottom are brutishly led by the nose to comply with the sacrifice. According to Smith, the men with beards may be identified with the House of Lords, which resisted the reinstitution of the heresy laws, while the lower group of compliant men may be identified with the House of Commons, which supported the heresy act.[18] The Commons so little resist this satanic Mass that they are portrayed as participants in it: the chain that leads them is redoubled in the Latin/English text: "*Tu solus sanctus, tu solus doctus, tu solus irremehesibius* / 'Thou only arte holye, thoue only arte learned, thou only irreprehesible,*"* a partial parodic echo of the *Gloria* in the Latin Mass.[19] From a Protestant perspective, this echo underscores their spiritual slavery. The Latin tag may be included in the English version of this engraving to emphasize the enslaving enchantment of the Commons in a way that also resonates with Reformist critiques of the Catholic Latin liturgy as obfuscating.

If this engraving is linked to the renewal of Marian heresy laws, then we can understand it as simultaneously a political cartoon and a caricature of theological controversy. It illustrates the extent to which the *corpus politicum* had become violently entangled with the *corpus mysticum* by this stage of the Tudor dynasty. This entanglement is particularly ironic given Mary Tudor's express desire to turn back the reforms of her father and half-brother, a task she could only undertake via the political mechanisms established by Henry's break with Rome.

It is the theological dimension of this disturbing, cartoonlike image, however, that makes the most vivid impression. The illustration clearly mocks Catholic doctrine and practice in the process of accusing the Marian theologico-political establishment of heavy crimes. To achieve its full impact, however, this Protestant propaganda must depend upon the logic of transubstantiation insofar as as it dramatizes the plight of English

Protestant martyrs by presenting it as the literalization of the sacrifice purportedly reenacted in the Roman Mass. In the Mass of the "romish wolves," the elevated host is conspicuously replaced with the image of the living lamb hung above the altar (which also, of course, evokes the crucifixion itself).[20] While it is good Protestant doctrine to deny the Real Presence of Christ in the sacrament, the engraving requires its readers to reconstruct imaginatively a curious, oxymoronic version of that doctrine to make sense of what is happening. The chief lamb *is* Christ, yet his speech also evokes some lines from the letter to the Hebrews that appear most strongly to support the Protestant view of the sacrament: "Why do you crucifie me agen. For with one oblation have I for ever made perfecte those that are sanctified."[21] The lamb echoes the insistence on the sufficiency of Christ's single sacrifice expressed in Hebrews; this verbal tag forms a counterpoint to the unscriptural scripture legible in the book on the altar: "Christ alone is not sufficient without our sacrifice," a sentence which conforms to the typical Protestant critique that the Catholic theology of the sacrifice of the altar denies the efficacy of Christ's original sacrifice. Curiously reversing confessional stereotypes, it is the "Catholic" doctrine that appears in the book, while the Protestant counter-assertion appears as the voice of the lamb subject to the sacrificial ritual.

The central act in the engraving clearly recapitulates the endless Reformation debate about the extent to which the celebration of the traditional Mass actually reenacts the sacrifice of Christ as an objective event: the question of the Real Presence of Christ in the Eucharist as some *thing* produced by the ritual at the altar.[22] However, in considering this image, it is important to also avoid the pitfall of Reformation and Counter-Reformation debates that obsess over the question of the presence of the body as an objective thing, either falsely or truly confected in the ritual, as the cost of neglecting the question of the community that coalesces in and through the ritual: the community that is itself the body of Christ and, according to the older ideals of the *corpus mysticum*, the most real presence at stake in the celebration.

The primary polemical thrust of this engraving is not fully legible outside the traditional codes of the medieval Christian community, even as it seeks to turn certain elements of this established doctrinal and representational system against themselves to justify the claims of a new, ostensibly purer English *corpus mysticum*. While the engraving clearly takes a specific argumentative stance in the ongoing Eucharistic debate that anticipates the stance of Foxe's myriad martyrs, it also harkens back to older ideas of the community as the body of Christ crystallized in the

Mass. It represents, simultaneously, both positive and negative versions of this mystical body. One negative dimension has already been noted: the body politic (represented in the Commons and Lords of Parliament) divided by its disagreements about the beliefs and practices that should constitute the mystical body. A further negative dimension is evident in the malevolent version of the mystical body materializing on the right side of the image: the blood of the Christ-lamb flies into the communion cups raised by Gardiner's fellow wolfish English Catholic bishops (each identified by names, such as Bonner, later made infamous by Foxe's work). This element of the image imagines the false church as a bestial counter-community. It overtly critiques the transubstantive doctrine and practice of the Catholic Church as viciously literal as it conveys the idea that those responsible for promoting belief in the Real Presence of Christ in the sacrifice of the altar actually seek to repeat this sacrifice in the executions that they engineer to silence the heresy of insisting on the fictional, empty character of the Mass. This negative community is cast as bloodthirsty and carnal in both belief and practice. Ironically, in its replacement of the host with the body of a lamb-Christ that literally bleeds into the communion cups of the dehumanized bishops, the engraving evokes the kind of sacrificial action associated with late medieval host desecration miracle narratives (such as the Croxton Play of the Sacrament), except that the negative role formerly occupied by the Jews has been partially remapped onto the hierarchy of Catholic bishops.[23] This echo of an older, seemingly opposite scheme of sacramental ordering underscores how much this work of sixteenth-century Protestant propaganda relies on inherited codes of representation to deliver its agonistic message.

On the positive side, we are presented with an image of the authentic "mystical body" not only in the sacrificial Christ-lamb, but also in his fellows, the martyr-lambs heaped on the killing floor, who not only visually echo the principal lamb, but also verbally recapitulate his predicament, as they appear to address him: "For thy names sake are we dayly put to death, as sheepe destinate to be slayne." The mystical body of the true church, the engraving argues, lies in these lambs fixed for slaughter, not in their priestly ritual sacrificers. These martyrs are the true sacrifice insofar as they actualize in their own bodily experience what is only imagined to happen in the Mass, the renewal or recapitulation of Christ's sacrifice.

In this affirmative referral of the mystical body to the experience of the Protestant martyr, *The Lambe Speaketh* closely anticipates the argument of *Actes and Monuments*. The most evident link between the engraving and Foxe's work is the fact that the principal participants explicitly labeled in the tableau are those later celebrated or derided by Foxe (Gardiner, Bonner, Cranmer, Latimer, and so on). The engraving's anticipation of *Actes and Monuments* is also strong insofar as Foxe also frequently refers to these very martyrs as "lambs": for example, Hooper (one of the lambs in the engraving) is led to the stake in Foxe's narrative as "a Lambe [led] to the place of slaughter."[24] Foxe, like the artist of the engraving, persistently plays upon conventional pastoral allegory (the sheep as the flock of the church, Christ as the Lamb of God) to deliver his polemical message. Most significantly, *The Lambe Speaketh* inculcates a mode of iconographic reading also demanded by the famous title page of Foxe's *Actes and Monuments:* it sets forth two versions of community for the viewer to compare, and it posits that these communities are (positively or negatively) formed around the Mass that they either celebrate or seek to negate. Foxe's frontispiece recalibrates the *corpus mysticum* in a much subtler manner, as we will see, but many of its conceptual moves are forecast by this earlier, more vulgar work of propaganda. Like *The Lambe Speaketh,* Foxe's martyrology seeks to harness and redirect the social-sacramental dynamic of the medieval *corpus mysticum,* rather than simply seeking to negate it.

To illustrate how strongly this sort of pastoral-sacrificial motif resonated in the reception of Foxe's martyrology and merged with emergent nationalist sentiment by the end of the sixteenth century, it is useful to look at an immediate successor to the editions of *Actes and Monuments* produced during Foxe's lifetime. Timothy Bright's *Abridgement* of *Actes and Monuments* (1589) lacks the visual sophistication of *The Lambe Speaketh* or the vivid woodcut apparatus of Foxe's larger volumes; it notably fails to reproduce the celebrated title page of Foxe's folio. Nonetheless, its title page illustration makes clear how the underlying logic of Foxe's martyrdom narratives is linked to the 1555 print, illuminating a clear conceptual link between the critique of the Mass, the image of the martyr, and the ambition to recollect the Protestant faithful into a reformed mystical and political body.

In Bright's title page, as in *The Lambe Speaketh,* the sacrificial ritual associated with the Catholic Mass dignifies Protestant martyrdom in traditional pastoral terms (figure 2). The thumbnail image on Bright's title page depicts the pope cutting the throat of a lamb, while martyrs burn at the stake behind him.[25] Again, as in the 1555 image, the Catholic sacrifice is literalized (although here not overtly cast in terms of the ritual Mass), as the corrupt bishop of Rome cuts the throat of the martyr-lamb. Again, the critique of transubstantiation is implicit in the charge that the same bloody-minded prelates who expect a literal sacrifice in a ritual celebration engage in murderous sacrifices of their doctrinal enemies. The martyr-lamb is the only true sacrifice that such religious leaders accomplish, but this conceptual move oddly continues to require the "false" religion to sanctify the members of the "true" church: not in the Eucharistic ritual, but by submitting the godly to the more gruesome rituals of martyrdom. The foregrounded sacrifice depicts the spiritual truth of the backgrounded burnings. Interestingly, the martyrs in flames, the supposedly iconic image of Foxe's book, are *not* what Bright chooses to foreground in the *Abridgement* title page. Rather, it is the image of the papal sacrifice of the martyr lamb that advertises the Foxe "brand." In using this woodcut as the title page image, Bright's *Abridgement* illustrates how a sixteenth-century audience may have received Foxe's narrative more overtly as a transference of the meaning of the sacrifice of the Mass to the sacrifice of the martyrs, adopting and adapting a Eucharistic literalism for Protestant national martyrology.

Bright's *Abridgement* is recognized as more overtly nationalistic than Foxe's original volume. Indeed, it has been argued that Bright's edition corresponds more closely to the Protestant nationalist agenda that Haller discerned in his influential study than Foxe's original editions.[26] The two churches motif of Foxe's title page, which we will examine more closely later, is recapitulated in a more obviously political key in the *Abridgement* as the image opposed to the "papal sacrifice" of the title page is a woodcut (first printed in the 1570 edition of *Actes and Monuments*) depicting Henry VIII's triumph over the pope. As Jesse Lander suggests, in the iconography of Bright's volume, "the struggle between the true and false church is . . . given a national specificity that is absent in the title-page of the larger book."[27] After these opening images, the *Abridgement* includes a list of all the "signs" of England's special, "elect" status as a Christian nation (figure 3). This list, titled "A Speciall Note of England," begins with the claim that England was "the first kingdome that vniuersallie embraced the Gospel" and ends with the reminder that it was also "the first reformed."[28] While it is this overt nationalism that has attracted the most critical commentary, I argue that Bright's *Abridgement* can only succeed in producing the sense that Protestant England was, in Haller's apt phrasing, "a mystical communion of chosen spirits,"[29] by drawing upon the deeper tradition of the *corpus mysticum* embedded in the emblem of the sacrificial lamb that transfers the cohesive force of the Mass to the figure of the martyr. As a closer reading of Foxe's original title page and text will show, these two elements necessarily reinforce each other as the politicized and Protestantized *corpus*

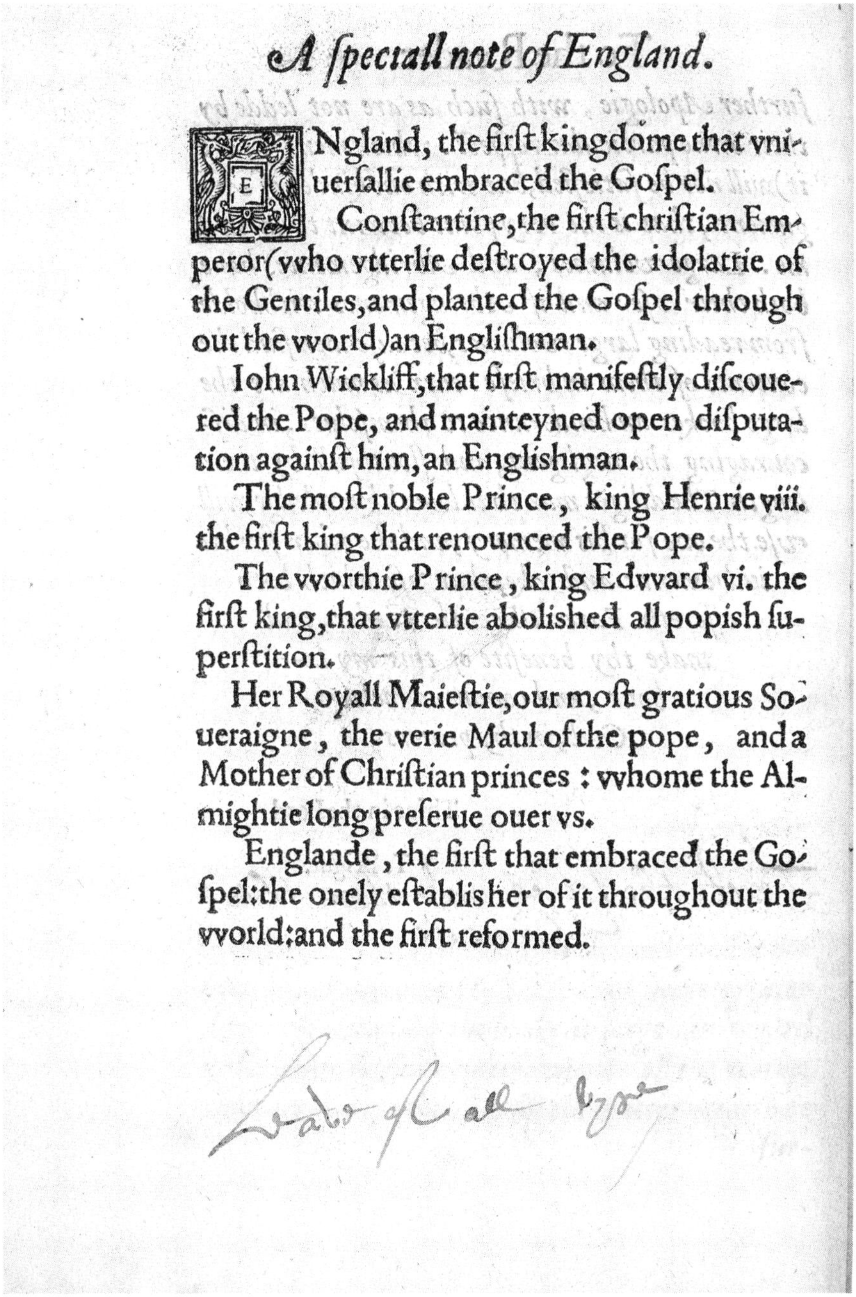

A speciall note of England.

Ngland, the first kingdome that vniuerfallie embraced the Gofpel.

Conftantine, the firft chriftian Emperor (vvho vtterlie deftroyed the idolatrie of the Gentiles, and planted the Gofpel through out the vvorld) an Englifhman.

Iohn Wickliff, that firft manifeftly difcouered the Pope, and mainteyned open difputation againft him, an Englishman.

The moft noble Prince, king Henrie viii. the firft king that renounced the Pope.

The vvorthie Prince, king Edvvard vi. the firft king, that vtterlie abolished all popish fuperftition.

Her Royall Maieftie, our moft gratious Soueraigne, the verie Maul of the pope, and a Mother of Chriftian princes : vvhome the Almightie long preferue ouer vs.

Englande, the firft that embraced the Gofpel: the onely eftablisher of it throughout the vvorld: and the firft reformed.

Figure 3. "A Speciall Note of England." *An Abridgement of the Booke of Acts and Monumentes of the Church* (London, 1589). Reproduced by permission of the Folger Shakespeare Library.

mysticum continues to allude to the sacramental schema of medieval Christianity even well into the era of the Reformation.

Remapping the Mystical Body:
The *Actes and Monuments* Title Page

Foxe's voluminous history of martyrdoms represents not only the trauma of Marian-era Protestant martyrs, but also the trauma of the pre-Reformation social-mystical body. It is this body, at least as it is imagined to coalesce in the Mass, that the martyrs assail with disputations about the efficacy of the rituals that traditionally composed it. That the debates that are central to Foxe's martyrological formula so frequently fixate on the Real Presence as if it were a hypostatized object or substance within the sacrament testifies to the decay in the early medieval performative, communal understanding of the sacrament detailed in the previous chapter. Yet it is also telling that the debates themselves must be obsessively reiterated in the form of a politically sanctioned textual *Monument*. These reiterations implicitly suggest that the sacramental celebration of the medieval church had maintained some socially cohesive force and that this force needed to be channeled in new ways rather than simply abolished by political authority. This claim can be elaborated through a close analysis of one of the most famous elements of Foxe's work: the iconic title page, first printed in 1563, and reprinted in all editions up to 1682 (figure 4). To early modernists, as much as to generations of English Protestants, this title page is a visual cliché, reproduced (as it is here) countless times. Yet the very clichéd character of the title page is a sign of its centrality: it speaks to the intertwining of theological and political forces at the inception of modern English national identity. If a burgeoning Protestant national identity is emblematized in the title page illustration, then this emblem is dependent upon depicting, in negative form, a prior mode of sacred and social order: the Catholic Mass. The title page illustrates how Foxe's project both perpetuates and realigns the *corpus mysticum* tradition formerly bound up with the celebration of the Mass.

In Foxe's title page, as in its precursor, *The Lambe Speaketh,* the Mass is captured at its high point, the central action of elevation, the moment of consecration that makes effective the Real Presence of Christ in the ceremony. In contrast to *The Lambe Speaketh,* however, the central visual representation of the Mass is rather straightforward and indeed maintains a clear integrity (the priests are not subhuman wolfish beings,

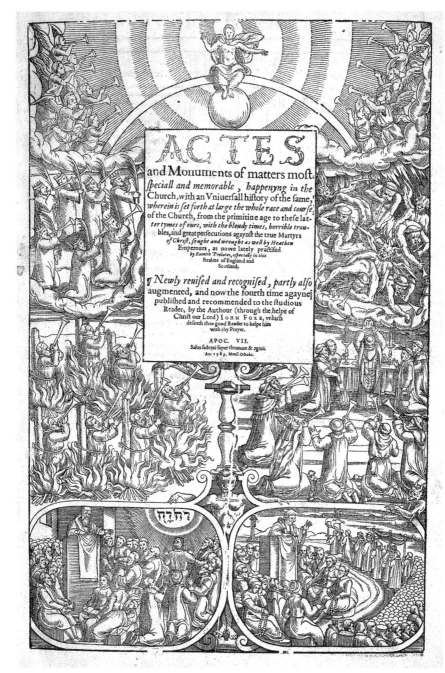

Figure 4. *Actes and Monuments of matters most speciall and memorable* (London, 1583). Title page. Reproduced by permission of the Folger Shakespeare Library.

the host is a wafer, not an actual lamb, the ritual is not the subject of parliamentary squabbling, and so on). By allowing a relative integrity to the image of the Mass on the frontispiece, Foxe's title page trains a community of readers used to this form of sacramental celebration to transfer the values associated with the Mass to a newer martyrological scheme of community. In reproducing the moment of consecration, Foxe's frontispiece emblematizes the tradition of the *corpus mysticum* as a central point of social and sacramental reference. The sacramental character of this ritual is, of course, precisely what Foxe and the ranks of Protestant martyrs he memorializes seek to contest, but nonetheless, in the title illustration, the image of Eucharistic celebration is granted the power to coalesce a distinct community. Foxe's illustration critiques the opposing tradition more subtly in the way the celebration itself is framed on the title page. This framing makes an argument about a fundamental division within Christendom that is encompassed by a larger awareness of how ritual religious performances gather, order, and shape human community. I want to linger on the visual impact of this framing in what follows, before delving into the text itself.

The *Actes and Monuments* title page remaps the spiritual life of England in oppositional terms, but this oppositional schema is more subtle and nuanced than usually acknowledged. The image of the Mass is reproduced on the right-hand side, at Christ's left hand, in the inverse visual logic of the illustration.[30] The central, crowning Christ-figure functions as the orienting axis of the complete tableau; previous critics have noted in the image the influence of the "medieval doom" with its representation of salvation and damnation at the gesture of the judging Christ.[31] If the image is read vertically, from top to bottom (an axis that can be conceived, as Thomas Betteridge has suggested, as descending from ideal to real),[32] three distinct layers emerge: an upper spiritual realm of either order or chaos, a middle "sacramental"[33] realm that mediates between eternity and history, which opposes the celebration of martyrdom to the celebration of the Catholic Mass, and the lower order of the ecclesiastical reality which results—an image of two worldly communities—two churches, two preachers, two congregations, only distinguishable at first glance by the difference in their devotional aids: books versus beads.

Previous critics have emphasized the fundamental duality of this image of two churches: a binary opposition between true and false churches, indebted to a larger tradition of Reformist visual polemic, organizes the horizontal axis of the woodcut.[34] While it is no doubt true that the title page envisions a conflict between opposed forces to teach the reader to recognize the visible, historical form of the true church,[35] I want to emphasize how it nonetheless conveys this lesson by a series of paradoxical juxtapositions that can prove disorienting. On the "false church" side, for example, the souls of the popish prelates are ascendant, yet also point downward and are intermixed with demons that emblematize their truly satanic nature, contradicting their apparently exalted position on the page. Betteridge's analysis notes that the oppositional theme is reinforced in this scheme insofar as the side of the "false" church is characterized by a subtle lack of integrity; its borders are persistently lapsed and broken by demonic intrusions in contrast to the static stability of the Protestant side of the page.[36] However, I believe that it is also important to note that, at first glance, the visual schema depends upon a logic of equivalency between the two sides that can provoke confusion in the reader untutored in the intricacies of Reformation controversy.

That such confusion may have been a concern even in Foxe's own day, when such controversies were far more vivid, is suggested by the glosses to the image provided in the 1570 edition (figure 5): the 1570 title page helpfully labels each side of the drawing, on both the top and the bottom of the page: on the left, "true church" side, in brackets, we are reminded that this is the "Image of the persecuted Church," while on the right, "false church" side, we find the bracketed reminder that this is the "Image of the persecutyng Church." The scriptural glosses at the top, from Matthew 25, reinforce the message, from left to right: "Come ye blessed. &c . . . Go ye cursed. &c." Such fussy glossing suggests a certain anxiousness that the reader get it right, as if the illustration itself does not entirely stake out a clear-cut claim about the relative truth and falsehood of the churches portrayed.

This ambivalence in the frontispiece, I argue, is a result of its deep engagement with the tradition of the *corpus mysticum,* which is represented in the sacramental sphere in the center of the page. The horizontal sacramental plane stages a migration of meaning and values from right to left, from Mass to martyr, across the image. This organization assumes a fundamental relationship between social and sacramental orders, an assumption inherited along with the iconography of martyrdom from the religious world of the Middle Ages. The lived experience of the martyr ideally occurs as a temporal sequence of events culminating in a spiritual transfiguration, but Foxe's title page represents this temporal sequence as a spatial juxtaposition oriented around a specific negative response to the performance of the Mass. Beginning at the top left, we find an orderly rank of ascended martyrs, who are evidently the heavenly avatars of the earthly martyrs, relocated out of daily life and into the ethereal realm of the cloudy heavens, carrying palms and trumpeting in holy triumph. This

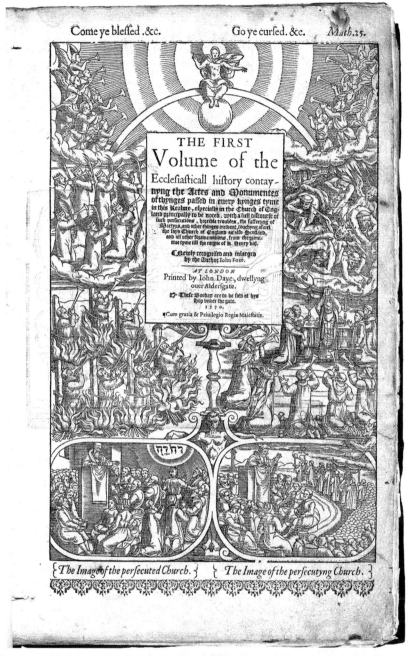

Figure 5. *The First Volume of the Ecclesiasticall history contaynyng the Actes and Monumentes of thynges passed in euery kynges tyme in this Realme* (London, 1570). Title page. Reproduced by permission of the Folger Shakespeare Library.

mystical community is positioned directly above the first example of the memorable image of martyrs in the process of being consumed by flames, an image compulsively reiterated throughout the vast text.[37] Upon closer examination, at least two of the martyrs in flames directly gesture with open hands at the idolatry of the Mass represented on the other side of the page, suggesting a religious community formed around a critique of this sacramental celebration, but also one that might invite identification with some of the ideal values formerly associated with this celebration. The structure of the image stresses how the community of immolated martyrs becomes the sacramental equivalent of the consecration that is supposed to happen in the Mass. Foxe's text reveals that the meaning of the Mass is precisely what the majority of martyrs die contesting. In contesting the significance of the sacrifice of the altar, and all its visible accoutrements, they themselves become the sacrifice, the true *imitatio Christi*.[38] In this sense, they form the new—or, as Foxe would have it, the real, heretofore repressed—*corpus mysticum* of the English community.

The title page image thus provides a map of the pattern of theological disputation in the text insofar as it locates the primary site of conflict at the sacramental level, the transitional zone where the martyrs on the left will have been transmuted into an ideal form of presence precisely by virtue of contesting the validity of the Real Presence confected in the Mass represented on the right. The title page visually transfers the act of merging the material and the transcendent, the secular time of the human here-and-now with sacred and eternal time, from the Mass to the martyr. The image engages in a translation of sacramental idioms that the subsequent text will also incessantly perform. Both title page and text construct a counter-ideal of mystical community that transposes, but does not quite efface, the dynamic of mystical performance associated with the Catholic Mass.

Whatever forms of incipient individualism may be associated with the Reformation, Foxe's title page highlights how for the early modern imagination, what was most vitally at stake in this conflict was not simply the fate of individual souls, but the integrity of wider communities as bodies of Christ. As the bottom of the title page makes clear, the opposing worldly ecclesiastical communities derive their respective coherence (or lack thereof) from the type of sacramental experience that superscribes them in this image. Beneath the celestial and sacramental levels, the two images of the church in the world illustrate how the dynamic of the higher orders results in the formation of specific devotional habits that constitute distinct ways of being-in-common-in-the-world: reading scripture versus saying the rosary (although both groups obediently listen to a dominant pastoral figure who stands in for the head of a larger hier-archical institution). The sacramental argument of the middle of the title page resolves at the bottom into a claim about how the dynamic relation between transcendent and immanent orders collects the diverse members of the church into a social body.

This lower level of the title page has been previously analyzed as an illustration of the print-oriented culture of early modern Protestantism in contrast to the less literate oral and material traditions of medieval Catholicism, an orientation captured by the oval representation of the godly community on the left.[39] The devout readers framed on the left side of the page are indeed a reminder that Foxe's volume seeks to sup-plant the mode of sacred sociality founded in the consecration of the Mass with one founded more soundly in scripture. However, the affin-ity between Protestantism and the relatively new technology of print on display here should not obscure the extent to which this title page, as much as Foxe's subsequent text, is an amalgam of modern and medi-eval elements.[40] Such an amalgam is evident even in this oval of godly readers. In the background, behind the studious congregation, other worshippers behold the radiant letters of the Tetragrammaton. While this reproduction of the Hebrew name of God in the midst of a Protes-tant congregation is certainly another testament to the scripturalism of a print-oriented religion,[41] it is also worth noting how the Tetragrammaton is framed in a round white aura, elevated above the crowd—reminiscent of the elevation of the host portrayed on the opposite side of the page. And, indeed, in the companion oval on the right side of the page, the background space parallel to that of the Protestant Tetragrammaton on the left is occupied by what appears to be a Corpus Christi procession, the public Eucharistic celebration that also expressed an imagined ideal of the social body in the late Middle Ages.[42] In keeping with the theo-logical thrust of the title page, this particular procession seems to lead to the gallows, toward a communion in death rather than life. Nonetheless, evoking almost subliminally the complex social and religious tradition of the Corpus Christi festival encourages the reader to transfer the affective resonance of the late medieval procession to the readerly reverence of the godly circle haloed by the Tetragrammaton on the left. These details suggest that the goal of *Actes and Monuments* is a fundamental reori-entation, rather than a complete erasure, of a social experience in vital connection with sacramental life.

The title page of Foxe's *Book of Martyrs* thus can be conceived as the Hegelian *Aufhebung* of the medieval *corpus mysticum:* it negates its image, yet also preserves some of its core sacramental and social principles (an extended sense of the Hegelian term). It preserves the image of the Mass as the central organizing point of the sacramental realm, either as the focus of misguided or even demonic celebrants or as the target of critique of the trumpeting martyrs, whose instruments point in the same upward direction as the elevated host, a detail reiterated on the Catholic side by the clerical trumpets heralding the consecration. Insofar as the image preserves, in its representation of martyrdom, the notion of a sacramentally constituted communal mystical body, it illustrates, even at the most extreme point of opposition, its dependence on its other, the abandoned (but clearly not forgotten) sacramental system of medieval Catholicism.

This double gesture continues even more intensely in the text of *Actes and Monuments*. At the same time that Foxe's martyrology attempts to claim the forces of cohesion formerly attributed to this Mass, it seeks to deconstruct the ritual itself to strip these forces away from their traditional form. Foxe seeks to transfer the power claimed for the performance of the Mass (the power to access the transcendent within the immanent to draw together a community as a body of Christ) to the Protestant martyr, to reinstantiate the mystical bonds that compose this body within the martyrological narrative. Foxe's martyrs are narrated—and narrate themselves—in an effort to form a community founded in a common faith.[43] However, the formulas through which this community articulates itself also demand persistent disputes about the status of the older ritual and communal order. The disputes themselves are a *performance* that seeks to draw upon and simultaneously overwrite the performance of the Mass. In *Actes and Monuments*, these performances are framed first of all visually, as we have seen, on the title page, but also verbally, in the text of the proem to the most immediate tales of martyrdom, those which occurred during the reign of Elizabeth's predecessor Mary. The next section will examine this textual framing, which dissects the text of the canon of the Mass as given in a medieval missal, before turning to the exemplary narratives of individual martyrs.

Deconstructing the Mass: The Preface to Book Ten of *Actes and Monuments*

In several editions of *Actes and Monuments*, Foxe prefaces the section in which he begins to recount the tales of the Marian martyrs (Book Five in 1563 and Book Ten in 1583) with an extended deconstruction of the canon of the Mass "after Salisbury use," which his fellow Reformer

Coverdale translated (and Foxe transcribed) "word by word out of Laten into English" (*Actes and Monuments* [1583], 1398). As Ryan Netzley has observed, Foxe's polemic against the Mass (in English as well as in Latin) has often been neglected in critical work in favor of a focus on the martyrological narratives themselves: "By ignoring this preface, modern scholarship tacitly accepts the conclusion that the mass is a 'vain' thing, reaffirming the text's polemic position. However, in the process, contemporary criticism also rejects the argument of Foxe's book ten preface by implicitly maintaining that the mass and conflicts about it are irrelevant for reading the *Actes and Monuments*."[44] My emphasis on the tradition of the *corpus mysticum* corrects this oversight by showing precisely how Foxe's engagement with the Mass itself is integral to the subsequent martyr narratives. In this section, as on the title page, Foxe sets up a conceptual framework that enables a transfer of communal sacramentality from the Mass to the martyr. In this sense, the "polyphony" of the text that appears perplexing to the modern critic is actually essential to Foxe's project.[45]

Foxe is careful to put into place in this preface a logic that transfers the sacramental value of the old rite to the experience and memory of the martyrs themselves. Foxe introduces this logic in the opening lines of Book Ten:

> Forasmuch as we are come now to the tyme of Queene Mary, when as so many were put to death for the cause especially of the Masse, and the sacrament of the Altar (as they cal it) I thought it conuenient upon the occasion geuen, in the ingresse of this forsayd story, first to prefixe before, by the way of Preface, some declaration collected out of dyuers writers and Authors, whereby to set foorth to the Reader the great absurditie, wicked abuse, and perilous idolatry of the popish Masse, declaring how and by whom it came in, clouted and patched up of diuers additions, to the intent that the Reader, seeing the vayne institution thereof, and waying the true causes why it is to be exploded out of all Churches, may the better thereby iudge of their death, which gaue their liues for the testimonie and word of truth. (1397)

Foxe explicitly links the martyrs of the Marian years to the Mass by positing an immediate relation of antagonism. The Mass is the "cause" of their death, "cause" echoing in a double sense: exposing its supposed falsehoods was the quintessential "cause" or purpose of the martyrs themselves, but also "cause" in the sense of direct causality, as if the ritual itself put them to death as sacrifices. This second sense is evocative of the gruesome scene of *The Lambe Speaketh*: the false sacrifice inevitably and incessantly demands real blood. This double sense of "cause" suggests a more complicated relation than straightforward antagonism between the martyrs and the Mass. While the sacramental value of the Mass is thrown into question by the sarcastic parenthetical aside—"(as they cal it)"—this value is relocated to the martyrs who "gaue their liues" contesting this "patched up" ritual. The Mass is ironically granted some measure of efficacy in this exchange: even if it has no other value, it does offer the opportunity for those who contest it as a sacrament to become sanctified as martyrs.

The main part of Foxe's preface focuses on the "Canon" of the Mass, the ritual of transubstantiation, with its overtly sacrificial elements. For Foxe, the accretions of tradition surrounding the Mass—which from the perspective of a social history informed by de Lubac could signify the ongoing development of a symbolic language expressive of a sacramentally invested collective life—are treated as mere theatrical "trinckets," a theater malevolently designed to mislead the Christian community to its damnation. Yet the theatrical performance of the Mass is in turn supplanted by another realm of performance in the pious theater of cruelty of martyrdom. Before turning to these performances however, Foxe's procedure is to render the Mass visible as a vernacular text and to anatomize it in a series of glosses crowding the right margin of the page, keyed to letters that insistently interrupt the body of the text. Such iconoclastic glossing was a common Reformist strategy, pursued as well by French Calvinists.[46] Foxe's text works to ensure that his English audience is alienated from the Mass; the ritual must be rendered foreign and fictional—the property of Rome and the pope, divorced from connection with the traditional lived experience of the people. Estranged, broken off from the rhythms of life, the Mass is fit to Foxe's project—its ideal aspirations can now be more easily transferred, absorbed into the martyrological narrative.

Foxe effects this alienation by insistently emphasizing the arbitrary nature of many of the aspects of the ritual, the historical contingency of its traditions, and the ways it deviates from scripture. However, for the present context, the most pertinent argument lies in the frequent critique that the traditional Mass fails in its aspiration to represent the unity of the Christian community.[47] Unlike Cranmer, who focuses on refashioning the liturgy itself,[48] Foxe, writing at a later moment of Protestant political ascendancy, seeks to achieve the medieval communal ideal through the martyrological narrative. Particularly striking in his treatment of the

Canon of the Mass are his marginal comments on the crucial moment of the elevation of the host, the "sacring" that was the focal point of collective attention in the traditional ritual.[49] At the invocation "this is my body"—the crux of Reformation debate, where the missal instructs "Lyfte it up aboue hys forehead, that it may be seene of the people"— Foxe interjects a gloss "(h)": "Yf it were the true Sacramentall bread of the body of the Lord it should be take & eaten and not lifte up to be gased vpo" (1399). Here, significantly, Foxe grounds his critique neither directly on the question of the Real Presence nor on the merits of the doctrine of transubstantiation, but rather on the grounds that the denial of participation to all, in the form of actual eating of the host as the body of Christ, exposes the inauthenticity of the ritual. The Mass falsifies itself in its emphasis on the visual over the visceral. The ritual's concentration on the performative acts of the priest comes at the expense of the spiritual well-being of the whole congregation. An earlier gloss also reinforces this argument: "(e)" (at "take ye," which draws attention to the singular role of the priest at the supposed expense of the many worshippers): "He (Christ) saith not let one of you take and eate it himself alone" (1399). A similar objection is raised in relation to the chalice "take, and drinke of this (i), yee all," where gloss "(i)" exclaims: "Why takest thou it then alone? Or why should not the lay people then drincke of the cup also? Be not they the Lords disciples? Scholars of his heauenly schoole?" (1399). Again, Foxe iterates another typical Reformist complaint: that communion "in both kinds" is withheld from the laity.[50] The Mass, far from producing a more closely knit Christian community, actually reinforces division; the traditional rituals deny true participation in the body of Christ.

Given this dim view of the social value of the Mass, it is not surprising to find that Foxe's gloss on the declaration of the "mystery of faith" reflects the degeneration of the term traced by de Lubac and outlined in the previous chapter. Foxe asserts: "These words (*misterium fidei*) haue ye here added declaring the cup to be but a misticall representation of the blood" (1399). While de Lubac shows that the earlier sense of "mystery" was a dynamic action interrelating the symbolic and the real (including multiple temporal dimensions: past, present, and future), and the Eucharist and the church as social and sacramental entities, for Foxe, writing after the long period of decline in this sense of "mystery," the idea of a "misticall" action immediately implies a merely fictional or fictionalizing gesture. In Foxe's rendition, the phrase becomes yet another example of the delusive quality of the larger tradition. From de Lubac's perspective, Foxe's derisive gloss would represent a late development of the trend toward rationalism and realism begun back in the twelfth century, yet it is nonetheless important to recognize that Foxe still aspires to achieve a version of the *corpus mysticum* through his martyrology.

Foxe reminds the audience of what the Mass is supposed to effect and the myriad ways, from a Reformed perspective, that it fails in this efficacy in order to construct an alternative sacramental edifice built on the sacrifice of martyrs whose relics consist in the collection of texts assembled as witness. He ends the preface to Book Ten by recapitulating the main themes of his attack on the Mass as a prelude to the stories of the Marian martyrs:

> And thus haue ye in sum the gatheringes of the masse, with the Chanon and all the appurtenaunce of the same, which, not much vnlike to the Crow of Esope being patched with the feathers of so manye byrdes, was so long a gethering, that the temple of Salomon was not so long in building, as the Popes Masse was in making. Whereby iudge now thy selfe (good Reader) whether this Masse did proceede from Iames and other Apostles or no. And yet this was one of the principall causes for which so much turmoyle was made in the Church, with the bloudshed of so many Godly men, suffering in so many quarters of this realme: some consumed by fire, some pined away with hunger, some hanged, some slayne, some racked, some tormented one way, some another: and that onely or chiefelye, for the cause of this aforesayd popish Masse, as by the reading of this story folowing, by the grace of Christ our Lord, shall appeare more at large. In whome I wyshe thee to continue in health and to perseuere in the trueth. (1405)

Foxe sums up his critique by associating the Mass with "gatheringes" that are not authentic social or communal occasions, but mere collections of falsehoods—a patchwork or false edifice comparable to the contraptions found in fables: "not much vnlike to the Crow of Esope being patched with the feathers of so manye byrdes." This false "gathering" of a "Masse" of disparate traditions in itself fails to produce the true body of Christ. However, the conceit of the Mass does perversely and indirectly work toward a spiritual end insofar as it provokes the community of the Reformed faithful to challenge it by staking their bodies against it in myriad ways: "some consumed by fire, some pined away with hunger, some hanged, some slayne, some racked, some tormented one way, some another." The martyrs who offer themselves as these sacrifices constitute the true *corpus mysticum* that paradoxically founds itself on the claim to efface the traditional means of assembling the *corpus mysti-cum,* the sacramental community, in the old Mass. The martyrs are those "in whome" the living faithful may "continue in health" and "perseuere in the trueth." To counter the attraction of the Mass, Foxe offers his text as the authentic experience of sacramental collectivity. His work does not reject the traditional goal of communal sacramentality—indeed, in a world still immersed in many ways in traditional collective experiences of Christendom, he could not hope to succeed in his polemical task if he did—but he does seek to achieve it via a different medium: the visceral liturgy of the martyr.

The Liturgy of Martyrdom in *Actes and Monuments*

With Foxe's larger theological, historical, and even satirical arguments against the Mass in mind, we can turn to the narratives of individual martyrs in Book Ten and beyond. The martyrs who are most interest-ing in this context are not only those who reiterate Foxe's conceptual theological arguments against the Mass, but also those who embody his efforts to relocate the ecstatic, affective devotional habits associated with the Mass within the experience of martyrdom. As the title page forecasts, this effort to re-situate devotion is driven by the project of reconstructing a community around the sacrificial image of the martyr. The Eucharistic overtones of these martyrological narratives, reminiscent of pre-Reformation martyrologies, also function effectively in Foxe's tell-ing to form or reinforce bonds between the martyrs and their immediate audience or community in the narrative—and also, implicitly, with the audience or community of ideal readers whom Foxe's work addresses.

Foxe's work develops a distinct liturgy of martyrdom that may be compared to Thomas Cranmer's revision of the Eucharistic liturgy in the early 1550s Book of Common Prayer, as Janel Mueller has observed. Mueller associates Foxe's martyrology with Cranmer's Reformed liturgy, which, in accord with the mainstream of Reformist theology,[51] replaces the "sacrificial" aspect of the old Mass with a prayer on the part of the worshippers to "offer and present unto thee (O Lorde) oure selfe, oure soules, and bodies to be a reasonable, holy and lively sacrifice unto thee."[52] According to Mueller's argument, both Foxe and Cranmer proj-ect "the sacramental incorporation of the subject's body into the body of Christ."[53] Like Cranmer's ideal congregation, Foxe's martyrs make them-selves the sacrifice. Mueller's connection between Foxe and Cranmer is compelling, but limited. As others have noted, she tends to underestimate

the continuity between medieval Catholic sacramental theology and martyrology and their Reformed variations, assuming a starker opposition
between religious adversaries than may actually have been the case.[54]
In the present context, I want to emphasize how both Cranmer and
Foxe evoke the larger, established concept of the *corpus mysticum*. The
notion that those present at a Eucharistic celebration or those subject
to martyrdom become part of Christ's sacrifice and, therefore, members of the body of Christ is not innovative but extremely traditional;
it echoes, for example, the Eucharistic theology of Augustine's *City of
God*, discussed at the end of the previous chapter. It is a notion essential to the long-standing concept of the *mystical body* as a sacramental
community.

Such a performative and communitarian view of the sacrament of
the Eucharist is also visible in medieval English religious drama. Sarah
Beckwith's account of the York Corpus Christi cycle in *Signifying God*
emphasizes how the sacramental aspect of these pre-Reformation dramas reinforces their communitarian import.[55] Beckwith reconstructs
the medieval milieu in which the Corpus Christi plays functioned as a
"complex kind of para-liturgy" in relation to the Mass, "a commentary
upon and interaction with the liturgy of the mass and its offices."[56] In
the medieval city of York, the community becomes the body of Christ
in the midst of performances that extend and complicate the performance of the Mass: "Through their rearticuation of the body of Christ
on the streets of York, the representations that organize social existence
in York are examined."[57] Beckwith shows that the integration between
sacrament and community posited by the idea of the *corpus mysticum*
remains vivid in an English context until the very eve of the Reformation, despite changes in the understanding of the Real Presence in the
Mass and the development of the church into a more centralized institution in the later Middle Ages. Similarly, Eamon Duffy has argued that an
enthusiastic "lay appropriation" of the sacrament of the altar emerges
in "para-liturgical" rituals such as the Pax board and the distribution of
unconsecrated, "blessed bread" at the Mass (as a substitute for the host
itself, traditionally consumed only at Easter). Such practices, which might
convey as well as contain social conflict, are evidence of a medieval laity
"which is alert to the sense in which the eucharist both symbolizes and
makes community."[58]

The proliferation of paraliturgies in the later Middle Ages is an ironic
precedent for the way in which Foxe's Protestant martyrs appropriate
the gestures of the liturgy of the Mass, even in the midst of their hostility
to it. There is a greater continuity between the paraliturgies of the late

Middle Ages and their early Protestant successors than has previously been recognized. We cannot read this continuity if we simply take Foxe and his martyrs at their literal word, concentrating on what they are saying (polemics against the Mass and the Real Presence) versus what they are doing. A shift in focus reveals in Foxe's work a considerably more complicated relation to the ritual life of the Middle Ages, a life in which the social is intimately bound up with the sacramental. In his martyrology, Foxe sought a narrative and visual form that would both fulfill the communitarian aspirations of the old Mass and its myriad paraliturgies and accomplish the theological goals of the Reformation (i.e., delegitimizing the Mass itself, exalting scriptural authority, empowering the political over the ecclesiastical). This contradiction, which becomes clear in historical hindsight, contributes to the compelling social and political force of Foxe's work: it allows its audience to recognize the martyr as embodying the corporate life of the *corpus mysticum,* even as it also encourages them to disavow the doctrines of the Catholic Church.

Foxe displaces the ideal of the Mass into the moment of martyrological apotheosis. This displacement is most visible in those moments in which the martyr mimics the gestures of the old Mass. In blending and refining into a distinct formula the liturgical and martyrological traditions that he inherited, and in exploiting the powerful resources of the press and political patronage to disseminate this formula, Foxe arguably achieves a more powerful reformation of the tradition of the *corpus mysticum* than Cranmer was able to achieve in his Reformed liturgy.[59] Foxe's work demonstrates how the center of gravity for the *corpus mysticum* shifts out of the realm of the liturgy during the English Reformation. Part of this shift, though, occurs precisely because Foxe incorporates the liturgical rhythms of the foresworn Mass into accounts of the martyrs' performances at the stake. Such incorporations orient these performances toward achieving a version of the social-sacramental bonding that was also the ideal of the medieval Mass. Several examples from the ranks of Foxe's martyrs vividly illustrate the paradoxical pattern in which denunciations of the Mass are juxtaposed with paraliturgical performances.

Thomas Haukes, a notable Protestant martyr of 1555, provides a particularly striking case of this contradictory rhythm in Foxe's work. Like most other martyrs in the final section of Foxe's volume, Haukes runs into trouble for resisting the reimposition of traditional sacramental practices during Mary Tudor's reign. Although Haukes initially comes to the attention of ecclesiastical authorities as a result of his refusal to have his child baptized "after the papistical maner" (*Actes and Monuments*

[1583], 1585), under interrogation, his recalcitrance is revealed, unsurprisingly, to extend to participation in the Mass. Haukes denounces the Mass as "detestable, abhominable, and profitable for nothing" (1587). Nonetheless, his final scene of martyrdom includes an element conspicuously reminiscent of the Mass. Before he is taken to the stake to be burned, he makes an arrangement with some friends to give them a sign or "token" if he is able to tolerate the flames: "so secretly betwene them it was agreed, that if the rage of the payne were tollerable and might be suffered, then he should lift vp his handes aboue his head toward heauen before he gaue vp the ghost" (1592). In raising his hands in the midst of flames as a "token" to the faithful, Haukes promises to perform a "true" elevation in contrast to the "false" elevation of the Mass pictured on the title page of *Actes and Monuments*. This act, arranged by a prior agreement with friends, is also a means of sealing a bond between a community of like-minded believers. As a successful martyr, Haukes performs the action promised as he is burned at the stake:

> And when his speech was taken away by violence of the flame, his skin also drawen together, and his fingers consumed with the fire, so that now all men thought certainly he had been gone, sodainely and contrary to all expectation, the blessed seruaunt of GOD, beyng myndefull of his promise afore made, reached vp his hands burning on a light fier (which was marueilous to behold) ouer his head to the liuing God, and with great reioysing, as seemed, strooke or clapped thē three tymes together. At the sight whereof there followed such applause & outcry of the people, and especially of them which vnderstode the matter: that the like hath not cōmonly bene heard: And so the blessed Martyr of Christ, straight way sinckyng downe into the fire, gaue vp his spirite. (1592–93)

Foxe casts Haukes's act of elevating his hands, virtually at the very moment that he "gaue vp his spirite," as a "marueilous" sight in the 1583 edition. The "marvel" of this moment is underscored further as it is visually portrayed in a woodcut of Haukes's martyrdom accompanying the text (figure 6).

The Eucharistic overtones of this scene are even more prominent in the earlier version of this account included in the 1563 edition of *Actes and Monuments,* where Haukes is described immediately prior to the burning as "the gentle sacrifice [that] standeth ready to receiue the fire" (*Actes and Monuments* [1563], 1162). Haukes's performance in the flames is also more reminiscent of the miracle of the Mass in the 1563 version:

Figure 6. "The Martirdome of Thomas Haukes in Essex, at a Towne called Coxehall. Anno. 1555, June 10," *Actes and Monuments of matters most speciall and memorable* (London, 1583), 1592. Reproduced by permission of the Folger Shakespeare Library.

> And when his breath was taken away by violence of the flame, his skynne with burning as it wer drawen together, his fingers consumed in the fire, and that al men did loke certainly that now he would geue vp the gost, he mindeful of hys promis made, dyd lift vp his hands halfe burned, & burning with heate aboue his head, to the liuing God, & euē in a sodain, and with great reioycing striketh them three tymes together: By which thing, contrary to all mens expectation beyng sene, there followed so great reioycing and crye of the multitude gathered together, that you would haue thought heauen & earth to haue com together. (1162)

Haukes's "token" brings "heauen & earth" together in the eyes of a publicly gathered "multitude"; in this sense, it acts as a kind of alternate liturgy to the Mass,[60] accomplishing its goals in even more dramatic circumstances, at the point of an actual death which the gestures and words mark as a sacrificial imitation of Christ. The resemblance to the Mass is heightened by the nature of Haukes's bodily gesture, which remains the same across the two versions. While Susannah Monta is correct to observe that Foxe's later version of the account is more cautiously phrased (it is most acclaimed by "them which understode the matter" in 1583),[61] in the context of the current argument, I want to stress the strong continuities between the 1563 and 1583 texts: both recount a performance that merges the material and the spiritual and reconstitutes a version of sacramental fellowship among the witnesses, who become a kind of a *corpus mysticum* in beholding this marvel. Indeed, the narrowing of community that occurs in changes in the textual account between 1563 and 1583 is countered by the visual impact of the woodcut that clearly depicts Haukes in the act of elevating his arms while exclaiming "O Lord receive my spirite."[62] Even though the immediate audience of knowing witnesses within the narrative is narrowed in the 1583 edition, the larger audience for Foxe's text (including a nonliterate audience who might still be able to read the woodcut illustration) is invited to read Haukes as offering himself as a true sacrifice in direct contradistinction to the "false" sacrifice of Christ in the elevated host of the Mass.

Another example of this miraculous elevation of the martyr's hands at the stake even while flames consume him occurs in the narrative of another Marian martyr, Christopher Waide, also burned for heresy in 1555. Waide's rejection of the Mass is even more central to his indictment. While Waide affirms himself as a member of "holy Church, that is, of the congregation or bodye of Christ," he resists identifying the "very body" of Christ in the sacrament: "only affirming the very body of him to be in heaven & in the sacrament to be a token or remembrance of Christes death." This Zwinglian sacramental theology leads Waide, like Haukes, to proclaim the Mass to be "abhominable" (*Actes and Monuments* [1583], 1679). Ironically, however, in an echo of the Haukes case, Waide performs a miraculous gesture at the stake that evokes the high point of the Mass, the very consecration that he denies before the authorities. Waide's final words at the stake, like Haukes's final utterance, evoke the precedent of the early church martyrs, but his bodily gesture is reminiscent of the Mass:

> Then fire being putte vnto him, he cried vnto God often, Lord Iesus receiue my soule, wythout any token or signe of impaciencie in the fire, till at lengthe, after the fire was once throughly kindled, he was hearde no man speake, still holding hys handes vp ouer hys head together towardes heauen, euen when he was dead and altogether

rosted, as though they had bene stayed vppe wyth a proppe standing vnder them. Thys signe did God shewe vppon hym, whereby
his very ennemies might perceiue, that God had according to hys
prayer, shewed such a token vppon hym, euen to their shame and
confusion. And this was the order of this godly Martyrs execution,
thys was his ende. Whereby God seemed to confound and strike
with the spirit of dumbnes, the Frier that Locuste which was risen
vp to haue spoken against hym: and also no lese woonderfully susteined those handes which he lifted vp to him for cōfort in his tor-
ment. (1680)

Even after it has been "rosted," Waide's corpse is evidently transfixed in a
posture that parallels that of the consecrating priest in the Mass, "hold-
ing hys handes vp ouer hys head together towardes heauen." While Foxe
cautiously revises his claims about the miraculous nature of Haukes's
raised arms between different editions of *Actes and Monuments,* in this
case, Foxe is more bold in implying a divine intervention in Waide's
bodily posture ("woonderfully susteined"), perhaps because it is coupled
with the anomalous silencing of a Friar who had arrived at the execution
site to preach against heresy, another occurrence that Foxe attributes to
God's will.

   Earlier in the passage, when the Friar originally arrives on the scene,
"Wade very mightily admonished the people to beware of that doctrine" (1679), setting himself up, despite his extreme circumstances, as
a counter-preacher, an alternative ecclesiastical authority. Foxe leaves
it somewhat up in the air why exactly the Friar leaves without preach-
ing: "whether he were amased, or could have no audience of the people,
[the Friar] withdrew himselfe" (1679), although, as noted, the wonder
of Waide's uplifted arms at the stake seems to give Foxe license to claim
a miraculous intervention a bit later on. Here, in contrast to Haukes,
the divine "token" is not arranged according to prior agreement among
friends. Nonetheless, the liturgical overtone of Waide's gesture is heightened by the fact that he is represented as successfully substituting himself
for the papist cleric, a move that also casts his burning as a kind of substitute Mass, again with an authentic, divinely sanctioned sacrifice in
place of a false and illusory one, with the power to gather the godly into
communion as witnesses of the event.

   Another kind of mimicry of the gestures of the Mass may be found in
the more briefly recounted martyrdom of Joyce Lewes, another Marian
martyr. Lewes's rejection of the Mass is explicitly the main cause of her
persecution. She is inspired to resist attendance at Mass (with which she

had previously complied) by the example of a martyr burned "because hee refused to receaue the Masse" (2012). After taking instruction from a Protestant neighbor, Lewes is inspired to follow the example of the earlier martyr: "because she had learned the masse to be evil & abhominable, she began to hate it," a hatred that becomes publicly manifest when she turns her back on the "blasphemous holy water, injurious to the bloud of christ" cast at her local church (2012). Lewes rejects the sacramental rituals authorized in her community, but in doing so, she makes an effort to build a counter-community of Protestant faithful. This effort is most visible in the scene of her martyrdom:

> She was brought to the place of execution: and because the place was farre off, and the throng of the people great, and she not acquaynted with the fresh ayre (being so long in prison) one of her frendes sent a messenger to the Sheriffes house for some drinke: and after she had prayed three seuerall times, in the whiche prayer she desired God most instantly to abolish the idolatrous Masse, and to delyuer this realme from Papistry (at the end of the whiche prayers the most parte of the people cryed Amen, yea, euen the Sheriffe that stoode harde by her, readye to cast her in the fire for not allowing the Masse, at this her prayers sayde with the rest of the people, Amen) when she had thus prayed, she tooke the cup into her handes saying: I drynke to all them that vnfaynedly loue the Gospell of Iesus Christ and wish for the abolishment of Papistry. When she had dronken, they that were her frends dranke also. After that a great number, specially the women of the towne dyd drynke with her: which afterward were put to open penaunce in the Churche by the cruel Papistes, for drinking with her. (2013)

Lewes's prayers, which focus on the abolition of the "idolatrous Masse," appear to have a contagious effect on her companions and bystanders (even the Sheriff), who find themselves assenting to her words (notably with the liturgical word "Amen"). Lewes's final act clinches this communal sentiment with a kind of travesty of the Eucharistic ritual. She takes up the cup that she has been given and emulates the priest's elevation of the chalice in the Mass, even while she proclaims a message that defies "Papistry." She conveys an "unfayned love" of Christ through a complex performance that simultaneously imitates and undoes the "feigned" ceremonies of the Mass. Foxe then emphasizes how her gesture is in turn imitated by her neighbors ("specially the women of the towne") who choose to "drynke with her" in a communal gesture. Foxe emphasizes how Lewes succeeds, at least momentarily, in establishing a godly counter-community through her ritualistic gesture.[63] It should be noted that this communal drinking goes beyond the actual practice of the medieval Mass, which consisted in communion in one kind only for the laity—although reformers advocated communion in both kinds for all as a regular practice, a belief that may be glanced at in this scene. The festive character of this scene also echoes the wider conviviality and feasting that occurred beyond the doors of the church, but was still closely associated with Eucharist-centered holidays such as Easter or Corpus Christi in the late Middle Ages, paraliturgical events which reinforced the ideal association of the community with the body of Christ.[64]

Ritualistic, convivial drinking in close proximity to the stake is also an element in a complex sequence of Henrician martyrdoms recorded earlier, in Book Eight of *Actes and Monuments*. In the 1583 edition of his volume, Foxe includes an extensive account of the persecution, trial, and execution of three martyrs in Windsor in 1544: Anthony Person, Henry Filmer, and Robert Testwood.[65] As with the Marian martyrs, the official accusations of heresy against these men focus in large part on their attitudes and statements about the sacrament of the Eucharist and the Mass. For example, among other blasphemies, Testwood is accused of failing to show sufficient devotion at the elevation of the host in the Mass: "that whē the Priest shoulde lift vp the Sacrament ouer hys heade, then wouldest thou looke downe vpon thy booke, or some other way, because thou wouldest not abide to looke vpon the blessed Sacrament" (1218–19). Testwood draws attention to himself by separating himself from the rest of the parishioners through this resistant behavior; his action is not only theologically suspicious but also socially disruptive.

Testwood's fellow martyr, the priest Anthony Person, is accused of more colorful irreverence in a similar vein, as he is cited for proclaiming in his sermons that "like as Christe was hanged betwene two theeues, euen so whē the priest is at masse, and hath cōsecrated and lifted him vp ouer hys head, then he hangeth betweene 2. theues" and that "yee shall not eate the body of Christ, as it did hang vpon the Crosse, gnawing it with your teeth, that the bloude runne aboute your lippes, but you shall eate him thys day, as ye eat him to morow, the next day, and euery day: for it refresheth not the body, but the soule" (1219). Person's "heresy" denies the doctrine of transubstantiation as it simultaneously mocks the ritual gestures of the Mass and questions the moral integrity of the priests who celebrate it. When faced with these charges, Person, far from recanting, pushes back against the ecclesiastical authorities with imagery that anticipates the caricatures of *The Lambe Speaketh*: "ye are become rather bitesheepes then true byshops, biting and deuouring the poore sheepe of Christ like rauening wolues neuer satisfied with bloud" (1219).[66] Here again, the adherents of the traditional Mass, which supposedly reenacts a real sacrifice, are cast as not simply negligent, but also bloodthirsty and cannibalistic, as if the "realist" theological doctrine of what happens in the Mass inspires corresponding habits of real viciousness in all other aspects of pastoral duty.

Yet the final scene of the martyrdom of these men is marked by several gestures reminiscent of traditional sacramental celebration, including the Eucharistic rituals of the Mass. When they are brought to the stake, Anthony Person, clearly the sauciest of the bunch, embraces the post lovingly with the words: "Nowe welcome myne owne sweete wife: for this day shalt thou and I be maried together in the loue and peace of God" (1220). While Person's gesture associates his incipient martyrdom with a wedding ceremony rather than with a Mass as such, it does affiliate the pending execution with a sacrament in the medieval church, the public celebration of which was usually followed by a nuptial Mass.[67] In this instance, Person's declaration of martyrological marriage is followed by a ritual of communal drinking that is evocative of Eucharistic celebration, in a way similar to the case of Joyce Lewes:

> And being all three bound to the post, a certaine young man of Filmers acquayntaunce, brought him a pot of drinke, asking if he woulde drinke. Yea quoth Filmer, I thanke you. And nowe my brother quoth he, I shall desire you in the name of the liuing Lord, to stand fast in the truth of the gospell of Iesus Christe, whyche you haue receaued, and so taking the pot at hys hande, asked hys brother Anthony, if he would drinke. Yea brother Filmer quoth he, I pledge you in the Lord. And when he had dronke, he gaue the pot to Anthonye & Anthony likewise gaue it to Testwoode. Of which drinking their aduersaries made a iuesting stocke, reportyng abrode that they were all dronke & wist not what they said, when as they were none otherwise dronke then as the Apostles were, when the people sayd they were full of newe wyne, as theyr deedes declared. For when Anthonye and Testwoode had both dronken, & geuen the pot from them, Filmer reioysing in the Lord, sayd: Be mery my brethren, & lift vp your hearts vnto God, for after this sharp breakfast, I trust we shall haue a good dinner in the kingdom of Christ our Lord and redeemer. At the which words Testwood lifting vp his handes and eyes to heauen, desired the Lorde aboue to receiue his spirite. (1220)

The martyrs turn the offer of a final drink before their demise into a ritual display of fellowship in Christ, a performance that highlights their status as a mystical body in the moments before they transcend earthly life. Each punctuates his drinking with a pledge or prayer to Christ, transforming the act of drinking into a quasi-liturgical gesture that seals them together "in the Lord." As he recounts this scene, Foxe interjects a rejoinder to some of the more skeptical onlookers who joke that the men are simply getting drunk: "they were none otherwise dronke then as the Apostles were, when the people sayd they were full of newe wyne," affiliating this spectacle with Pentecost as it is narrated in the Acts of the Apostles (2:13–17). Foxe's allusion works, on one hand, to frame the scene in specifically scriptural terms, referring his readers to the text of the Bible for a full comprehension of its significance, while, on the other hand, it insists on heightening the dignity of the martyr's actions, identifying their act of drinking as a performance that marries spiritual and physical dimensions in a manner reminiscent of the sacrament of the Eucharist. Person's further references in the passage to the "sharp breakfast" of the stake to be followed by the "good dinner" in heaven and Testwood's "lifting vp his handes . . . to heauen" accentuate the potential Eucharistic resonance of this episode. Testwood's gesture is particularly interesting, as he had earlier been accused of disregarding the elevation in the Mass; here, at the point of his martyrdom, he performs a gesture of elevation, that, like others we have seen, asks to be read as a sign of true, rather than false, Christian sacrifice.

As these examples from the text illustrate, Foxe makes available to the burgeoning Protestant political order of Elizabeth a powerful rearticulation of the *corpus mysticum* grounded in martyrdom rather than the Mass. That this reorientation and rechanneling benefit—at least initially—the Protestant English political structure is made clear by the Elizabethan regime's sponsorship and promotion of Foxe's volume, often at key moments of crisis in the emergent English Protestant nation of the sixteenth and early seventeenth century: for example, the rebellion of the Catholic northern earls in 1569 was followed closely by the 1570 edition of *Actes and Monuments*. This tradition was carried through after the infamous Gunpowder Plot of 1605, which inspired another posthumous edition of Foxe's book in 1610. The next edition, 1641, appeared in the midst of fraught circumstances for the English monarchy and the state church on the eve of the outbreak of civil conflict.[68] The connection between moments of political and religious crisis and reprintings of *Actes and Monuments* suggests that the English nation cohered most closely as a *corpus mysticum* when it saw itself as the threatened sacrificial victim of a papistical enemy, a logic first encoded in Foxe's magisterial volume, which displaces the sacrifice of the altar to the sacrifice of the martyr. At the same time, however, this identification of the English nation with the "Persecuted Church" also instantiated a notion of an English *corpus mysticum* that proved difficult for future rulers to control, as the papistical enemy could morph readily into the legitimate sovereign, particularly in the theo-political imagination of more forward Protestants who found the national church insufficiently reformed. The most vivid instance of this reversal is, of course, the case of Charles I—but there too, the fundamental pliability of Foxe's narrative schema is also evident, as the last chapter of this book will explore. To briefly anticipate the argument of the final chapter, in *Eikon Basilike,* published at the very moment of the king's execution by Parliament in 1649, the monarch is again able to inhabit the role of the martyr, becoming the focus of a new series of national devotions that ultimately thwart the dream of a Puritan Commonwealth.

Foxe inaugurated a powerful discourse that competing religious and political factions attempted to harness for their own ends through the Restoration.[69] The "contradictory elements" in Foxe's work have been understood in temporal or apocalyptic terms, as when Damian Nussbaum describes the struggle between moderate and radical reformers in the Church of England in the 1580s: "To some the trajectory of [Foxe's] narrative pointed back: to the deliverance of the English church from forces of superstition and idolatry which had already been secured. To others his message also pointed forward: to a struggle in the cause of the gospel, which was yet to be won."[70] As I have argued in this chapter, however, this temporal "ambiguity" is also intertwined with a sacramental theology and a liturgy of martyrdom marked by another set of internal contradictions: a sacrificial performance that simultaneously evokes and effaces the rituals of its opponent, the "false church." These contradictions are written into Foxe's narrative in response to the pressure to formulate a reformed sense of the English mystical body. The fact that Foxe's martyrology was repeatedly resurrected at moments of collective crisis is a sign that this work did manage in some measure to construct a discourse with the resonant power to bind a larger community around the figure of Christian sacrifice.

The ritualized discourse of martyrdom that emerges from Foxe's work, however, also continued to exist alongside—as well as in tension with—older traditional notions of the *corpus mysticum* aligned with the Eucharistic celebration of the Mass. These conflicting concepts of the mystical body also intermingle with the commonplace allegory of the body politic—the comparison of the state to an organic body. As we have seen, the relationship between the body politic and the body mystical was often fraught, uneasy, and potentially violent, particularly after the Reformation. This uneasiness was heightened by the persistent ambiguity of the *corpus mysticum,* which is conceived and expressed in two idioms—Eucharistic and martyrological—intrinsically linked yet outwardly inimical to each other.

These tensions—between bodies politic and mystical, and between competing notions of the *corpus mysticum* itself—are most vividly exposed not in polemical religious literature, but in the tragic drama of the era. Shakespeare's *Titus Andronicus,* while nominally set in a pre-Christian Roman past, is intimately concerned with analyzing, through its extreme violence and multiple performances of bodily dismemberment, the paradoxical state of the mystical body in the aftermath of Foxe and the English Reformation. The language of the play is suffused with a metaphorics of the body politic that refers individual dismemberments to a larger state of communal disjunction. The designation of "martyr" is assigned to the victims of the play's most intensely violent episodes, inviting the audience to view these spectacles of violence as travesties of Foxean sacramental martyrdom. Further travesties of Eucharistic celebration are juxtaposed with these debased variations of martyrdom throughout the play. The interpenetration of both forms of travesty make it difficult to assign a clear religious allegiance to the play, but, taken together, they reveal a drama preoccupied with the trauma of an overdetermined yet dislocated mystical body. Reminders of England's own more recent religious trauma uncannily and anachronistically intrude throughout the play, opening the possibility for the audience to read the play's performance in terms of contemporary English religious crisis.

CHAPTER THREE

~

"Ruinous" Monasteries and "Martyred Signs"

Sacramental Travesty and the
Corpus Mysticum in *Titus Andronicus*

Critics have long sensed an intrinsic connection between Shakespeare's early Roman tragedy *Titus Andronicus* and Foxe's *Actes and Monuments*. As his history plays demonstrate, Shakespeare surely knew Foxe's book well, although, as most spectacularly illustrated in the Oldcastle/ *Henry IV* controversy, he was also quite willing to critique and revise Foxe's polemical representations of English history.[1] In its frequent evocations of the idea of the "martyr" and the act of "martyring" as analogues for its violence, *Titus Andronicus* has appeared to critics to invite its audiences to connect its theatrical spectacles to the spectacles of martyrdom portrayed in Foxe's masterwork.[2] The affiliation between *Titus* and Foxe's *Book of Martyrs* has usually been explored less in terms of topical references or historical source material,[3] and more in terms of general allusiveness: both works consist of repetitive, spectacular acts of violence, resulting in an impressive volume of tortured and dismembered bodies. Yet it is not only the sheer quantity of violence that links the works. Shakespeare's play expands the performative dimension of martyrological violence: it bodies forth live, on stage, myriad scenes reminiscent of Foxe's narratives, and, as a consequence, exposes fissures in the conventional martyrological formula.[4] In this bodying forth, I argue, *Titus Andronicus* implicitly critiques Foxe's martyrological mutation of the tradition of the *corpus mysticum*.

Such a critique can be traced in the degeneration of all the sacramental systems that potentially function as ordering forces in the world of the play. This encroaching degeneracy of sacramental order is not exactly, yet, a mode of secularization; the world of the play is not a secular one. It is notably a world where rituals of sacrifice and invocations of martyrdom still have a purchase, an effective and affective force. But this force is consistently turned awry; it disintegrates, rather than integrates, provoking violence instead of coherence. *Titus Andronicus* portrays a world where clashing, parodic sacramental performances produce travesties of a mystical body, a deviant *corpus mysticum* intimately bound up with the *corpus politicum* of Rome, and more obliquely, also with that of early modern England. Although its presentation of the mystical body is deformed, the play's insistent reiteration of sacramental motifs testifies to the continuing vitality of the idea of the *corpus mysticum* in the social and political milieu from which Shakespeare's theater emerges.

As previous critics have observed, Shakespeare's play is replete with mangled bodies that literalize metaphorical images of the body politic, usually in a state of disarray. This literalization of the traditional body politic metaphor begins at the opening of the play itself: the initial metaphor of a "headless Rome" (1.1.186)[5] is later rendered grotesquely literal in the fate of Titus's beheaded sons and mutilated daughter. Titus himself furthers this literalizing process at the outset in an ominous manner when he refuses to act as "head" of Rome ("a better head her glorious body fits / Than his that shakes for age and feebleness" [1.1.187–88]).[6]

In the most recent study to explore the affiliation between Foxe and Shakespeare's *Titus*, Thomas Anderson tellingly focuses on how the scenes of Eucharistic debate repetitively recounted in Foxe's volume form the subtext of religious trauma in Shakespeare's early tragedy.[7] For Anderson, what matters in these passages is a debate over the fundamental nature of performative language and signification: "The bloody battle over signifying practices was an encounter with crisis for a generation not able to process completely the drastic social and religious alterations as they occurred. The battle over signification that is repeated again and again in *Actes and Monuments* appears a generation later on the early modern stage. In the play's concern with vows, promises, and oaths, *Titus Andronicus* is haunted by the residue of what Foxe hoped to present as a tectonic shift."[8] Anderson substantiates this claim with subtle analysis of the way performative speech acts go awry throughout the play and contribute to its multiple vivid scenes of violence. In what follows, I seek to highlight how the rituals in which these wayward performatives occur are linked to the play's underlying preoccupation with a disoriented *corpus mysticum*.

In this chapter, I demonstrate how the much-noted, disturbed and disturbing relationship between literal bodies and figures of the body politic is intimately linked to the religious anachronism that pervades the play; taken together, I argue, these motifs allude to the derangement of a traditional *corpus mysticum*. The play unflinchingly explores the effects of this derangement even as it carefully displaces them into an uncanny, decadent Roman setting. The play is strewn with moments of sacramental travesty, where precisely the sacrifice of the body—the making sacred of the body—becomes a site of confusion and conflict.[9] These travesties insistently couple religious and political trauma throughout the play. *Titus* obsessively stages rituals that produce distortedly sanctified bodies that signal the disintegration rather than the reintegration of collective bodies (familial, social, and political), conjuring a perverse kind of *corpus mysticum* at odds with the older medieval Christian tradition.

From a perspective that seeks to limn the *corpus mysticum* haunting the play's dismembered body politic, what is most striking is the fact that the arguments that Anderson reproduces from Foxe all concern the status of the sacrament of the altar, the status of this body in the Mass.[10] As we have seen, such debates do not *only* concern the issue of signification. More precisely, as I have argued in the previous chapter, the issue of performative signification played out in these debates is intimately intertwined with a sense of the sacrament as a communal bond, with a whole notion of society produced in and through sacramental performances. Viewed in this light, the trauma permeating the play is also a trauma of the social-mystical body rent by disputes over the efficacy of the rituals that have traditionally composed it. As we have seen, Foxe's martyrs are witnesses for an English *corpus mysticum;* they form a counter-hierarchy grounded in performances of martyrdom that act as displaced versions of the Mass, a technique that enables this effort at an English history to assimilate the weight of traditional belief and practice at the same time that it seeks to obliterate it. In my argument, *Actes and Monuments* stands as an ironic testimony to the cohesive social force of the traditional sacramental celebration, even as it makes a strenuous effort to negate that force by substituting its martyrological narratives for it. *Titus Andronicus* is another document of this trauma, haunted equally by Foxe's martyrs and the sacramental world of traditional religion. *Titus* stages the tensions that strain Foxe's reformed *corpus mysticum,* as neither martyrological nor sacramental performances induce social cohesion or charity among citizens; instead, they are implicated in spasmodic outbursts of violence that produce the "shattering" effect of the play.[11]

The crisis of performative speech that runs throughout the play is intertwined with figures of a ritually constituted mystical body. This is discernible in the defaced yet still quasi-legible motifs of a medieval and Christian sacramental corporate body, which intrude anachronistically at key moments in the action. While this anachronistic mystical body shadows the dismembered individual bodies in the play (Lavinia, of course, and others), it also subtly pervades the figures of speech, the ritual actions, and even the imaginative settings of the play. Despite a nominally pagan setting in Rome, the play is littered with anachronistic allusions to sixteenth-century Christianity in crisis. Such allusions are deeply woven into the revenge plot: Tamora's accusation of "irreligious piety" (1.1.133), provoked by the sacrifice of her son, is followed by the deaths of Titus's sons (the first at the hands of his father) and, ultimately, the deaths and cannibalistic consumption of yet more Goth sons, a sequence that introduces a strain of Eucharistic travesty into some of the most urgent and memorable moments of the play. Titus in particular increasingly emerges as a master of sacramental travesty as the revenge plot develops, most notably in his killing of Chiron and Demetrius, which is, in certain aspects, staged as a mock sacrifice of the altar.[12] Yet earlier Titus also, like his extravagantly mutilated daughter, is fleetingly associated with the ruined structure of the body of the church, a trope that turns these traumatized bodies into indexes of theological and political trauma. These central events are further embellished with references to "martyred signs" (3.2.36), "limbo" and [heavenly] "bliss" (3.1.150), and a "ruinous monastery" (5.1.21) and "popish tricks" (5.1.76), allusive emblems of religious and political controversy in Reformation England.[13]

These intrusive anachronisms can invite readings of the play as a topical allegory that encodes messages of allegiance to one party or another, Protestant or Catholic. For example, Jonathan Bate finds a pro-Reformation allegory in the ruined monastery that anomalously materializes in act 5, an intrusion that will be addressed at greater length later in this chapter. Bate makes much of the fact that it is a Goth who beholds the "ruinous monastery" (5.1.21): "The Goth's meditation upon Henry VIII's dissolution of the monasteries, the most drastic consequence of England's break with Rome, carries forward the *translatio imperii ad Teutonicos* . . . 'the idea that humanity was twice ransomed from Roman tyranny and depravity—in antiquity by the Goths, in modern times by their descendants, the German reformers.'"[14] Bate assumes that this incident shows how the play favors the changes wrought by the Reformation in England. Lukas Erne, however, suggests a radically different reading of the same evidence, noting that the "Reformation context" that Bate identifies in the "ruinous monastery" seems to be colored by a distinctly Catholic perspective. Erne frames the monastery with a review of well-known points of biographical speculation about Shakespeare's own Catholic background to justify connecting the collapse of metaphorical and literal bodies in the play to the schism of the Reformation. He finds an echo of "the Pauline metaphor of the body as the universal church" in one of the final body images in the play, Marcus's expressed desire to heal the shattered community of Rome: "to knit again . . . These broken limbs again into one body" (5.3.69–71).[15] Erne's claim identifies the body of Christ, the Pauline figure for the church, derived most famously from 1 Corinthians 12, and a major source for the medieval concept of the *corpus mysticum,* as a crucial conceptual subtext for the play. If the play is imagined to harbor some distinct Catholic sympathies, the mutilated bodies on stage, most notably the play's "central visual image," the dismembered Lavinia, figure a more general dismemberment of the church "as several members cut themselves off from" it.[16] Erne's intuition that the play's violence is somehow obscurely related to a larger trauma to the Christian *corpus mysticum* is provocative and will be developed at greater length in what follows. However, the claim that the play depicts a mystical body in crisis need not be justified—as Erne does—by speculating about Shakespeare's own religious allegiances. As my argument will show, one effect of the play's shattered *corpus mysticum* is that it renders impossible any definitive religious identification of characters and actions; the impossibility of determining religious identity extends to the author of the play as well.

Whether one assumes Shakespeare was writing from a predominately Protestant or Catholic perspective, theological trauma powerfully underwrites some of the most visceral language in the play. Both of these arguments have some persuasive power, but, in crucial ways, they are irreconcilable. This irreconcilability highlights the inadequacy of any simple topical reading of the play. The play's pervasive concern with bodily mutilation, along with the much-noted tendency of individual bodies in the play to signify collective as well as individual identity, urge a recontextualization of the play's religious concerns that both draws upon and also goes beyond what previous criticism has already illuminated about the historical and religious content of the play. What emerges from this recontextualization is less a tragedy that takes sides in the religious controversies of the sixteenth century, and more one that gives expression to a deeper shattering of social and spiritual experience in the wake of the English Reformation.[17]

The play's engagement with the state of religious and political fragmentation in the early modern era is illustrated not only by its popularity in the late sixteenth century, but also by its revival later on, in the uneasy aftermath of the Civil Wars of the mid-seventeenth century, of a conflict in part stoked by the lingering religious tensions that inflect Shakespeare's play. Edward Ravenscroft granted *Titus Andronicus* a notable afterlife in the Restoration with his 1686 adaptation, which curiously begins by disavowing the essential structure of the play at the same time that it revives its vivid spectacles of violence to serve a new political agenda. On one hand, it is Ravenscroft who famously proclaims the original play "the most incorrect and indigested piece in all his Works; It seems rather a heap of Rubbish then a Structure," an oft-quoted remark that links Shakespeare's earliest tragedy with the idea of ruins for the subsequent history of criticism.[18] On the other hand, unlike later critics, Ravenscroft evidently understood the value of the "Rubbish" of *Titus* as a vehicle for trenchant religious and political critique, as his adapted script attempts to address the lingering wounds of civil conflict and religious hysteria in Restoration England. Ravenscroft's *Titus* specifically positions itself as a critique of the notorious "Popish Plot" and the closely related effort to "exclude" the Catholic James II from the English throne.[19] That Shakespeare's late sixteenth-century tragedy proves adaptable to the post-Civil War circumstances of late seventeenth-century politics suggests that the play's representation of civil conflict, including phantasmic plots that produce spirals of self-consuming, religiously inflected violence, touches on a deeper vein of trauma that runs throughout the history of Reformation England.

A "Sacrifice of Expiation": *Titus Andronicus,* Act 1

The difficulty of pinning down the play's religious politics is exemplified in the opening act, which stages a propulsive "sacrifice of expiation" (1.1.37) framed by fraternal and filial violence, through which Titus the classical Roman becomes shadowed by "a travesty of Abraham's submissive faith in God."[20] Long before the contested monastery looms in the background, the tragedy opens with a sacrificial ritual that simultaneously travesties medieval sacramental practices and the martyrological performances familiar from Foxe as it sets the stage for the subsequent cascade of violence. Previous critics have suggested that the opening sacrifice of Alarbus, which marks Titus's fleetingly triumphant reentrance into Rome, contains a dark parody of the Catholic Mass that is evocative of the polemical assaults of the Reformers.[21] As in Reformist parodies of the supposed literalism of the Catholic Mass, the sacrifice of Alarbus in 1.1 consists in physical, bloody violence performed in the name of a communion with a supernatural order. The play invests this quasi-sacramental ritual with a power that puts bodies—in the individual as well as collective sense—in relation to the sacred to protect their integrity.[22] Alarbus is a living body sacrificed to make the dead work for the living instead of against them.

That this sacrifice does not ultimately work toward its stated end potentially echoes a Protestant critique of Catholic "works" as misdirected; more broadly, however, the sacrifice of Alarbus conjures the specter of a negative *corpus mysticum* emerging from the misappropriation of religious rituals. Typical Protestant critiques of the sacrifice of the Mass (such as those reiterated continuously in Foxe's *Book of Martyrs*) often argued for the total inefficacy of the ritual, its status as a fraud or fiction. The sacrifice of Alarbus, by contrast, is not exactly inefficacious, but rather all too efficacious insofar as it initiates a contagion of violence, inspiring acts that repeat the mutilation and consumption of this initial victim. This sacrifice does work to ensure a continual communication between political and mystical bodies, but in a mode of contaminating violence rather than peaceful reconciliation. Moreover, the sacrifice of Alarbus, which from one perspective looks like a parodic Mass, from another perspective can seem like a parody of a typical scaffold scene in Foxe's *Actes and Monuments*. The potential association with *Actes and Monuments* is heightened by the scene's curious emphasis on burning the remains of the victim, a detail which conspicuously recalls the Marian martyrdoms recorded by Foxe.[23] If the sacrifice of Alarbus enacts a version of the conflated spectacles of Mass and martyrdom that suffuse Foxe's work, then it is this conflation that the play implicitly critiques through the larger arc of its plot. This overdetermined sacrificial ceremony provokes a violence that ultimately consumes nearly everyone in the play; it rends rather than binds a community, the fractured Rome of the play, which the audience is intermittently invited to identify with Reformation England.

The sacrifice is inserted into the opening of the play in a curiously stuttering manner. It is first referenced as if already completed in a long speech by Marcus, which looks toward the naming of Titus as emperor to forestall the civil strife between the brothers Bassianus and Saturninus, whose conflict threatens to tear apart Rome. Marcus acting in his role as tribune first announces the will of the body politic:

> Know that the people of Rome, for whom we stand
> A special party, have by common voice
> In election for the Roman empery
> Chosen Andronicus, surnamed Pius
> For many good and great deserts to Rome. (1.1.20–24)

The fraternal feud, reminiscent of the biblical conflict between Cain and Abel, is to be healed by the candidate chosen by the "common voice," the incorporate will of "the people of Rome." Titus's "surname Pius" evokes simultaneously associations with the Virgilian "Pius Aeneas" and the often-taken name in the papacy, the most recent of whom, Pope Pius V, excommunicated Elizabeth I.[24]

In a textual anomaly that may or may not be the result of an authorial oversight, Marcus goes on to report Titus's ritual actions upon his return to Rome: "at this day / To the monument of the Andronici / Done sacrifice of expiation, / And slain the noblest prisoner of the Goths" (1.1.35–38). Marcus's report of the "sacrifice" of the Goth as something that has already happened appears to contradict the staging of the sacrifice of Alarbus later in the scene, a detail which has led some critics to view these lines as a "false start" in the text.[25] For the current argument, it appears most significant that even in its initial reportage, the sacrifice opens a gap in the coherence of the action in the play. Its status in time and space is indeterminate, as what seemingly has been performed offstage will almost immediately be performed again onstage before the audience.

The textual problem of the repetitive, self-canceling sacrifice is symptomatic of its connection to the larger problem of sacramental travesty, rituals turned awry, in the play overall. Marcus's peculiar phrasing compounds the instability of the sacrifice in the text: "sacrifice of expiation" raises again (as with "Pius") overtones of Christian anachronism. As Helga Duncan observes, for the earliest audiences of the play, the phrase "must have hinted at the debate over the nature of the sacrifice of the Mass and the space in which the Eucharist was celebrated."[26] In this regard, the reference to the sacrifice as a fait accompli that is then canceled by a repetitive staging, at virtually the same moment that Titus is hailed as the savior of the corporate body of Rome, has ominous implications: the sacrifice is a warp in the fabric of the play and potentially the social world of Rome in which it is set. The repetition and uncertainty of the sacrifice mark it as potentially divisive, rather than healing. This is a quality that the subsequent, strangely redundant and compulsive staging of the ritual will expand upon. As the scene unfolds once the rest of the Andronici have appeared on stage, the instigator of this ritual travesty turns out to be, significantly, Titus's son Lucius. The last of the Andronici left standing at the end of the play—the surviving son, charged with the task of "knit[ing] again . . . these broken limbs" of Rome "into one body" (5.3.69–71)—Lucius is the character who will be ultimately responsible for restoring the *corpus politicum* of Rome. At the beginning of act 1, it is this same Lucius who appears as the guardian of a peculiar kind of *corpus mysticum*. Even more precisely, he functions in a quasi-priestly role, explicitly concerned with the interface between bodies mystical, natural, and political. In this capacity, Lucius takes on the role of the initiator of a ritual of sacrificial violence—the very ritual that sets in motion the cycle of violence that tears apart the body of his family as well as the body of the state.

This ritual consists of literally sacrificing an enemy Goth to heal the wounds incurred by the body of Rome in the most recent war:

> Give us the proudest prisoner of the Goths,
> That we may hew his limbs and on a pile
> *Ad manes fratrum* sacrifice his flesh
> Before this earthly prison of their bones,
> That so the shadows be not unappeased,
> Nor we disturbed with prodigies on earth. (1.1.99–104)

According to Lucius's demand, the proper body of the family extends from the realm of the living to the realm of "the shadows." It is this spectral family that must feed, vampirically, on the living body of the foreign Goth. This spectral family is granted a mystical dignity as it is renamed in "*Ad manes fratrum*," a sliding into Latin that enhances the sense that this scene belongs simultaneously to the world of classical heroism and cryptic liturgical ritual. Without the sustenance of the sacrifice, the spectral brothers threaten to turn on their living kin, to "disturb" them with "prodigies"—unnatural or supernatural forms of persecution. The sacrifice of Alarbus's "flesh" is designed to forestall the disintegration of this vulnerable haunted body.[27] Lucius's immediate concern centers on the welfare of a collective entity, the Andronici family, united by a common blood and a shared kinship. This family is metonymically related to the larger body politic of Rome, as Titus the patriarch signals in his first oxymoronic line of the play, addressed to the corporate body of the city, which includes Marcus and Lavinia, members of his immediate family: "Hail, Rome, victorious in thy mourning weeds!" (1.1.73). Lucius seeks to perform a ritual sacrifice to protect the integrity of the living corporate body of his family (and, by extension, Rome) from disruption by quasi-mystical "shadows," whose existence is nonetheless intimately tied to both family and city.

This sacrifice, however, does not stabilize the relationship between the mystical body and the living corporate body; instead, it compromises the body of the family further. Titus reinforces Lucius's conception of the relationship between the living and dead family when he turns aside Tamora's plea for the life of her son:

> These are their brethren whom your Goths beheld
> Alive and dead, and for their brethren slain,
> Religiously they ask a sacrifice.
> To this your son is marked, and die he must,
> T'appease their groaning shadows that are gone. (1.1.125–29)

Titus's insistence on going forward with the sacrifice ironically binds the Andronici to the alien Goths at the most intimate level from the beginning; the Goths simultaneously divide and connect the "brethren" (both "alive and dead"). Despite its professed goal of reconciling natural and supernatural bodies, an irresolvable principle of divisive violence is inscribed in the "religiously" demanded "sacrifice" from the outset. The crimes that must be "appeased" are displaced onto the Goths, but are in fact shared by the Romans who fear the "groaning shadows" that seem to persist in a purgatorial state.[28] This "sacrifice of expiation," which resonates in some ways superficially with Christian notions of sacrifice, ultimately becomes a travesty of Christian sacrifice—featuring motivations that are at best mixed as well as an unwilling victim and supernatural overseers who are shadowy and sinister.

In his description of the act of sacrificing Alarbus, Lucius inadvertently forecasts the manner in which travesties of sacrificial violence afflict both individual and collective bodies in the rest of the play. Lucius urges: "Let's hew his limbs till they be clean consumed" (1.1.132). Lucius's command, of course, eerily anticipates the fate of the mutilated Lavinia. His desire to have the body "clean consumed," however, has wider implications, for the "consumption" of bodies does not end with the "lopped" Alarbus, but rather only expands to other victims, as the significance of this sacrifice moves from a restricted to a general economy.[29] Worse than futile, the sacrifice actually spreads mutilating violence like an infection to the other bodies in the play. These performances of violence insistently blur distinctions between interior and exterior aspects of the civic body of Rome, pushing the logic that Lucius articulates to justify the sacrifice of Alarbus to the extreme limit. By the end of act 1, Titus has sacrificed his own son Mutius as well as Tamora's, in a rage inspired by a lack of submission to a code of family honor (a sacrificial rage which some have seen as a parody of the biblical Abraham).[30] At the same time, Tamora replaces Lavinia as Saturninus's bride and has become "incorporate"

(1.1.467) in Rome, moving from enemy to citizen in the space of a scene. By the end, act 5, there is no meaningful difference between Romans and Goths; indeed they have switched positions, becoming the army of the "true" Romans. In an anticipation of the trajectory of *Coriolanus,* the Andronici ultimately must merge with the Goths to retake Rome.[31]

In this initial act, then, the sacrifice, which is initially cast as a form of work that will stabilize relations between social, political, and "mystical" bodies (the supernatural "shadows" that Lucius invokes), instead becomes a means of unworking or undoing the coherence of these bodies. This sacrifice ironically represents a means of disassembling and dismembering bodies as well as investing them with political and theological significance: it inaugurates the generalized dislocation of ritual and ceremony that represents the disintegration of the *corpus mysticum* throughout the play. Tamora's desperate outburst in response to the prospect of her son's ritual murder—"O cruel, irreligious piety!" (1.1.133)—articulates a critique of Titus's relentless drive to sacrifice that subverts the very sense of Titus's surname "Pius." It also evokes a general condition of theological and political crisis, which, as the play will go on to imply, also afflicts Shakespeare's historical moment. This interchangeability of piety and irreligion is bound up with a larger interchangeability of suffering that is evident before the end of the first act of the play, as the bodies of Roman and Goth sons are chiastically exchanged in episodes of ritual killing. Tamora's exclamation on the verge of her son's sacrifice may represent, as Robert Miola has argued, an appeal to a universal "humanity,"[32] but it may also have a more specific resonance. If Alarbus can be cast as a type of martyr (a term freely used to describe later victims in the play), then this martyrdom in turn references the state of martyrdom in Shakespeare's England, as both Protestant martyrologies such as Foxe's *Actes and Monuments* and Catholic martyrologies such as Richard Verstegan's *Theatrum Crudelitatum Haereticorum Nostri Temporis (A Presentation of the Cruelty of Heretics in Our Time,* 1587)[33] publicized sacrificial victims of religious schism as a mechanism for reassembling a form of *corpus mysticum* in the midst of Reformation tensions.

When it is shared across confessional divisions, the rhetoric of martyrdom implies a general failure of traditional ritual performances to achieve a minimal level of social and religious coherence. In the world of *Titus,* failed or misaligned rituals always exacerbate, and never contain, violence. The disjointed character of the opening sacrificial episode—and its status as a Christian anachronism that invites audiences to connect the staged spectacle to more contemporary traumas—is underscored by a telling detail in Lucius's final commentary on the end of Alarbus. Returning to the stage following Tamora's outburst, Lucius proclaims:

> See, lord and father, how we have performed
> Our Roman rites: Alarbus' limbs are lopped
> And entrails feed the sacrificing fire,
> Whose smoke like incense doth perfume the sky. (1.1.145–48)

In conflating the smell of incense with the smell of burning human flesh, Jonathan Gil Harris suggests, Shakespeare is not offering a "doctrinaire debunking of Catholic ritual" but rather enabling a manifestation— a "symptom"—of a larger theological trauma: "a widespread sense of confusion and loss generated by the abolition of censing and the pathologization of smell."[34] Harris focuses on the relatively neglected aspect of smell in tracking the shifting borders between theater and religion in Shakespeare's work. I would like to emphasize, in turn, that the sensory confusion that Harris reads as a metonym for wider religious disarray is explicitly framed in terms of sacramental travesty and encompassed within a perversion of the larger tradition of the *corpus mysticum*. This incensed smoke exudes from the "perfor[mance]" of "our Roman rites" which are submitted to our "lord and father" for approval. Lucius, the character performing the "lopping" and burning, proceeds to the burial ritual without a trace of irony about figuring the "smoke" of burnt flesh as "incense," as if he had lost all coordinates for distinguishing sacred ritual from its travesty. This confusion of "incense" and martyrological "smoke" also indexes the conflation of the sacrifice of the altar in the Catholic rite with the sacrifice of the Protestant martyr burned at the stake that Foxe promotes throughout *Actes and Monuments*. That such a conflation is referenced—and cast as a form of travesty—at this initial crisis point in Shakespeare's drama suggests that the play is profoundly concerned with the ill effects of sacramental confusion. This sacrificial performance spectacularly fails to deliver the promised beneficial dynamic between the human and supernatural worlds; instead, it promises further civil violence. In this regard, the sacrifice of Alarbus initiates a persistent pattern of allusions to a dangerously deranged Roman *corpus mysticum* that runs throughout the play.

Scrambled parallels to the sacred history of Christian scripture as well as variations on Christian ritual in pagan trappings thus abound in this opening scene. In contrast to revenge tragedies like Kyd's influential *Spanish Tragedy,* or Shakespeare's later *Hamlet,* however, the supernatural or transcendent dimension never itself directly intervenes

in the play. In lieu of the representation of direct supernatural intervention, ever more explicit religious anachronisms intrude in the course of
events. These anachronisms anchor the free-floating spiritual anxiety and
dislocation of the initial act of *Titus Andronicus* in a specifically English
sixteenth-century scene of religious trauma.

Although the text is usually dated from the early 1590s, the play's pattern of anachronisms references a somewhat earlier trauma—the 1530s
Henrician Reformation. These references heighten the play's concern
with the fate of the *corpus mysticum,* as its final events unfold against a
background defined by the absorption of the *corpus mysticum* into the
corpus politicum. This is the development we traced in detail in chapter 1's analysis of Henry VIII's break with Rome. In *Titus,* then, we can
see how classical Roman archaism is actually interwoven with references
to a trauma of the more recent past, the upheavals of the early English
Reformation. The most vivid of these references is the perplexing ruined
monastery that marks the opening of act 5 of *Titus Andronicus.*

"A Ruinous Monastery": *Titus Andronicus,* Act 5

Although *Titus Andronicus* is set in a Rome on the brink of ruin, the
ruins that actually materialize in the play are the anachronistic ruins of
the Roman church in England. The anomalous "ruinous monastery"
(5.1.21) that materializes at the beginning of the final act refers the
relentless rending of particular, individual bodies throughout the play to
the larger trauma of the English Reformation even more overtly than
the sacrifice of Alarbus. This ruined monastery emblematizes the Dissolution of the Monasteries that marked the beginning of the Reformation
in England in the late 1530s and left scars on the physical landscape of
England that are visible even today. As an emblem of confused agency
and degraded spiritual life, the "ruinous monastery" becomes a metonym for the lost coherence of the English *corpus mysticum* in the era of
the Reformation. The adjective "ruinous," which hovers between active
and passive forms of destruction and decay,[35] can imply a force that
ruins itself, an agent as much as object of ruin. The image of a "wasted"
religious house reinscribes the figurative network of maimed rites, martyrdom, and mangled bodies of the preceding acts into a more proximate
historical trauma for Shakespeare's audience.

The monastery that evokes this trauma materializes in the play in the
gaze of a curiously wayward Goth soldier. As we have seen, the possible
religious identity of this Goth has been the occasion for some substantial

critical commentary. Less noted, however, is how the Goth's narration conveys a phenomenology for the intrusion of religious anachronism in the play. The Goth is given several lines to narrate his offstage discovery of the main villain, Aaron, and his newborn son. Before moving to the story of the discovery, he briefly describes the perverse impulse that leads him to the site:

> Renowned Lucius, from our troops I strayed
> To gaze upon a ruinous monastery,
> And as I earnestly did fix mine eye
> Upon the wasted building, suddenly
> I heard a child cry underneath a wall. (5.1.20–24)

While Philip Schwyzer argues that the Goth looks at the monastery with an interest "similar to that of a tourist in a strange country,"[36] the act of "stray[ing]" casts the Goth's "gaze" as subtly transgressive. The Goth describes an act of contemplation that involves cutting himself off from the main body of his comrades, a gesture that mimics in miniature the relation of the resistant Catholic community to the larger English body politic during the Reformation. The Goth "stray[s]" from his companions as if irresistibly drawn to the spectacle of the ruined religious edifice. This "straying" culminates in a quasi-devotional "earnest" and "fix[ed]" gaze, a pose of reverence rather than simple curiosity. He approaches this strange relic of religious turmoil with a kind of quiet awe. At the same time, he emphasizes the disintegrated state of the structure by renaming the "ruinous monastery" a desacramentalized "wasted building." The Goth's captivation with the dissolved religious house allows him to penetrate the secret tableau at the heart of the devastated building to perceive a scene of corruption, Aaron and his bastard son, within the "waste."

Aaron's sudden and abrasive shift into a distinct Puritan idiom upon discovery further heightens the sense that the "ruinous monastery" has opened a strange zone of temporal dislocation in the play. Aaron's discourse reinforces the anachronism of the "ruinous monastery" insofar as it also registers the pressure of a peculiarly English Reformation trauma. While Aaron's language throughout the play consists of a shifting pastiche of styles (ranging from parodies of Virgilian epic to Marlovian bombast), this particular idiom, which we might call "reprobate Puritan," does not emerge until late in the play, when he is discovered amid a scene of religious ruin. Aaron adopts this Puritan mode of expression when negotiating with Lucius over the fate of his son, as he insists on oaths that he portrays as empty and idolatrous:

> Yet I for know thou art religious
> And hast a thing within thee called conscience,
> With twenty popish tricks and ceremonies
> Which I have seen thee careful to observe,
> Therefore I urge thy oath; for that I know
> An idiot holds his bauble for a god,
> And keeps the oath which by that god he swears,
> To that I'll urge him, therefore shalt thou vow
> By that same god, what god soe'er it be
> That thou adorest and hast in reverence. (5.1.74–83)

In this tirade, Aaron lapses into pseudo-Puritan jargon, the language of radical purifiers who sought to purge England of its "popish" past, often through acts of iconoclastic violence. Aaron's discourse echoes the rhetoric of disenchantment associated with Reformed theology.[37] The Reformist elements in this speech lie not simply in the pejorative "popish" but also in the implicit critique of the idea that "oaths" and "baubles" have any supernatural efficacy. Yet, in the hyperbole of Aaron's ranting, the "religious" is assimilated to the "popish" as "god" is reduced to a "bauble," a rhetorical flourish that implicitly equates the discourse of radical Protestantism with a general dismissal of the divine as such.[38] Aaron's extremism suggests that such discourse destroys the idea of divinity, rather than protecting it from idolatrous corruption, as Reformers would have it. Juxtaposed with the "ruinous monastery," Aaron's heretical language reinforces the sense that a shattered *corpus mysticum* shadows the actions of the archaic characters at this moment in the play.

These intrusions—Aaron's Puritan cant and the eerie ruins of religious dissolution—enable an early modern audience to transpose the play's general violence into terms that reflect a profound spiritual disorientation afflicting Elizabethan England. Framed by religious ruin, Aaron and his son embody this disorientation. Previous critics have attempted to wrench this peculiar father and son into a coherent allegory. For example, Clare Asquith has suggested that if Aaron represents a radical Puritan and Tamora in crucial ways functions as a double for Elizabeth, the black child in the ruined monastery represents the English church after the Elizabethan Settlement.[39] While Aaron's discourse at this moment in the play is inflected with radical Protestant clichés, as noted, it does not necessarily follow that the scene yields such a clear-cut allegory. The cumulative effect of the juxtaposition is to underscore the transformation of religious spaces and "ceremonies" into politic schemes—a transformation in alignment with the thrust of Aaron's corrosive rhetoric. In other words, the ruined monastery and the disenchanted "bauble" of the religious oath are both contiguous with a *corpus politicum* that inhabits the empty shell of a formerly "reverenced" *corpus mysticum*. Lucius's compliance with Aaron's demand ("Even by my god I swear to thee I will" [5.1.86]) does not so much reinforce his identity as a crypto-Catholic Roman as demonstrate his fundamental inability (like that of all other figures in the play) to maintain any meaningful spiritual orientation in a reality defined in such politic terms.

Shakespeare merges Aaron's parody of Protestant anti-ceremonialism with the theatrical typology of Marlowe's Barabas to emphasize the politic schemes that deform the implicit *corpus mysticum* in the play. Another possible frame of reference for Aaron's emergence from the monastery is the milieu of his acknowledged theatrical predecessor, Barabas, *The Jew of Malta*.[40] Even more than Aaron, Barabas moves within a range of sanctified spaces—not only the monastery where his final act of revenge turns into his own undoing, but also the convent created by the Christian absorption of his former home in Malta. Aaron, like Barabas, the anti-Christian Machiavel, resists assimilation to Christian forms; his echo of Barabas again draws attention (in a negative way) to the anachronistic religious subtext of the tragedy. Aaron's discourse goes beyond Barabas's, however, in its erosion of the linguistic forms in and through which the mystical body might take shape. This erosive force is linked to Aaron's weird vitality in the play. In striking contrast to Barabas, who murders his own daughter after her conversion to Christianity, Aaron is notoriously concerned with protecting the future of his progeny. Indeed, Aaron's will to empty out "ceremonies" into mere forms is undertaken for the benefit of his son, the beneficiary of the "oath" that he demands, a son who does indeed live on, curiously exempt from the sacrificial spectacles that consume nearly every other child in the play.[41] Aaron's notable desire to save his son via feigned religious devices contrasts sharply with the aged patriarch, "Pius" Titus, who demands the sacrifice of his own children as well as Tamora's. Despite their antagonisms, however, Titus and Aaron ironically converge by the close of the play: Titus's arrangement of the final action of the play in ritualistic terms (the "martyrdom" of Chiron and Demetrius and the subsequent banquet) mirrors Aaron's politic contempt for the purported transcendent ends of "ceremony" more than it does the flawed aspiration to reconcile natural and supernatural bodies in the sacrificial opening of the play. Aaron's diatribe thus exemplifies a larger, relentless process through which the figures for the mystical body are distorted and hollowed out by politic rhetoric in the play.

The monastery in *Titus* may be understood as meta-theatrical in the sense that it evokes the milieu of Marlowe's Malta as much as Reformation England. However, as Julia Lupton has shown, the conditions of theatrical performance in London (in the liberties, the grounds of dissolved monasteries that persist outside normal legal jurisdiction) serve to merge the scenes of Malta and sixteenth-century England—both enact the "expropriation" of religious capital (and religious difference) into political ("politic") schemes.[42] The monastery in *Titus* is more unassignable—it is not clear that it properly belongs to anyone, but neither is it entirely neutral. In this obscurity we can perhaps measure the distance between Marlowe's overt anti-Catholic satire (of which Barabas is the primary exponent) and Shakespeare's more elliptical relation to the contemporary state of religious schism in England. Aaron's relation to the ruined monastery is more associative than instrumental.

In summary, Aaron's diatribe, which casts "popish tricks" as politic devices, mirrors the spiritual emptiness of the "wasted" monastery. Together, these emblems at the opening of act 5 reflect into each other to form a mise en abyme. Here, the remnants of a medieval mystical body are reconfigured as constituent elements in a sequence of politic machinations. The emergence of this constellation of religious anachronisms at this late point in the play is foreshadowed not only by the sacrificial travesty of act 1, discussed in the previous section, but also by more subtle allusions to the dissolution of medieval religious life in prior acts. In these earlier instances, as well as in the final denouement of the Theyestian banquet, it is Titus himself who most forcefully articulates the disarticulation of the mystical body. This occurs most particularly in a previously overlooked allusive interlude in act 3, where, in a prelude to the onslaught of bodily dismemberment, Titus cryptically casts himself as a foresworn Catholic pilgrim.

Titus's Cryptic Pilgrimage: Chaucerian Baroque and the Dismembered *Corpus Mysticum*

Act 3, scene 1 is perhaps the scene most rife with bodily mutilation in the tragedy. Titus embarks on a fruitless intercession on behalf of his deviously imprisoned sons near the beginning of this act, and the scene will culminate in the revelation of Lavinia's multiple mutilations, Titus's own lost (self-mutilated) hand, and two headless sons. This excessive dismemberment overtly reflects the disintegrating effect of Saturninus's reign of tyranny, particularly as it has "incorporated" Tamora's Gothic drive to revenge herself on the Andronici for the sacrifice of Alarbus. From this perspective, the rent bodies of Titus and his children allegorically stand in for the mutilations of the body politic by an unjust regime. However, the speech with which Titus opens the scene seems keyed to an anachronistic religious register that invites audiences to find the fate of the body mystical intertwined with that of the body political. As with the subsequent enigmatic appearance of the ruined monastery, as it was cross-referenced with Aaron's rabid Reformist speech, the *corpus mysticum* implied by the religious anachronism appears fatally compromised by politic schism.

Indeed, there is a subtle anticipation of the later reference to the "ruinous" religious house in the complex initial speech of 3.1. Titus's speech conflates ruined bodies with ruined buildings in a way that expands into a larger conflation of individual suffering with collective spiritual trauma:

> For all my blood in Rome's great quarrel shed,
> For all the frosty nights that I have watched,
> And for these bitter tears which now you see
> Filling the aged wrinkles in my cheeks,
> Be pitiful to my condemned sons,
> Whose souls is not corrupted as 'tis thought.
> For two-and-twenty sons I never wept,
> Because they died in honour's lofty bed.
> For these two, tribunes, in the dust I write
> My heart's deep languor and my soul's sad tears.
> Let my tears staunch the earth's dry appetite;
> My sons' sweet blood will make it shame and blush.
> O earth, I will befriend thee more with rain
> That shall distil from these two ancient [ruins][43]
> Than youthful April shall with all his showers.
> In summer's drought I'll drop upon thee still;
> In winter with warm tears I'll melt the snow
> And keep eternal springtime on thy face,
> So thou refuse to drink my dear sons' blood. (3.1.4–22)

As he engages in a futile effort to save his sons from the deadly judgment of a Roman tribunal, Titus incongruously compares his eyes to "ruins" that will "distil" a rain of tears to outface all the seasons of the year; later in this same scene, Titus also promises to "bow this feeble ruin to the earth" (3.1.208), comparing his entire body to a ravaged building collapsing into base matter under the burden of its age and abuse.

These embodied "ruins" are embellished in the baroque style of the poetry of tears: in lines that vividly evoke the sacramental poetics of the Counter-Reformation, Titus establishes a chiastic exchange of tears for blood, one bodily fluid supplanting the other. Titus pleads to forestall the "earth" who seeks to "drink my dear sons' blood." This image of Eucharistic travesty is echoed later in the more literal corrupt sacrifice of Chiron and Demetrius, in which Titus promises that Tamora will "like to the earth swallow her own increase" (5.2.191) when she is served the "pasties" concocted from her sons' flesh. In the latter case, the "earth" provides an image of the devouring mother, consuming herself in the form of her own progeny. Each scenario presents an inversion of the ideal Mass insofar as the sacrificial imagery is oriented toward a form of absolute destruction rather than a hope of salvation. Nonetheless, both instances function as antitypes that also recapitulate the central elements of the type in distorted form. The sacramental undercurrent in both passages refers the performance of violence beyond the physical realm to convey a state of spiritual disintegration; in this sense, both correspond to the dissolution of the *corpus mysticum.*

The blood and tears figuratively issuing from Titus's "ruin[ed]" eyes organize the lament for his sons according to the coordinates of both medieval religious ritual and newer devotional practice. "Blood" as the substance of Christian salvation and Eucharistic celebration and the fluid medium of martyrdom, past and present, persistently crosses into "tears," emblems of religious devotion and penitence associated with the Counter-Reformation poetics imported into England in the 1590s by Jesuit missionary martyrs such as Robert Southwell. Southwell's "poetry of tears" was designed, in part, to offer consolation for the persecuted English Catholic minority of the time.[44] Most specifically, his verse seeks to imaginatively reconstruct an English *corpus mysticum* in the face of the loss of access to traditional sacramental life.[45] In contrast, Titus's tears appear to lack even the efficacy to console, much less to perform effective intercession on the part of the doomed sons. The inefficacy of these tears and the apparent rejection of weeping itself by the end of this scene may be read as "a critique of Catholic tearfulness at a time when it was of very little practical or political help," as Anna Swärdh, the critic who has gone the furthest in drawing out the Southwellian resonances of this scene, has suggested.[46] As with other instances of religious anachronism, however, this speech cannot be easily reduced to a straightforward political allegory.

The literary dimension of this speech's response to contemporary English Catholic crisis enfolds a secondary allusion, one which refers back to a relevant point of medieval political and religious conflict. It contains a scrambled but nonetheless legible imitation of the famous opening of the "General Prologue" to *The Canterbury Tales,* which emerges in the midst of Titus's hyperbolic chiasm of tears and blood:

> For these two, tribunes, in the dust *I write*
> My heart's deep languor and my soul's sad tears.
> Let my *tears* staunch the earth's dry appetite;
> My sons' sweet *blood* will make it shame and blush.
> O earth, I will befriend thee more with rain
> That shall distil from these two ancient *ruins*
> *Than youthful April shall with all his showers.*
> *In summer's drought I'll drop upon thee still;*
> In winter with warm *tears* I'll melt the snow
> And keep eternal springtime on thy face,
> So thou refuse to drink my dear sons' *blood.* (3.1.12–22,
> emphasis mine)

The allusion is signaled in this section of the plea by the lines that refer to "tears" that "write," which anticipate the intertextual character of the lament that follows. In the subsequent lines, Shakespeare's text encodes an echo of Chaucer's setting for the fourteenth-century pilgrimage to the shrine of the "hooly blisful martir," Thomas Becket, in *The Canterbury Tales:*

> Whan that Aprill with his shoures soote
> The drogute of March hath perced to the roote,
> And bathed every veyne in swich licour
> Of which vertu engendred is the flour;
> Whan Zephirus eek with his sweete breeth
> Inspired hath in every holt and heeth
> The tender croppes, and the yonge soone
> Hath in the Ram his half cours yronne. (1–4)[47]

This verbal echo has not, to my knowledge, been previously noted. However, the resonance between the two texts is striking. Titus imagines his tears in Chaucerian terms; his grief cites the cosmic frame of Chaucer's "Aprill," only to wrench it out of joint.[48] The "shoures" or "showers" of April that Titus promises to outface are "youthful," recapitulating the "yonge sonne" in the sign of Aries in Chaucer's text. Shakespeare's lament displaces the "drought" from "March" to "summer," thereby disrupting the temporal coordinates of Chaucer's "Prologue." Titus's distressed monologue also contains the idea of being "bathed": in tears (rather than rain) that perpetually "drop" on a seasonally dislocated landscape. This incongruous allusion fits into the larger pattern of anachronism in the play which gestures toward an English Catholic world in fragmentation.[49] While this evocation could be read as nostalgia for the lost coherence of a medieval world, it also functions as a reminder that this lost world crystallized around a prior eruption of violence contesting the relative integrity of the *corpus mysticum,* although one with a different outcome and effect.

This Chaucerian allusion sutures Titus's chiasm of tears and blood to a specifically English Catholic past of pilgrimages and martyrs' shrines. The shrine of Thomas Becket, the destination of Chaucer's pilgrims, is the site of a prior conflict between political and religious powers. Here, the *corpus politicum,* as championed by Henry II, failed in its effort to overcome the immunity of the institution of the church, the provenance of the *corpus mysticum.*[50] The martyr of Canterbury marks an earlier episode of the conflict between bodies of church and state that returned with a vengeance in the reign of Henry VIII in the mid-sixteenth century. The cryptic reference to Chaucer's medieval springtime pilgrimage in Shakespeare's scrambled citation simultaneously reveals and conceals a critique of this later attack.

If the dismembered Chaucerian allusion represents the impossibility of a return to the conditions of fourteenth-century religious life, it also memorializes the site of this loss somewhere between the blood and tears of Titus's futile supplication. By the early 1590s, the time of the first performances of *Titus,* the destination of Chaucer's pilgrims had been razed, its shrine ruined, its martyr disavowed and literally dismembered.[51] The principle of church immunity intimately linked to the autonomy of the mystical body of the church, that Becket's shrine once represented, had been thoroughly nullified by another King Henry, in a more successful and lasting challenge. From this perspective, the dismemberment within the Chaucer allusion could recall the irrevocable loss of a prior sacramental order. Nonetheless, this allusion, it is essential to recognize, fails finally to coalesce into either a sustained memorial or a coherent critique. The language of the lament mimics the self-destructive logic of this larger historical turmoil. The text dismantles the full force of the allusion at almost the same moment that it appears. Titus drowns this allusion out within a few lines with the even more charged vivid imagery of his own "warm tears" replacing "my dear son's blood." While this final chiasm masks the literary allusion, it actually amplifies, rather than dilutes, the sense of sacramental disorientation inflecting Titus's speech. In this sense, the self-disintegrating allusion to Chaucer, as embedded in Titus's intercessory speech, corresponds to the pattern found in the sacrifice of Alarbus and the "ruinous monastery"; taken together, these elements constitute a constellation of moments that are also symptoms of a breakdown in the coherence of traditional religious signification. The remainders of traditional religion maintain an expressive force, however, even as their spiritual content is partially obscured by the explicit crisis of the revenge plot.

Lavinia becomes the locus of the sacramental breakdown implied in Titus's futile lament upon her entrance with Marcus shortly after these lines. The dislocated allusiveness of Titus's complaint prepares the audience for the spectacle of the "ravish'd" and dismembered Lavinia. Her appearance immediately and repeatedly provokes the question "who hath martyred thee?" (3.1.82; 105) from both Titus and his son Lucius. This persistent query casts sexual violation as a trope for spiritual devastation. The invocation of "martyrdom" for Lavinia's state is, in strictly Christian terms, inappropriate.[52] However, the obsessive casting of Lavinia as a "martyr" functions in a similar way to the other instances of religious anachronism in the play. It lends an intensity of expression to a crisis that is personal and political, but not explicitly religious; it draws attention to the way a religious figure of speech or motif may be wrenched away from its original context and applied to an alien circumstance. In this process, perhaps most vividly in the case of the dismembered Lavinia, this usage summons the image of a distorted *corpus mysticum* shadowing the stage performance, particularly if we recall the way Foxe adapts the ideals of the sacramental *corpus mysticum* to Protestant martyrology. Titus reinforces the association between Lavinia and a shattered *corpus mysticum* later in the scene, as he purports to make an empathetic connection to her plight: "O, what a sympathy of woe is this; / As far from help as limbo is from bliss" (3.1.149–50). Again, Titus articulates trauma in anachronistically Christian terms: Lavinia is exiled from "bliss," and she instead inhabits "limbo"—the supposed sphere of the sacramentally bereft, unbaptized infants. Yet even in this broken state, Titus posits a "sympathy"—an affective, unspeakable connection that links Lavinia to those around her. All present (actors as well as audience) become, in this "sympathy," a community "of woe." Titus emphasizes her debased state with religiously tinged language that reassembles, fleetingly, a kind of mystical body, yet one conjoined around the image of the loss of a sacramental world, rather than its achievement. Lavinia may most terrifyingly embody a ravaged mystical body, but her ability to occupy such a position depends on the audience's ability to read the network of subtle, cryptic religious anachronism that envelops her disfiguration. In inviting such a reading, the play ironically offers to reconstitute a negative approximation of the *corpus mysticum* among the audience.

The play's use of Lavinia to evoke a negative mystical body most vividly emerges in the next scene, when Titus explicitly portrays Lavinia as a defaced religious image. As in the previous scene, Titus adopts the posture of penitent pilgrim, deprived, however, of an unspoiled devotional destination. This pose is struck in the midst of a "banquet," as the Andronici family has withdrawn into the home to tend to its wounds:

> Come, let's fall to, and, gentle girl, eat this.
> Here there is no drink! Hark, Marcus, what she says:
> I can interpret all her martyred signs—
> She says she drinks no other drink but tears,
> Brewed with her sorrow, mashed upon her cheeks.
> Speechless complainer, I will learn thy thought.
> In thy dumb action will I be as perfect
> As begging hermits in their holy prayers.
> Thou shalt not sigh, nor hold thy stumps to heaven,
> Nor wink, nor nod, nor kneel, nor make a sign,
> But I of these will wrest an alphabet
> And by still practice learn to know thy meaning. (3.2.34–45)

Titus frames the problem of interpreting the inner life of the mute Lavinia in language saturated with religious trauma. He imaginatively constructs a shrine around his daughter's iconic mutilated body, positioning Lavinia as a saint's image as he casts himself as a worshipful devotee, a "hermit" at "holy prayer." Titus portrays the effort to make Lavinia legible within a sacramental system as curiously both violent (a matter of "wrest[ing] an alphabet") and passive ("still practice"). In either case, Lavinia's broken gestures represent a language that must be relearned precariously, if at all, under extreme circumstances. Her mutilated condition not only outdoes that of her classical precursor, Ovid's Philomel, but also invokes the sixteenth-century phenomenon of saints' images marred by iconoclastic violence: images with lopped hands and scarred faces that, like monastic ruins, littered the landscape of Shakespeare's England.[53] With this religiously charged conceit, Titus transposes Lavinia's visible injuries, the "stumps" that she "hold[s] . . . to heaven" in a mutilated gesture of prayer, into marks of a wider communal experience of desecration.

The same speech in which Titus draws attention to the indecipherable character of Lavinia's "martyred signs" occurs in the midst of a "banquet" marked by signs of sacramental impoverishment: Titus enters his quasi-devotional address to Lavinia as he urges her to "eat" and highlights a lack of "drink" at the table ("Here there is no drink!"). Indeed, some critics have suggested that the scene mimics elements of the celebration of the Mass.[54] This "banquet," however, is marked by the absence of the Eucharistic sustenance conventionally associated with the *corpus mysticum*. Instead, Titus, the "begging hermit," a lost pilgrim or poor substitute for a priest, can only gesture toward "martyred signs." These "signs" turn out to convey that, for Lavinia as well as her family, there is "no other drink than tears," a figure which again evokes the Southwellian poetry of tears. As suggested in the discussion of Titus's tears in 3.1, this trope marks the loss or lack of the body of Christ in the Mass and the common body of believers, the community in Christ, centered around it (Southwell's Magdalene weeps in an exemplary manner over the absent body of Christ, doubling the position of English Catholics who have lost the "real body" of Christ in the Mass).[55] Here, however, it is Lavinia's shattered body that is the locus of sorrow, a body that Titus momentarily casts as a ruined religious icon and fleeting emblem of a disintegrated *corpus mysticum*.

Titus's address hints at an allegorical significance that, like Lavinia's indecipherable "martyred signs," ultimately cannot coalesce into a coherent, consoling religious message. It signifies, most tellingly and expressively, a mystical body communally joined around loss and absence. As in previous episodes, the signifiers of a shattered sacramental body in the play cannot resolve themselves into a consistent allegory. The focus of act 3, scene 2 abruptly shifts after this speech to a parodic, quasi-sacrificial victim, the fly. Marcus's announcement, "Alas, my lord, I have but killed a fly" (3.2.59), provokes a brief tragicomic exchange at the end of the scene that anticipates the final sequence of sacramental travesty in the play, even as it blurs the allegorical implications of Titus's address to Lavinia.

The Two Banquets of Titus: Travesties of Communion

Imagery of hunger and self-consumption underscores the isolation of the Andronici family in the "banquet" scene of 3.2: there "is no drink" and Lavinia only drinks her "tears." The communal meal is also empty otherwise; the family ultimately sustains itself on "old stories chanced in the times of old" (3.2.84) and on "false shadows" rather than "true substances" (3.2.81). This emptiness reflects the exile of the family from the larger body politic of Rome at this point in the play. Given the overtones of sacramental deprivation, this desolation may more generally reflect the spiritual isolation of Catholic families in the Reformed world of Elizabethan England,[56] cut off equally from regular participation in the sacraments that constitute the traditional *corpus mysticum* and full social relations with the wider world around them. This state of famine is, however, briefly forestalled by the arrival of a fantastic sacrificial victim: the fly. The fly provides the minimal occasion to revive a semblance of ritual life within the family, however fleeting and ridiculous, an occasion that again conflates the liturgies of the Mass and the martyr. A further exploration of this unlikely figure will reveal its relevance to the larger network of allusions to the concept of the mystical body in the play.

If the dolorous "banquet" evokes in some ways a disjointed, sacramentally bereft Mass, then the "fly" constitutes a miniature sacrifice at the center of this debased ritual, a comic version of the more serious ritual travesties that take place throughout the play.[57] The absurdity obscures the potentially critical edge of Titus's earlier deployment of religious imagery. In this way, the play protects itself from being read as a straightforward allegory of religious politics. However, on another level, this absurdist episode exposes a deeper disorientation of religious ritual that is pertinent to the more serious moments in the tragedy. Marcus initiates the comic sequence by stabbing at the table:

> TITUS: What dost thou strike at, Marcus, with thy knife?
> MARCUS: At that that I have kill'd, my lord—a fly.
> TITUS: Out on thee, murderer. Thou kill'st my heart.
>   Mine eyes are cloyed with view of tyranny;
>   A deed of death done on the innocent
>   Becomes not Titus' brother. Get thee gone;
>   I see thou art not for my company.
> MARCUS: Alas, my lord, I have but killed a fly.
> TITUS: "But"?
>   How if that fly had a father and a mother?
>   How would he hang his slender gilded wings
>   And buzz lamenting doings in the air.
>   Poor harmless fly,
>   That with his pretty buzzing melody
>   Came here to make us merry, and thou hast kill'd him.

MARCUS: Pardon me, sir, it was a black ill-favoured fly,
    Like to the empress' Moor. Therefore I killed him.
TITUS: Oh, Oh, Oh!
    Then pardon me for reprehending thee,
    For thou hast done a charitable deed.
    Give me thy knife; I will insult on him,
    Flattering myself, as if it were the Moor
    Come hither purposely to poison me.
    There's for thyself, and that's for Tamora.
    Ah, sirrah!
    Yet I think we are not brought so low,
    But that between us we can kill a fly
    That comes in likeness of a coal-black Moor. (3.2.52–79)

In this exchange, the fly embodies the cryptic, self-effacing rhetoric of the play by appearing first as a creature that is an innocent victim ("poor harmless fly"), who then abruptly becomes the deserving enemy ("Pardon me, sir, it was a black ill-favoured fly, / Like to the empress' Moor. Therefore, I kill'd him"). Although this comic banter about the fly seemingly distracts from the play's intermittent representation of the effects of Reformation trauma, it more profoundly embodies and illustrates the disjointed logic driving such violence, as the arbitrary collides with the absolute in the rapid redescription of the fly as innocent, then guilty. The fly embodies, in miniature, the contested figure of the Reformation martyr, whose status as holy victim or heretic was the subject of endless debate among religious adversaries.

As it recapitulates such debates, the figure of the fly here recalls, in parodic form, the play's initial sacrifice of the Goth Alarbus—the play's initial martyr—to the specters of the Andronici. In parodying itself, the play at this instant also consumes itself; it destroys itself as pure tragedy or coherent allegory. Like the fly, Alarbus at the point of his death conjures directly conflicting redescriptions; he is cast, in turn, as the blameless victim of cruel and empty ritualism ("cruel, irreligious piety" [1.1.133]) and an expiating sacrifice to dangerous spiritual forces ("t'appease their groaning shadows" [1.1.129]). Despite the elaborate ritual surrounding it, Alarbus's end, like the fly's, appears arbitrary as a result of these shifting registers of meaning. To paraphrase Marx, the fly repeats the pattern of Alarbus's sacrifice: if the first instance is tragic, the second is farcical. The fly paradoxically disrupts and reinforces the genre of the play; the comic and trivial intrude on the scene of high tragedy but also recapitulate this tragedy in diminished form. The echo effect of the fly episode—in particular, its repetition of key aspects of the opening ritual sacrifice—highlights how ritualistic action has become even more alienated from any reference to a coherent spiritual or social dimension by this point in the play. In this regard, in addition to glancing back at the opening of the tragedy, the banquet of 3.2 foreshadows the final apocalyptic sacrificial meal of act 5. This culmination of ritual travesty marks the violent progress of events in the play from the sacrifice and child-killing at the beginning.

The play ends with a recapitulation of the opening sacrifice of Gothic son(s) and an Andronici child. Despite Robert Miola's assertion that the concluding Thyestean banquet of *Titus Andronicus* "has nothing to do with the Eucharist,"[58] many other critics have discerned Eucharistic overtones in the banquet sequence of 5.2 and 5.3, "where the flesh of sons is consumed in a ghastly parody rather than an echo of the body and blood of Christ."[59] The critical tendency to find allusions to the Eucharist in the culminating banquet calls attention to the underlying paradigm of the *corpus mysticum* in the play. It is true, however, that the most obvious "precedent, pattern and lively warrant" (5.3.43) for Titus's plan is the Ovidian tale of Procne and Philomel, the myth repeatedly cited throughout the play and recalled again by Titus himself in his address to Chiron and Demetrius. Another classical text, the Senecan revenge tragedy *Thyestes,* is also a recognized influence, however, one that potentially reinforces the play's allusions to sacramental crisis.[60] Jasper Heywood's English translation of *Thyestes* (1560) suggests a vantage point from which the Thyestes allusion in *Titus* can function as an image of the havoc wrought on the commensalism of the traditional *corpus mysticum* in the wake of the Reformation.[61]

Heywood, a future English Catholic exile and Jesuit, was militantly Catholic—Thomas More's nephew and John Donne's uncle—in the highly charged circumstance of Reformation England. His translation of *Thyestes* was completed at a particularly tumultuous time: during the transition from Mary Tudor to Elizabeth, 1558–60, in the midst of the Elizabethan Settlement, which reinstated the Tudor Reformation. Thyestes's enforced cannibalism resonates with related, ongoing controversies about the status of the Eucharist—the issue of Real Presence in the sacrament of the sacrifice of the altar. On one hand, the tragedy's portrayal of ritualized cannibalism could be read as reinforcing a Protestant parody of the Mass, which was ridiculed as cannibalistic in concept by Reformers. However, from another angle, *Thyestes* could be read as a portrait of religious tyranny, one which enforces a kind of sacramental travesty on an unwitting subject: Atreus's ritual slaughter and preparation of Thyestes's sons are clearly cast as twisted perversions of religious sacrifice in both the Senecan text and Heywood's translation. More particularly, Thyestes is the victim of a tyrant, his brother Atreus, who is conspicuously willing to twist sacrificial rituals to his political advantage—to destroy his brother's competing claim to power. In its portrayal of a tyranny that becomes manifest through a grotesque parody of a fundamental religious ritual, then, the tragedy may speak to English Catholic concerns at the moment that the Marian Counter-Reformation was on the brink of being turned back in favor of a return to a Reformed Church of England. The English translation includes subtle indications that such a reading is possible. In act 4 of Heywood's translation (third scene), for example, the translation gestures more strongly than the original toward the feast as one of communion, as Atreus frames the meal as a bond between brothers, again taking the play toward ritual travesty—the horrible feast grotesquely subverts the very bond that it is supposed to reinforce. Atreus proclaims: "Let us this daie with one consent (o brother) celebrate. This day my steptors may confirm and stablyshe my estate, / And faythfull bond of peace and love between us ratifye" (*Thyestes*, Heywood translation [1560], 2398–2402).[62] The translation adds the idea of "love" to the "pacem" of the original, a Christianizing touch. The actual feast, of course, carries exactly the opposite meaning—it is divisive and destructive. Thyestes's position as the unwitting victim of Atreus's false "bond of peace and love" could also be related to the experience of English Catholics enduring, yet again, the replacement of the Catholic Mass with the communion service mandated by the Protestant Book of Common Prayer.

The entire final scene added by Heywood himself (not in the Latin original), is, as John Kerrigan notes, a kind of prayer for divine vengeance.[63] It begins, however, with Thyestes evoking a place reminiscent of purgatory, notably "lothsome Lymbo lakes" (2700), where Thyestes himself—who "makes his broode his cursed foode" (2705)—is still too monstrous to be admitted. Thyestes is exiled from even the horrors of the afterlife (foreshadowing also, strikingly, Heywood's own incipient exile). Heywood's Thyestes underscores how he has outdone even his grandfather Tantalus, who attempted to feed his son to the gods, and who appears as the inciting Fury at the beginning of Seneca's tragedy: "Thou [Tantalus] slewst thy son, but I my sons, alas have made my meate" (2745). Thyestes's "wombe" as his children's "tombe" has displaced hell itself in its atrocity. Yet even this displacement seems to fail: the "gates of hell" do not swallow Thyestes as he seems to wish or request. Supernatural response is withheld: "Why do ye thus thy infernall feendes, / so long from hens witholde?" (2783–84). Interestingly, this is a reversal of stoic *sympatheia,* as the natural and supernatural worlds fail, in this final supplement, to respond to the horrible condition of Thyestes. It is in response to this perceived failure or lack of divine response that Thyestes frames his prayer for vengeance. It is possible to understand this exiled Thyestes, subject of sacrificial travesty, as figuring a sense of desolation and spiritual abandonment on the eve of the recommencement of the English Reformation in 1559–60.

Heywood's translation thus potentially offers a model for the processing of ongoing religious trauma through an ambivalent engagement with classical texts, a model Shakespeare elaborates on in *Titus Andronicus.* The conflict between the brothers in Seneca's tragedy is mapped onto Titus's character in some complex and interesting ways; these resemblances underscore the fundamental ambiguity of Titus's character in relation to the religious subtext of the play in the final act. Thyestes's plight as an exile from both political power and divine recognition mirrors Titus's situation in some ways; although Titus does not literally consume his children (the fate reserved for Tamora), he does kill them at several points in the play. Titus also mirrors Atreus, however, particularly toward the end of the play and most specifically in his maniacal plotting of the sacrifice and preparation of Tamora's sons. Titus may be a more sympathetic figure than Seneca's Atreus, but in planning his banquet, he shows himself to be equally willing to travesty sacrificial rituals, rituals that are cast even more overtly as akin to Christian practice than in Heywood's translation.

Titus conflates the idea of "martyrdom" with ritual elements and gestures reminiscent of a Mass as he prepares Chiron and Demetrius to be ritually sacrificed. This conflation evokes a dynamic similar to that of the opening sacrifice of Alarbus, and it heightens the repetitive, ritualistic undercurrent of Titus's actions. However, this very repetition also draws attention to a degeneration of the motive and purpose of the ritual activity. While the earlier sacrifice was "cruel," it at least purported to achieve the higher goal of appeasing the purgatorial spirits of the dead Andronici. In this final sacrifice, the cruelty is heightened, but so is the vacancy of purpose. Titus uses the trappings of religion and sacramental ritual paradoxically to enhance the debasement of his victims. His plan aspires to exceed their prior violence with a carefully plotted theater of cruelty, which turns out to be a repertoire of performative gestures borrowed (again, anachronistically) from Christian practice. Thus, he addresses Chiron and Demetrius:

What would you say if I should let you speak?
Villains, for shame you could not beg for grace.
Hark, wretches, how I mean to martyr you:
This one hand yet is left to cut your throats,
Whiles that Lavinia 'tween her stumps doth hold
The basin that receives your guilty blood.
You know your mother means to feast with me,
And calls herself Revenge and thinks me mad.
Hark, villains, I will grind your bones to dust,
And with your blood and it I'll make a paste,
And of the paste a coffin I will rear
And make two pasties of your shameful heads,
And bid that strumpet, your unhallowed dam,
Like to the earth swallow her own increase.
This is the feast that I have bid her to,
And this the banquet she shall surfeit on:
For worse than Philomel you used my daughter,
And worse than Progne I will be revenged.
And now prepare your throats. Lavinia, come,
Receive the blood, and when that they are dead
Let me go grind their bones to powder small,
And with this hateful liquor temper it,
And in that paste let their vile heads be baked.
Come, come, be everyone officious
To make this banquet, which I wish may prove
More stern and bloody than the Centaurs' feast. (5.2.178–203)

The sons are forced to occupy the same position that they have imposed
on Lavinia: bound, with mouths "stop[ped]," deprived of the ability to
respond or communicate. Titus heightens the affinity between the position
of these "villains" and Lavinia by referring to the act he intends to commit
with the infinitive "to martyr," applying the same term evoked by Lavinia's plight in an earlier scene ("Speak, gentle sister: who hath martyred
thee?" [3.1.82]). Both situations perversely play upon the original meaning of "martyr" as "witness."[64] While in the earlier instance, "martyred"
in the strictly Christian sense is an inappropriate adjective for Lavinia—
whose condition gives witness to a crime, rather than a spiritual truth—it
does emphasize Lavinia's position as one who suffers violence out of pro-
portion to her relative innocence. The term "martyr" applied to Chiron
and Demetrius in this situation more fully aligns with a juridical sense
of "witness," as Titus's treatment of their bodies will make their criminal

guilt manifest to all. The invocation of "martyrdom" here highlights not only the terrible symmetry Titus seeks to impose upon the victimizers of his daughter; it also signals how Titus will pursue his vengeance using religious rituals emptied of their spiritual significance and turned into deadly, politic weapons. This implication is reinforced by the line immediately preceding the allusion to martyring: even if they could speak, Titus claims, they would be unable to "beg for grace," a phrase which equates their enforced silence with an inability to participate legitimately in the ritual prayer that opens the celebration of a Mass. Thus, Titus positions the brothers as both mock sacrificial victims and deficient members of a mystical body; this positioning emphasizes how their fate functions as a parody of the body of Christ in both its pre- and post-Reformation forms.

Previous critics have noted that Titus's repeated injunction to "receive the blood" echoes the consecration of the Mass,[65] but recognizing how Shakespeare draws upon the tradition of the *corpus mysticum* in this speech, as elsewhere in the play, enables a more complete appreciation of the significance of these sacramental intimations. The invocation of the possibility of praying for "grace" ironically casts Titus as a type of priest, assembling a set of rituals that mimic the Mass, yet oppose its spirit. The injunction to "receive the blood" also casts Lavinia in a curious role: as, in part, a grim communicant but also a dutiful altar boy, facilitating the ceremony. Titus's subsequent command: "Come, come, be everyone officious / To make this banquet" casts efficacious action in terms of the fulfilling of a duty, or "office," in the sense of the term commonly applied to political and ecclesiastical positions. More significantly in the context of Titus's anti-Mass, "officious" evokes the liturgical sense of "office" as an "authorized form of divine service or worship," traditionally associated with the service of Holy Communion.[66] Titus thus seeks to expunge the evil of Tamora's sons through a ritual that both literalizes and travesties the elements of the Mass, as bodies devoid of "grace" nonetheless become subject to the "office" of ritual preparation for a communal meal. Like the transubstantiated Eucharistic wafer, the "paste" that Titus confects conceals the real presence of a body, but this confection will defile the communicant, exclude her from proper human society and ultimately affirm Titus as the politic master of ritual travesty.[67]

As in other instances in the play, these allusions to traditional Christian practice are mingled with classical allusions that make the ultimate point of reference obscure. As expected, Titus cites Ovid's tale of Procne and Philomel as the classical precedent for the violence that he seeks equally to imitate and surpass, an allusion and aspiration that seem to draw Titus's actions away from a Christian frame of reference. However, at the very end of this passage, Titus alludes to another episode from Ovid, the Centaurs' Feast (*Metamorphoses*, 12.239–592).[68] In Ovid's account of the feast, as translated by Shakespeare's contemporary, Arthur Golding, the violent breakdown of communal celebration is emphasized as cups and implements of eating are thrown about: "Things serving late for meate and drinke, and then for bluddy frayes" (12.273).[69] The Centaurs' Feast is also a wedding feast, a feast associated with what would be a sacramental event (usually including a Mass) in a medieval Christian frame of reference. This secondary Ovidian allusion thus reinforces the sense that Titus seeks to stage a debased quasi-sacramental ritual. Imagining the banquet to come as a chaotic wedding feast strengthens the idea that Titus looks forward to performing an aberrant "sacrifice of the altar" in his long speech to Chiron and Demetrius.

The full effect of this sacrifice will only become evident in the midst of the social event, the "feast I have bid her to," the communal meal.[70] The truth of the feast is conveyed to the audience prior to the meal itself, in Titus's incorporation of the sons' "guilty blood" into "pasties," but it is the social ceremony of the banquet that must become the final vehicle of Tamora's destruction. At the beginning of the banquet scene, as Lucius and his Goths prepare to join their Roman hosts, Aaron is conspicuously excluded from participation; he is assigned "no sustenance" (5.3.6), marking his status as an outsider to the social and political order of the feast (and anticipating his final sentence of starvation). Marcus also draws attention to the supposed pacific purpose of the feast: "The feast is ready which the careful Titus / Hath ordained to an honourable end, / For peace, for love, for league and good to Rome" (5.3.21–23). The echoes of Atreus's false hospitality in *Thyestes* are particularly strong in Marcus's lines (although it is not clear that Marcus is aware of Titus's plan). Marcus envisions the feast as a communion that will heal wounds between rivals, encourage charity, "peace," and "love" and ultimately work for the benefit of the collective body politic ("good to Rome"). The actual feast that ensues, of course, achieves exactly the reverse of nearly all of these goals, although the purging of Tamora and Saturninus may be considered a "good to Rome." The unsettling question remains, however, whether the means of this purging—by travesties of sacrifice that empty out the "grace" or spiritual content of sacramental rituals in order to weaponize them to achieve revenge and political dominance—will indeed secure the corporate "good" of Rome. This is a question which the play raises implicitly, but to which it refuses to give a straightforward or reassuring answer. The indeterminacy reflects a subsistent and continuing tension in the political history of early modern England.

The speeches that Marcus and Lucius give immediately after the violent climax of the feast underscore the religious and political connotations of this cannibalistic banquet and its potential reference to a larger *corpus mysticum*. In the same imaginative and literal space as the banquet itself, Marcus recapitulates his position as tribune at the beginning of the play as he addresses himself to

> You sad-faced men, people and sons of Rome,
> By uproars severed, as a flight of fowl
> Scattered by winds and high tempestuous gusts,
> O let me teach you how to knit again
> This scattered corn into one mutual sheaf,
> These broken limbs again into one body. (5.3.66–71)

The resonance of these lines with the Pauline concept of the body of Christ and the medieval *corpus mysticum* tradition has already been noted at the beginning of this chapter.[71] The image of a reconstituted *corpus mysticum* at the end of *Titus Andronicus* may now be seen to be darkened by the multiple acts of sacramental travesty that have preceded it. Marcus's language does draw upon the traditional allegorical figures for the community of the church collected in the rite of communion. Most notably, the image of "scattered corn" to be joined in "one mutual sheaf" evokes the commonplace image, familiar from medieval commentary, of the bread of the Eucharist made of many grains symbolizing the gathering of many members of the church into the church as the body of Christ.[72] However, this traditional image of the *corpus mysticum* follows closely upon its grotesque travesty in the banquet, where the sons "baked in this pie" become themselves the food for their parent, "eating the flesh that she herself hath bred" (5.3.59–61), in a scene that culminates in violent death, not redemption. Given the way that Titus's travestied ritual killing and feast invert the traditional Mass and the institution of martyrdom, Marcus's immediate turn toward a language of reconciliation steeped in Christian tradition seems somewhat empty. It is not clear that the sacramental means for assembling "one body" in a mystical as well as political sense remain available after Titus's vengeful killing spree. Shakespeare's play evokes a longing for a "mutual," communitarian order at virtually the same moment that it evacuates the very forms for constituting such an order familiar to an Elizabethan audience.

The figurative exile of Aaron and Tamora appears to be an inevitable aspect of the sacramental refoundation of the community of Rome that Marcus projects, yet it also disturbingly shadows it in significant ways.

There is a curious symmetry to their fates, again, as they both turn on the question of eating or being eaten as a marker of belonging to the human community. In effect, in imposing these penalties, Lucius continues his father's project of wreaking revenge through crypto-religious rituals of consumption and burial.[73] The still-living Aaron is condemned to be deprived of food: "Set him breast-deep in earth and famish him / There let him stand and rave and cry for food" (5.3.178–79). Lucius's command also forbids any relief of this condition upon pain of death; feeding Aaron is equated with reintegrating him into the community.[74] Strikingly, Aaron's response to this sentence relapses into the Reformist-tinged discourse introduced earlier in act 5:

> I am no baby, I, that with base prayers
> I should repent the evils I have done.
> Ten thousand worse than ever yet I did
> Would I perform if I might have my will.
> If one good deed in all my life I did
> I do repent it from my very soul. (5.3.184–89)

Aaron reacts to Lucius's sentence by summoning again some curiously Puritanical atheistic vitriol. He rejects the idea that he will utter "base prayers" to "repent" in response to Lucius's condemnation—instead, he insists he will only repent "good deeds," an absurdist parody of the common Reformist argument against the salvific value of "good works." As with Aaron's earlier diatribe, it is difficult to grasp the precise significance of this lapse into parodic Puritan cant. It again represents an intrusion of the language of contemporary religious controversy into the archaic world of the play, inviting audiences to see the characters through a Reformation prism. One possible effect of Aaron's rhetoric is to delegitimize the force of Lucius's punishment—by refusing "base prayers" and "good deeds," Aaron exempts himself from the *corpus mysticum* of Rome—and, in this very contrast, draws attention to the possibility that this theological concept underlies the concluding sequence of the tragedy. His discourse casts the potential spiritual import of his "starvation" as an empty, merely politic device, a base power play that he would overwhelm with "ten thousand worse" if he had his way. Thus, Aaron's final curses ironically reinforce the implications of Titus's ritual travesty earlier in the final act; these curses allude to the possibility of a larger mystical body even as they also seek to obliterate it as an actuality.

Tamora, on the other hand, is conspicuously deprived of burial "rites" by Lucius's command, in explicit contrast to Titus and Lavinia (who are, like Foxe's martyrs, to be "closed in our household's monument" [5.3.193]):

> No funeral rite, nor man in mourning weed,
> No mournful bell shall ring her burial,
> But throw her forth to beasts and birds to prey. (5.3.195–97)

The forbidden "funeral rite" and particularly the "bell" again appear to refer to a religious context outside the classical world. Previous commentators have noted how Lucius's sentence recapitulates religious controversy about burial rites between Protestant and Catholic factions in Reformation England,[75] but these observations should be integrated with a recognition of the significance of the underlying paradigm of the mystical body in the play. As Tamora is deprived of a burial that is marked in traditional Christian terms, she is rendered food for animals, for "beasts and birds to prey" (with a possible pun on "pray"—the beasts will "prey" on her body, in lieu of Romans who will "pray" for her soul). Both punishments underscore how Aaron and Tamora are to be deprived of means to be "knit" into the "one body" of the Roman community. The fact that each of these punishments carries both physical and metaphysical implications suggests again that the body of Rome is imagined to be a *corpus politicum* enmeshed with a *corpus mysticum*. However, insofar as each punishment refers back in some way to Titus's vengeful banquet, each also functions as a reminder of how this *corpus* has only been reassembled through travesties that have turned quasi-Christian rituals into means of political destruction. The notable lack of charity in Lucius's sentences, as well as Aaron's resistant final mockery of the very premise of his punishment, undermine the certainty that this version of Rome will achieve redemption or even lasting stability.

Shakespeare's play obsessively summons forth figures evocative of a Christian *corpus mysticum* in the midst of a bloody and debased classical Rome. In doing so, his play underscores not an alternative spiritual universe, but, perversely, the present-absence of a salvific Christian horizon to transcend vengeful pagan Rome. The Roman setting acts as a screen that allows the play to reveal how the traditional tropes that figure the *corpus mysticum* have been dislocated in the aftermath of the Reformation. Thinly veiled by the screen of this fractured classical setting, *Titus* explicitly foregrounds, and sheds a critical light upon, the mechanisms through which the liturgical forms of the *corpus mysticum* are transposed into a martyrological idiom by Protestant writers such as Foxe after the Reformation. Through myriad scenes of sacramental travesty,

Titus argues that this transposition risks disintegrating the socially unifying principle of the mystical body.

Titus is notorious for its raw quality: its bombastic rhetoric and shocking violence—which reflect the vogue for revenge tragedy in the late sixteenth century—led critics for many years to dismiss it from the Shakespearean canon entirely or marginalize it as the inexpert product of a still-developing talent. However, insofar as this provocative, hyperbolic play displays traces of a deeper concern with the integrity of the mystical body as a social and sacramental concept, it can be connected in some unexpected ways to later Shakespearean dramas. The degenerate Roman world of Shakespeare's early tragedy, on the surface, seems quite distant from the cosmopolitan, urban milieu of Vienna in Shakespeare's early seventeenth-century comedy *Measure for Measure*. Yet *Measure* is a play that is also significantly concerned with the fate of the concept of the *corpus mysticum* in the Reformation, although the later work's engagement takes place in a different key. While *Titus* focuses on the spectacular conflation of the Mass and the martyr in its multiple, bloody stagings of sacramental travesty, this idiom is moved to the margins in the comic commercial world of Shakespeare's Vienna. While in the later play issues of social and sacramental integration are just as significant, due to changes in genre and political-theological context, they are articulated via a different set of tropes: in the language of economics and marriage. Although these tropes lack the visceral impact of the vivid martyrological spectacle of *Titus,* insofar as they also layer pre- and post-Reformation social and sacramental significance, they equally convey a sense of crisis, a crisis that emerges in the metaphoric language of money, debt, and trade, and is provisionally resolved—in uneasy tragicomic terms—in strained vows of marriage.

~

CHAPTER FOUR

"Coining God's Image"

The Fiscal Theology of the
Mystical Body in *Measure for Measure*

In his commentary on de Lubac's history of Eucharistic theology, Michel de Certeau suggests that the *corpus mysticum* constituted an "absent third term" in the evolving structure of the church.[1] According to his account, the *corpus mysticum* had bound the historical past of the church (embodied primarily in scripture) to its contemporary manifestation (enacted in the sacraments), but this suture slowly disintegrated until the religious crisis of the sixteenth century, when it was canceled out by the opposition between a scriptural Protestantism and sacramental Catholicism.[2] In the great interview scenes of act 2 of *Measure for Measure*, the Puritan Angelo and the Catholic Isabella play out a version of this effacement of the *corpus mysticum*, but the crossing of their positions takes place amidst an insistent rhetoric of economics and coinage that enables a third position between extremes to come back into view. The language of coinage represents the *res nullius* of the mystical body in the play, the "property of none," no proper single person, but rather a suprapersonal entity—God or the body politic. In other words, and beyond the particular bodies of Angelo or Isabella, the rhetoric of coinage emblematizes the larger, communitarian body at stake in this debate.

In her initial exchange with Angelo, Isabella argues for life and mercy for her brother, who has been condemned for fornication, in opposition to Angelo's "precise" insistence on his death according to the justice demanded by the letter of the law. In this interview (2.2), Isabella bases her arguments for mercy on a higher-order economic exchange, which is associated with the mystery of Christ's incarnation:

ANGELO: Your brother is a forfeit of the law,
    And you but waste your words.
ISABELLA: Alas, alas!
    Why all the souls that were were forfeit once,
    And He that might the vantage best have took
    Found out the remedy. How would you be
    If He which is the top of judgment should
    But judge you as you are? O, think on that,
    And mercy then will breathe within your lips
    Like man new-made. (2.2.94–104)[3]

Isabella generalizes the sense of transgression inherent in Angelo's legalistic "forfeit" to express metaphorically the common bonds of sinfulness binding together "all the souls" as spiritual debtors. In this rhetorical turn, Isabella also recasts the nature of the "law" that is the reference point of Angelo's original claim; in Angelo's formulation, Claudio is "forfeit" to an absolute law with power over life or death. In Isabella's twist, this law is simultaneously universalized and ameliorated: "all souls" are "forfeit," thus no human law produced in this fallen state can emulate the absoluteness of divine law.

Isabella's economic rhetoric in this passage reflects the traditional doctrine of the Atonement as formulated by Saint Anselm, which imagined the redemption of Christ in terms of a transaction or exchange between God and man, as mediated by Christ. Original sin amounts to a "debt" (something "forfeit") that humans themselves cannot pay. According to John Bossy's account of the doctrine, payment "could only be made by someone who was both God and man." Through his suffering and death, Christ, this God-man, restores the relation between the two parties "by an act of retributive compensation equal in weight to the offence committed."[4] The sacrifice that pays the debt is the "remedy" that replaces "vantage" in Isabella's argument. Isabella's economic language establishes a sense of the relation between divine and human as one of community or "kinship" (as Bossy puts it) disrupted and then restored: "all the souls" are the human community joined, through Christ, in a common destiny of sin and redemption, ideally moving toward a restored, more perfect relation with God. The terms of the economic transaction render the universe of divine judgment legible, as comprehensible as relations in the human commonwealth: community with God reinforces a sense of human community. Understood in this sense, economic language does not alienate, but actually deepens, the redemptive telos of Isabella's Catholic argument, which can also be read as consistent with Augustine's efforts to map out the City of God as a more sublime version of the City of Man. This conception of an economic relation between the divine and the human is consistent with the sacramental sociality of the *corpus mysticum,* a concept of Christian community also deeply rooted in Augustine's theology, as described in chapter 1. Indeed, we may understand this theo-economic concept of community as another idiom for describing the dynamic of the *corpus mysticum.*

Tensions between this Augustinian theology of the mystical body and more recent Reformation theologies of salvation and grace run throughout the exchange between Isabella and Angelo. In her next sentence, Isabella asks Angelo to locate himself within this wider scheme or community of divine-human relations: "How would you be . . ." Angelo, however, refuses to be personally located within such a scheme. Instead he resituates himself as the avatar of the impersonal law: "It is the law, not I, condemn your brother" (2.2.105). Retreating into this juridical figure and refusing to engage in the sacred economy that Isabella evokes, Angelo expresses his position as a logical extension of the Reformation theological stance that rejected the traditional conception of the Atonement. The idea of redemption as a clear economic transaction between God and man was significantly altered in Luther's doctrine of justification: faith alone justifies. Although Luther continues to accept the fundamental transaction between God and Christ to redeem humankind, he explicates this transaction in markedly more juridical, less communitarian terms.[5] God's decision about whom to save and whom to damn becomes incomprehensible and arbitrary from this perspective: "In Luther's penal or criminal theory of the Atonement, there was no transaction, the parties were not reconciled . . . since the act was purely one-sided. There was no natural or social axiom to explain God's accepting Christ as a substitute for man in general . . . it remained an impenetrable decision."[6] Angelo ventriloquizes this "impenetrable" juridical God in his line about the law. Consistent with the Puritan stereotype that shadows his persona, as an agent of judgment, he refuses to be located on a relational, economic continuum.

Isabella counters the inscrutability of Angelo's legalistic theology with an appeal to a more transparent economy of grace. She attempts to ameliorate Angelo's law by shifting his perspective to the supersession of the old law, a past under which all souls "were forfeit." The new law is actually closer to an economic contract, a deed sealed in the incarnation and sacrifice of Christ, the "remedy" offered by a "creditor" God.[7] However, Isabella's conceit interferes with the straightforward economic expectation of an exchange governed by the logic of profit or fiscal advantage, as it insists on a profit or "vantage" deferred, passed over in favor of the "remedy" of Christ's sacrifice (the original substitution that is the pattern for the play's series of "tricks"). Isabella imagines a fiscal theology of immediate loss and perpetual gain, in which God stands as the ultimate creditor and judge. Her argument about the "forfeit" souls attempts to level Angelo's authority, posing it in contrast, rather than continuity, with God's own authority, a point she emphasizes with her next move, to put this creditor God at the "top of judgment." Isabella presumes that provoking Angelo to dwell on his own sinfulness will lead to a spiritual rebirth from which he will emerge as the Pauline "New Man" ("O think on that, / And mercy then will breathe within your lips / Like man new-made") dwelling in the life of mercy rather than the death of the law ("For the Law of the Spirit of life *which is* in Christ Jesus, hath freed me from the Law of sinne and of death" [Rom. 8:2]).[8] "New-made" is not only reminiscent of Paul's rhetoric, but it also subtly continues the overtly economic language of the previous sentence insofar as it evokes an idea of "making" or fashioning akin to that involved in minting, stamping, and forming inchoate metal into the shape of a coin.

Measure for Measure is replete with images of men as coins, which are part of a larger pattern of economic imagery that interconnects the play's political and theological concerns. Isabella's use of economic language to describe a universal scheme of salvation and the emergence of the Pauline "man new-made" harkens back to the coinage language in the opening scene in which the Duke originally "elects" Angelo as his substitute (1.1), and it also anticipates Angelo's later imagery of coining as making or counterfeiting men (2.4.44–51). Although much of the criticism on *Measure for Measure* continues to focus on variations on the "King James version" of the play (the idea that the comedy addresses itself to issues of particular concern to the new ruler, King James),[9] the pervasiveness of economic tropes in the play has not escaped critical notice.[10] Indeed, attention to economic figures has appeared in some accounts as key to understanding how the play engages with some vexing social disorders of the early seventeenth century.[11] The topos of *economy* in the play might invite a version of Marxist analysis that seeks to reveal the divine face of the sovereign (corresponding to the divinely ordained kingship championed by James) as a mere façade for a more earthly concern with economic control. According to some variants of Marxist critique, any claims to divinity might appear as only an obfuscating superstructure veiling the material economic base that is the true driver of history. However, the concept of fiscal theology shows how a more subtle operation is at work, as the crucial substructure is *not only* material, *but also* mystical or theological.[12] The *corpus mysticum* translated into terms of fiscal theology shows how materialism and mysticism were inextricably intertwined in the premodern imagination. My argument stands in accord with Marx's claims that economic figures reveal fundamental structures of social relations. On the other hand, I insist that the structure of social relations revealed by economic tropes cannot be simply characterized as those of the material conditions of production. For the early modern imagination, as illustrated by Isabella's argument about the "forfeit" souls, economic language also conveys powerful traditional ideas about the integrity of the social world as a *mystical body*, a sacramentally constituted form of life.

It is nonetheless the case that *Measure for Measure* belongs to a hybrid era in which emergent secular notions of economic life, encouraged by Reformation critiques of medieval theological assumptions, exist in tension with older tropes of mystical economy. In this chapter, I argue that figures of coinage or economy register a debt to the older corporate tradition of the *corpus mysticum* and to related theo-political traditions that parallel *Christus* and *fiscus* (terms that referred, respectively, to the church and to the royal "purse" or treasury administered by the sovereign). Attention to patterns of economic language can deepen our understanding of how the play interrogates the nature of the social bonds that constitute the commonwealth of fictional Vienna and historical seventeenth-century London.

The rhetoric of coinage in the play gestures toward two distinct schemes of value that perpetually contaminate each other throughout: sovereign authority (political) and mystical community (spiritual or sacramental). As Kantorowicz shows, the conceptual link between the *Christus* (church) and the *fiscus* of the state lies in their status as *res nullius* (property of no one and everyone). And indeed, figures of coinage in the play amount to a rhetorical *res nullius*, a common rhetorical property that characters use to shape their agendas, but which also always escapes their purposes, taking them in directions away from their intentions, whether toward materialistic or mystical schemes of value.

The discussion of "fiscal theology" in this chapter extends my engagement with Kantorowicz's account of the mystical body through an analysis of economically charged sacramental tropes. It is distinct from Agamben's analysis of the "mystery of the economy" in Trinitarian theology,[13] although, as I suggest in the introduction to this volume, I believe it is complementary to this analysis. Agamben's discussion of the Trinity, which ultimately extends into a larger account of glory and liturgy as political and theological "signatures," seeks to recover a dynamic articulation of a transcendent divine economy within an immanent, profane economy. I believe a similar interplay of transcendence and immanence may be traced through the economic motifs of *Measure for Measure*. I differ from Agamben's account insofar as I claim that the interplay between economy and Christian theology in *Measure* frequently occurs in tropes that are intimately related to the communitarian aspects of the sacramental *corpus mysticum*.

The Vienna of *Measure* is a commonwealth in which signifiers of the sacramental order of the mystical body continue to have currency, even as they are insistently transformed by emergent schemes of material value. This sacramental economy is shown to be the "mysterious materiality"[14] that, transposed into another key, sustains the usurious commerce of the city. Thus, the play opens with a ritual transfer of sovereignty that is conflated with the issuing of a coin, as the Duke appeals to Angelo to stop hoarding his virtues and spend them freely in the commonwealth. As he draws Angelo into a closer engagement with the city, the Duke uses economic language to imply an idea of the community as a mystical body that resonates with Isabella's fiscal theology.

Angelo's engagement with the city as a sacramental economy is perpetually awkward, however, an awkwardness that reveals both the continued vitality of sacramental forms and their ongoing mutation into another kind of economic logic. On one hand, he overreacts to Claudio and Juliet's unauthorized, but relatively mild, exploitation of the protocols of sacramental marriage by imposing the draconian death sentence that inspires Isabella's plea for mercy. On the other hand, he not only fails to address, but also actively succumbs to the logic of the city's sex trade, which, in the discourse of Lucio and others, is cast as a debased variant of Isabella's economy of grace. The awakening of Angelo's sexual desire during his debates with Isabella appears as even more pernicious than this trade, however. The "devilish mercy" (3.1.71) that he offers Isabella (the exchange of her chastity for her brother's life) is cast as a desacramentalizing counter-rhythm, an iconoclastic impulse linked to a dark parody of Reformation theology. In the ultimately comic world of the play, this travesty of Puritanism cannot triumph, but this defeat does not amount to a full restoration of an authentically sacramental economy. The Duke salvages a simulacrum of the mystical body of Vienna in the final sequence of marriages and pardons in the play; in this same sequence, however, he also uses the marriage bond to convert Isabella's sacramental value into political capital. The Duke's prospective marriage to Isabella is the final example of the play's representation of a transvaluation of values, a reordering of relations between mystical and material bodies in the urban space of early modernity.

In the political sense, the figure of the coin represents an extension of a problem within the concept of the sovereign's two bodies, specifically, a division between contradictory and even antagonistic spheres: law and economic value. In the first half of the play, the body of laws that is the first mark of the sovereign is conspicuously undermined by a second body, the body of coins, bearing the mark of sovereign value, that enable the play's myriad sexual transactions. The numismatic authority of the Duke enables an expanding horizontal economy that threatens to dissolve his legal efficacy; this horizontal economy is figured, on the one hand, by the sex trade embodied by Lucio, Pompey, and their fellow bawds and whores, and on the other, by Claudio and Juliet's usurious misappropriation of sacramental marriage. This dilemma inspires the Duke to initiate a further fissuring of his personal authority: the apparent separation of "name" (marker of political authority) and "nature" (natural body). This split paradoxically interjects the natural body of the Duke into the spiritual and sexual life of the body politic; he mimics the circulation of a curious Eucharistic coin in the disguise of Friar, while Angelo as a hollowed-out figure of authority counterfeits justice in the Duke's name.

The figure of the coin, and the trope of economic exchange in general, also represents a contested site of spiritual value, a dimension that emerges most starkly, as we have already seen, in the private interviews between Angelo and Isabella. At stake in this insistent economic rhetoric is the health of the commonwealth as both a body politic and a *corpus mysticum,* a double identity, which is introduced as a problem from the opening scenes of the play. These may be framed by a review of some of the major conceptualizations of the political and theological forces at work from the premodern to early modern periods.

Political Theology and Economy: "Marks of Sovereignty" and "Fiscal Theology"

The political aspect of coinage is illuminated by reference to an influential chapter of the *République* (1583) on the "marks of sovereignty." Jean Bodin identifies the "right of coining money" as one of the fundamental properties of the sovereign, an entitlement that is "of the same nature as law, and only he who has the power to make the law can regulate the coinage."[15] For Bodin, these marks of sovereignty are inscribed within a larger political theology that assumes an analogical relationship between earthly sovereign and God. Elsewhere in the *République,* Bodin asserts:

"For if justice is the end of the law, law the work of the prince, and the prince the image of God; then by this reasoning, the law of the prince must be modeled on the law of God."[16] Bodin's chain of analogical associations, a commonplace in early modern political discourse, implies a vertical structure of power: a hierarchy with God enthroned at the highest level; directly below, his "image" and deputy, the king; and further down, the father as the head of the household. These vertical layers of power ideally reflect and mutually reinforce one another, guaranteeing the stability and coherence of the existing political and social order.

Bodin's sixteenth-century articulation of the political economy of sovereignty as another form of vertical hierarchy is an important intellectual background for *Measure*, but to link the economic rhetoric of the play to the spiritual dynamic of the *corpus mysticum*, another detour through Kantorowicz is in order. In the section of *The King's Two Bodies* immediately prior to his engagement with de Lubac's treatise on the *corpus mysticum*, Kantorowicz explores a curious intersection between the economic and the theological as it emerges from the thirteenth-century legal treatises of Bracton (chapter 4: "Law-Centered Kingship," section 3: Bracton, *Christus-Fiscus*). Again, insofar as this merging of theological and economic concepts occurs in the midst of an effort to make distinctions between the king's personal interests and the wider interests of the polity, Kantorowicz treats it, like the *corpus mysticum*, as a precursor to a fully articulated doctrine of the king's two bodies. In this capacity, Kantorowicz explores the commonplace linkage between *Christus* and *fiscus* in the Middle Ages and the Renaissance. The pairing of *fiscus* and *Christus* ultimately derives from Augustine: *Si non habet rem suam [rem]publicam Christus, non habet fiscum suum*, "Unless Christ has his state [or community] he lacks his fisc" (qtd. in Kantorowicz, *King's Two Bodies*, 176). Kantorowicz glosses Augustine's commentary thus: "the political notions of *res publica* and *fiscus* were used in a figurative and spiritualized sense: the community of mutual love and charity depended upon the spiritual treasure, and the one who practiced charity and gave alms thereby contributed to the 'fisc' of Christ without needing to fear the temporal 'fiscal dragon,' that is, the 'exactor of the fisc' of the empire" (176).

While Kantorowicz cites this idea as it appears in Augustine's commentary on Psalm 146, the idea is also further developed in *City of God*, where Augustine clearly seeks to develop a concept of Christian commonwealth that is both analogous to pagan Roman political ideals and superior to them. Augustine praises the Roman republican tradition of personal poverty for the enrichment of the "commonwealth," but he emphasizes that even though the ideals of the Christian community appear superficially similar, the extent of their concern with the common good is greater: "The Christians make a common property of their riches with a far more excellent purpose: namely, so that they may distribute to each according to his need . . . with no one calling anything his own and all things being held in common."[17] Augustine describes something akin to a Christian socialism, obviously in subsequent history, more often worked out as an ideal than an actuality, but not necessarily without imaginative force. As in his commentary on the sacrament of the Eucharist (discussed in chapter 1), Augustine develops an ideal of community bound together by recognition of mutual obligation and affective investment: Augustine's notion of the "*fisc* of Christ" is a logical extension of his Eucharistic theology, insofar as it conceptually and performatively extends the fellowship between Christians that initiated in the sacramental celebration. In this regard, the "fisc" of Christ is another figure for the *corpus mysticum* as the body of Christ. This is the link, frequently overlooked by modern readers, that bequeaths a spiritual dimension to fiscal metaphors in premodern texts.

Thus, Kantorowicz actually has the *fiscus-Christus* and the *corpus mysticum* situation reversed in terms of the organization of his argument in *The King's Two Bodies*. Although medieval conceptions of the *fiscus* and the *corpus mysticum* both appear as precursors to a fully developed idea of the "politic" body of the king in Kantorowicz's work, he does not understand the concept of the *fisc* in itself as fully participating in traditions of corporate thought. It appears instead as an open question: "did the fisc have an independent existence all by itself as a body corporate?" (179). However, the *corpus mysticum* necessarily complements and completes the *fiscus*. The fiscal theology developed in the wake of Augustine, although foreign to the modern imagination, shows how the fiscal dimension—as a collective network—was imagined on analogy with the mystical body. In the Christian era, the *fisc* or "royal purse" (the fiscal resources of the sovereign) gradually becomes a metonym for the "public sphere at large": "The perpetuity of the suprapersonal king began to depend also on the perpetuity of the impersonal public sphere to which the *fisc* belonged" (191).[18] This very impersonality and perpetuity, however, are traits that also bring the *fisc* into the realm of the divine—*Christus* (as church) and *fiscus* (as state) are paralleled in aphorisms circulating into the sixteenth century, for example, in Alciati's *Emblemata* (1531): "*Quod non capit Christus, rapit fiscus*" (qtd. in Kantorowicz, *King's Two Bodies,* 174). Kantorowicz cites medieval legal doctrine that traces this parallel back to the concept of "*res nullius*" as the basis of the analogy between *Christus* and *fiscus*. The *res nullius* is at the heart of the political and theological conceptions that Kantorowicz describes as a "fiscal theology": "Bracton fell in with the budding fiscal theology of his age" when he defined the sacred resources of the church and the public resources of the state by the common term *res nullius*: "'That is, they are not property of any single person, but only property *of God or the fisc*' . . . the common denominator for *Deus* and *fiscus*, was, in his case, the *res nullius*" (186). The *res nullius* is that property of being-in-common that defines economy as a sphere where politics and theology can coincide in the premodern imagination.

Significantly for the interpretation of *Measure for Measure*, Kantorowicz finds in the figure of marriage the link between the idea of the royal *fisc* and the corporate notion of the *corpus mysticum*. Marriage was a traditional emblem for relations between sovereign and subject in the Middle Ages and early modern period. Kantorowicz describes how this emblem was doubly powerful insofar as it also showed the joining of the *corpus mysticum* and the *fiscus* through the imagined dowry of the body politic. According to Kantorowicz: "The analogy of the *corpus mysticum* served to clarify the relations between the estates of the body politic and their king, and the marriage metaphor served to describe the peculiar nature of the fisc" (218). The ruler was imagined as joined to the realm in a mystical marriage, modeled on that imagined between Christ and his church, and also deployed to convey the relation between a bishop and his see. The complex political theology of this dowry was conveyed in ceremonies with both sacramental and economic elements: coronation ceremonies were frequently likened to weddings (212–15). James I used this analogy to express his relation to the English nation, borrowing the language of Ephesians 5 (the scriptural passage traditionally cited to justify the marriage metaphors involving sovereigns as well as bishops) to reinforce his headship as husband-sovereign: "I am the husband and the whole island is my lawful wife; I am the head, and it is my body" (qtd. in Kantorowicz, *King's Two Bodies*, 223). James I's notion of the dowry as an expression of divine right sovereignty plays a role in the final act of *Measure for Measure*, as will be shown later in this chapter.

While the figurative dowry of Isabella's chastity proves crucial to the resolution of the comedy, less exalted dowries contracted among the members of bodies politic and mystical are equally crucial to establishing the political and spiritual issues at the heart of the play. The erotic economies of Vienna rely on a stable standard of value determined by the coin which derives its "law and value" from the sovereign, according to Bodin.[19] However, "law" and "value" contradict each other insofar as the image of the lawful sovereign is the same "figure" of value that enables the erotic commerce overrunning the body politic of Vienna and eroding the Duke's patriarchal authority, rendering him little more than a "fond father" (1.3.24). In terms of James's marriage analogy, such tensions can be imagined as a contradiction between "head" and "body," or, more precisely, between the alternate models of sovereignty (vertical and horizontal, respectively) that each represents. To perform its designated function in the economic life of the body politic, the coin must circulate as a free-floating material object, the medium of myriad transactions between all levels of society. The coin, rather than the law, is the primary zone of contact between erotic life and sovereign authority in the play; the numismatic efficacy of the Duke ultimately challenges his spiritual and legal efficacy. The body of laws that is the first mark of the sovereign is continuously undermined and eroded by a second body, the body of the coin bearing the "mark" of sovereign value, the multiple, scattered body into which sovereignty divides itself to ensure the stability of both licit (dowry) and illicit (brothel) sexual transactions.

Despite the plague of the sex trade and its attendant ills, evident throughout the play, the main focus of the legal action actually turns on a seemingly marginal case of transgression: the handfast marriage of Claudio and Juliet. This contested marriage reveals how a traditional sacramental economy emerges in tension with political economy early in the play. The handfast wedding is emblematic of the pre-Reformation sacramental order, in which a priest and church service was optional, and sometimes only an afterthought, as the sacrament could be truly contracted on the basis of a simple agreement between two baptized Christians.[20] This theology of sacramental marriage was coextensive with the concept of the sacramental community of the *corpus mysticum.* Like the dynamic reciprocity between the vertical authority of the priest and the gathered community of the church in the ritual of the Eucharist, this theology of marriage posits a more fluid relationship between laity and ecclesiastical authority: indeed, the handfast as a legitimate form of marriage is only coherent and conceivable when the wider society is understood as a *corpus mysticum,* joined together through the sacraments and, ideally, as Augustine would have it, through bonds of charity, into the body of Christ. This was the concept of marriage that reigned until the Council of Trent (1563), when the Catholic Church, under pressure from the Reformers (who denied the sacramental character of marriage altogether) and civil authorities (who sought to regulate marriage more strictly in the interest of parental desires and inheritance rights), instituted a series of new requirements for the "outward order" of marriage rites.[21]

The case of Claudio and Juliet represents the larger problem of "fiscal theology" in the play insofar as it corresponds to the curious rhythm in which sacramental traditions appear in tension with seemingly modern or "secular" economic interests. Claudio describes his relationship with Juliet in terms that both evoke and contradict the older understanding of sacramental marriage:

> Thus it stands with me: upon a true contract
> I got possession of Julietta's bed.
> You know the lady. She is fast my wife,
> Save that we do the denunciation lack
> Of outward order. This we came not to
> Only for the propagation of a dower
> Remaining in the coffer of her friends,
> From whom we thought it meet to hide our love
> Till time had made them for us. But it chances
> The stealth of our most mutual entertainment
> With character too gross is writ on Juliet. (1.2.142–52)

Claudio and Juliet consummate their "most mutual" relation without the benefit of a visible ceremony, evoking an older ideal of sacramental marriage: a relationship established by mutual accord between two consenting, baptized partners, who engage in sexual union, was considered the essence of the sacrament, with formal, public ceremonies technically superfluous to the theological validity of the match. However, no sooner is this sacramental ideal invoked than it is revealed to be enmeshed in the emergent concerns of an economy oriented toward usurious rather than communitarian ends: Claudio and Juliet have put off the formal ceremony in the interest of "the propagation of a dower" which remains "in the coffers of her friends," waiting for long-term private advantage or interest. Claudio and Juliet appear at first to enter into their handfast marriage in the spirit of the sacramental ideal, but almost immediately proceed to muddle that spirit with a more mundane agenda, as they engage in a form of erotic usury that anticipates others (including that pursued by Claudio's persecutor, Angelo) throughout the body politic of Vienna. By attempting to hide their "mutual entertainment" to gain the favor and financial support of Juliet's family, they transpose their marriage bond into a usurious arrangement, an agreement to exploit their union for financial profit. This bid to generate money from their erotic bond is, however, ironically thwarted by the more natural form of generation that is the expected outcome of marriage: a visible pregnancy, which frustrates their attempt to win the dowry, and, more immediately, puts Claudio's life in jeopardy.

As Julia Lupton observes, Claudio and Juliet's union may be seen as threatening to authority in the play because it suggests, "in the equality and mutuality of their bond, an image of civil relation distinct from the one that authorizes absolute sovereignty." Lupton's view that such a match "dangerously separates the purely contractual dimension of marriage from its sacramental and communal mediations"[22] requires some tempering, though. If the dowry problem is set aside, the manner of this marriage is exactly in accord with the traditional sacramental theology of marriage and emblematizes the ideal of the sacramental mystical body. However, if the dowry problem is foregrounded, the match is indeed in danger of slipping into the "purely contractual." The motivation for keeping the marriage private turns out to be the desire to profit from a larger dowry. Insofar as the match is conceived in usurious terms, as a matter of monetary profit rather than sacramental bonds, the marriage is consistent with other lower-order economic transactions of the play. What appears to be of *Christus* is actually a matter of *fiscus*.

The initial conditions of Claudio's transgression establish a rhythm that pervades the play, as marriage as a figure for sacramental sociality of the *corpus mysticum* collapses into a contract that is a harbinger of a civil society constituted as a network of materialistic economic transactions. The play continually reminds its audience of this double face of the coin by repeating this rhythm throughout. Even before we are introduced to Claudio's dilemma, we can discern such a rhythm in the economic metaphors that pervade the opening scene of the Duke's "election" of Angelo. Economic language is so prominent in this initial scene that Angelo becomes literally identified with the image of a coin. In this instance, however, the rhythm works in reverse: Duke's stamping of Angelo's "mettle" into a rhetorical coin to be circulated as a signifier of sovereign authority is not necessarily an act of materialistic debasement, but a demand for his subordinate to engage more fully with the mystical body of the city.

"So Noble and So Great a Figure": Coinage, Sovereignty, and Community

The numismatic language, which embellishes the opening scene of the Duke's delegation of authority to Angelo, elevates the significance of the coin as a symbol of a mystical conception of the body politic. The mystical body which concerns the Duke initially seems to be that of the classic two bodies doctrine: a transcendent form of sovereign authority temporarily incorporated into the natural body of the ruler. As the scene progresses, and particularly in his comments on Angelo's disconnection from his fellow citizens, it emerges that the Duke is also concerned with a broader sense of the *corpus mysticum* of Vienna as a spiritually coherent collective body.

In his initial address to Escalus, the Duke plays upon the early modern ruler's aura of mystical authority by conflating spiritual and political "election," invoking a mark of election that also implies a "figure" of economic value:

> What figure of us think you he will bear?
> For you must know, we have with special soul,
> Elected him our absence to supply
> Lent him our terror, dressed him with our love. (1.1.17–20)

The Duke assimilates his role as a sovereign selecting a political representative to the action of a Calvinist God, who stamps the souls of the elect with an eternal grace that will guarantee redemption at the Last Judgment. While the Calvinist theology of election posits a deeply embedded, internal, and invisible mark of election, which is written or "grafted" in the heart, the Duke's election of Angelo is more external: he has been graced with the divinely sovereign qualities of affecting "terror" and "love," but these are only "lent," a matter of "dress" or outward show. The Duke's initial question ("What figure of us think you he will bear?") suggests that Angelo's "election" might be more properly understood as a test or trial of Angelo than an assured affirmation of his inherent quality. By speculating on the "figure" who will "supply" his absence, the Duke questions not simply the image of authority that Angelo will project, but also his intrinsic worth: will he be capable of "bearing" (much less capitalizing on) the value with which he has been invested? The Duke's initial posture as a mock version of a Calvinist God has the effect of drawing attention to Angelo (whom the play consistently casts as a type of Puritan) as a figure associated with Reformation theology while at the same time undermining the meaning of this theology—especially as it applies to Angelo—by conflating it with economic tropes that move in a different theological direction.

The Duke also mimics the Protestant doctrine of the *Deus Absconditus* insofar as his entrance is simultaneously an exit; yet, again, his direct address to Angelo merges the abstract voice of biblical authority with a more dynamic fiscal theology that implicitly puts Angelo's integrity into question. For the Duke imaginatively dispossesses Angelo as he draws the younger man into the *res nullius* of the political economy of Vienna. This is a zone where theological, economic, and erotic values coincide and clash, and the possibility of a sovereign individuality is thrown into question:

> Thyself and thy belongings
> Are not thine own so proper as to waste
> Thyself upon thy virtues, they on thee.
> Heaven doth with us as we with torches do,
> Not light them for themselves; for if our virtues
> Did not go forth of us, 'twere all alike,
> As if we had them not. Spirits are not finely touched
> But to fine issues, nor nature never lends
> The smallest scruple of her excellence
> But, like a thrifty goddess, she determines
> Herself the glory of a creditor,
> Both thanks and use. (1.1.32–43)

If Claudio and Juliet's casual marriage represents a threat to social order and sovereignty in the form of a usurious variation on the sacramental mystical body, the Duke implies in this speech that the Puritan Angelo represents the opposite challenge: his godly hoarding of his own "virtues" threatens implicitly the root meaning of "common-wealth," whether understood as a mystical or politic body. Paradoxically, the Duke dispossesses Angelo at the same moment he supposedly puts his deputy in possession of the powers of "mortality" and "mercy" (1.1.47). He assigns Angelo to act as the strict arbiter of civil behavior in his absence by curiously admonishing him for his peculiar failings, specifically, his overly "proper" relationship to himself. The Duke implies that his act of election is equally an act of expropriation, sanctioned by the scriptural precedent for his sententious emblem: "No man when he lighteth a candle covereth it under a vessel . . . but setteth it on a candlestick that they that enter may see the light" (Luke 8:16).[23] The creation of Angelo as substitute ruler entails an engagement with the body politic that will disrupt any tautological relationship between Angelo and his "virtues" that might correspond to the individualizing thrust of a belief in justification by faith alone or the doctrine of election. The Duke's admonition is a call to public service: by acting as the Duke's representative, Angelo will give himself and his withheld "virtues" to the community, rather than continuing to nurture them solipsistically in ascetic isolation, as an individual assured of his own election might choose to do in a body politic that is decidedly mixed with reprobate members.

The Duke's address to Angelo thus incorporates the deputy into a sphere of sovereignty characterized by tensions between political and sacramental economies, tensions further figured in his speech by the conflation of economic artifacts (in their production) and sanctified relics. The Duke reinforces his merging of politics and theology by continuing to combine numismatic and religious imagery: "Spirits are not finely touched / But to fine issues." The Duke's "touch" suggests the touchstone and the stamp used in the technical production of coinage. Ideally, this technology was a monopoly of the Renaissance sovereign. Furthermore, this line suggests that the Duke's "election" of Angelo is similar to the "issuing" of an "Angel," the English coin peculiarly linked to the mystical aura of sovereignty as the gold coin employed in the ritual cure of scrofula, the disease also known as the "King's Evil."[24] The Angel as "touched gold" represents the quintessential gesture of the sacral sovereign with healing powers.[25] The Duke's words thus curiously identify Angelo the Puritan with the golden Angel, the efficacious relic of sovereign miracles. The Duke maps out, albeit in somewhat obscure terms, the spiritual and material contradictions that Angelo will be required to negotiate in the remainder of the play. For Angelo's "spirit" is "touched" into service—translated from an immaterial or affective quality into a material substance—as it becomes the "fine issue" of the Duke's authorizing mint.

The vision of "nature" in the concluding lines of the Duke's speech appears on the surface to contradict the Aristotelian tradition of conceiving of "use" (or usury) as an *unnatural* activity—the basis for medieval church prohibitions against earning interest on loans—but this evident contradiction more profoundly alludes to a transactional economy of Christianity similar to Isabella's fiscal theology, discussed at the beginning of this chapter. Again, the economic register of the Duke's speech carries a theological and scriptural dimension that further develops the argument that Angelo must share himself more generously with the mystical body of the commonwealth. Marc Shell observes that the "Duke's remark [about "nature"] is not directly about sexual procreation . . . Yet . . . the product of monetary generation, or use, and the product of sexual generation, or a child, have been compared."[26] Sexual and monetary generation are not simply compared, but actually conflated in the Duke's reference to the "smallest scruple." The most minute portion of natural "excellence"—the "loan" that is ideally recompensed through erotic union and biological reproduction—is also the measure of a fraction of an ounce of gold, a technical term of the goldsmith.[27] From a naturalistic angle, the Duke identifies in Angelo an obstruction that is simultaneously erotic and economic, a dysfunction that he will subsequently remedy in his arrangement of the "bed trick." But the Duke's remarks also have a significant religious dimension insofar as they subtly reference the scriptural "parable of the talents," as several critics have observed.[28] In this parable, which Marc Shell characterizes as characteristic of the common Christian "topos of God as banker,"[29] a master rewards those servants who turn a profit on the gold (or "talents") that he distributes to them, but casts out the servant who hoards the gold, rather than investing it in the world and returning it with interest (Matt. 25:14–30). The parable challenges Christ's followers to share their gifts with the wider world and return profits of grace to their lord and creator. Insofar as the Duke is indeed subtly alluding to this scriptural tradition—despite his classicizing reference to the goddess "Nature"—he evokes a tradition of spiritualizing economic language that recurs in Isabella's later appeals. This language works not only to define an ideal of Christian community, and the investments in this community expected of its citizens, but also to pinpoint the problem that Angelo's version of Reformed religion represents for this communitarian tradition: to mark his elect status, he separates himself from the mixed mystical body of the commonwealth, hoarding his "talents" from contact with potentially reprobate fellow citizens. The Duke's address implicitly argues that this type of Calvinist separatism challenges older notions of charity and reciprocity that had been understood to bind the community together in Christ.

Angelo's response subtly alters the Duke's communitarian economic tropes by turning them more overtly into marks of absolutist civil sovereignty and expressing resistance to the Duke's appeal to him to engage more fully with the community. He argues that the Duke's sudden "election" threatens to degrade the intrinsic value, the "great and noble figure," of sovereign authority: "Let there be some more test made of my mettle / Before so noble and great a figure / Be stamped upon it" (1.1.53–55). By "electing" a representative of doubtful substance, Angelo implies that the Duke risks producing only a mere counterfeit, a figure of false value. Angelo resists the Duke's appeal to enter into the wider economy of the mystical body by implying that this "election," which is cast as an act of coining, may be an act of fraud—"stamping" the inferior "mettle" of "Angelo" into a false "angel"—and so, in effect, the production of a counterfeit coin. Angelo subtly argues that the Duke's delegation of authority, the sudden substitution that transforms Angelo into both the

Duke's counterfeit coin and bastard son, could be seen as an act of *ille-gitimation* on the part of the rightful ruler, the source of legitimacy itself. In this reply, which is simultaneously self-effacing and subtly critical of the Duke's initiative, Angelo articulates a discernible discomfort with the Duke's efforts to put his "talents" into wider circulation. Angelo's resistance foreshadows his later inability to negotiate the balance between "mortality" and "mercy" necessary for maintaining the integrity of the city as a mystical body.

While the initial scene in which Angelo is "elected" as a substitute authority implies also that he is being put into circulation as a coin in the mystical economy of the commonwealth, it is the Duke himself, in the crypto-religious guise of a Friar, who will ultimately circulate more widely through the body politic as he attempts to reorder schemes of spiritual and material value. Detached from his obligation to determine "mortality and mercy" through the law (1.1.47), the Duke continues to exercise a peculiar form of sovereignty, playing on his assumed spiritual authority to effect a series of exchanges (the "bed trick" and the "head trick") that ultimately reveal the debased character of the counterfeit deputy and challenge the larger set of legal and religious principles that he represents.

In this process, the Duke appears to redefine the doctrine of the ruler's two bodies in terms that emphasize the fiscal character of the *corpus mysticum,* the second, mystical body of the ruler in Kantorowicz's account. In announcing his plans to Friar Thomas in a later scene, the Duke draws a distinction between "name" and "nature" that reflects a particular interpretation of the doctrine of the king's two bodies: "I have on Angelo imposed the office, / Who may in th' ambush of my name strike home, / And yet my nature never in the fight / To do in slander" (1.3.44–47). Angelo takes on the "office" and "name" of the ruler—the *legal* and *politic* function of the sovereign—while the Duke withdraws his *natural* body into the disguise of a "true friar" to "behold" the "sway" of his substitute (1.3.47). However, the Duke as Friar encompasses two bodies, political and spiritual.[30] Insofar as his subsequent trajectory mimics in some ways that of a coin circulating through the body politic, he also embodies the conceit of fiscal theology—the dynamic through which worldly economy may also signify the sacramental form of the mystical body.

That the Duke imagines his role as Friar to be concerned explicitly with testing Angelo's resolve to remain separate and apart from the mystical body of the commonwealth is suggested by the secondary rationale that the Duke offers to Friar Thomas for his election of Angelo. Thus, at the end of the scene, the Duke adds:

> Lord Angelo is precise,
> Stands at a guard with envy, scarce confesses
> That his blood flows or that his appetite
> Is more to bread than stone. Hence shall we see,
> If power change purpose, what our seemers be. (1.3.54–57)

If the Duke begins his account of the reasons for his absence from the point of view of a "fond father" (1.3.24), a tattered *imago dei,* he has shifted by the end of his explanation from the role of a mortal, imperfectly merciful God to that of the tempting Devil who challenges Christ to "tell these stones to become bread" (Matt. 4:3). Angelo, however, is not quite Christ. The Duke's reference to Angelo as "precise" explicitly links him to the zealous religious habits of a Puritan.[31] As in the Duke's earlier speeches, we see here hints of the problems inherent in such a form of zealotry. Angelo's imagined desire to be "stone" suggests an idolatry of self as much self-deceiving as self-perpetuating, vulnerable to the hypocrisy of "seeming." Furthermore, in addition to its scriptural resonance with the Temptation of Christ, "bread" may have Eucharistic overtones; according to this implication, Angelo exempts himself from the mystical body of the community gathered in sacramental celebration. Thus, the Duke may also be taken to imply that Angelo insists on staying outside the sacramental economy as well as the erotic economy of Vienna. The suggestion that the Angelo of the flesh may contradict the Angelo of stone suggests that the Duke's abdication and disguise are a way of disrupting a solipsistic idolatry that not only withholds erotic and economic value from the body politic, but also hoards a carefully cultivated form of personal sanctity in a sphere of existence isolated from social experience.

The counterpoint to Angelo's parsimony in the play is the social world of Lucio and his compatriots on display in the scene following Angelo's election (1.2). While the Duke continually uses economic metaphors to emphasize Angelo's hoarding of his "talents" as a problem, similar economic language in this scene underscores the debased character of the commonwealth that Angelo is urged to engage. The intimations of a sacramental mystical body in Lucio's social world are skewed, here as everywhere, by more worldly impulses. While Angelo's solipsism is a problem because it is in danger of completely denying the value of community, Lucio and his friends show that the values that bind together the life of the community of Vienna are also deeply troubled, and troubling, to the extent that the audience seems invited to sympathize, to some extent, with Angelo's impulse to withdraw from it altogether (an impulse, it might be noted, seemingly shared by the Catholic Isabella, who first appears in the midst of withdrawing into a cloister). The economic values of Shakespeare's Vienna appear as the corrupt, overly materialistic, and even diseased variants of the tropes of fiscal theology. Nonetheless, even in this dissolute milieu, the play incorporates glimmers of a notion of the sacramental mystical body that temper the vision of an economy of utterly degraded values. The discourse of Lucio and his companions recapitulates—in a lower key—the tensions between sacramental and materialistic conceptions of the commonwealth as a mystical body that pervade the play.

The coins that Lucio and his fellow Gentlemen pass between them are signifiers of debauchery and disease rather than of sovereign value or sacramental community. Thus, in the second scene of the play, Lucio hails the entrance of Mistress Overdone ("a Bawd") in the following terms:

> LUCIO: Behold, behold, where Madame Mitigation comes!
>   I have purchased as many diseases under her roof as
>   come to—
> SECOND GENTLEMAN: To what, I pray?
> LUCIO: Judge.
> SECOND GENTLEMAN: To three thousand dolors a year.
> FIRST GENTLEMAN: Ay, and more.
> LUCIO: A French crown more.
> FIRST GENTLEMAN: Thou are always figuring diseases in me, but
>   thou art full of error. I am sound. (1.2.44–53)

Lucio introduces the coin into the conversation as the agent of sexual exchange in the brothel of "Madame Mitigation" and, simultaneously, the agent of syphilitic infection. Physical decay wrought by sexual excess becomes an index of wealth to such an extent that denominations of currency become indistinguishable from the symptoms they enable ("dollars" are also "dolors" or pains; a "French crown" is both the coin issued by the French sovereign and the bald head associated with the "French disease").[32] Lucio's conceit sets off a curious contest in which his economic extravagance is "judged" by the degree to which he appears ravaged by the number of diseases that he has "purchased."

Yet coins also embody lateral relations between citizens that are potentially structural analogues to the bonds of the *corpus mysticum*. Indeed, even in terms of their physical appearance, coins were sometimes compared to the holy hosts of Eucharistic ritual through which the *corpus mysticum* was traditionally gathered. The high medieval church designed the host to project an appearance of sanctity appropriate to a material object charged with bearing the spiritual body of Christ into the world: it was "to be white, round, thin and was usually inscribed with a cross, the letters IHS, and from the twelfth century, a crucifixion scene or the lamb of God."[33] As Marc Shell observes, to fulfill this mandate, the Eucharistic "wafer was expressly manufactured like [a] coin: it was pressed between wafer irons and impressed with insignia like those of coins."[34] The potential analogy between host and coin, in the context of brothel jokes that instead associate coins with sex and disease, enables these "crowns" and "dolors" to appear also as symptoms of degeneration in the spiritual *corpus.*

While analogies between coins and hosts may seem distant from Lucio's bawdy banter, the initial framing of this discourse in the scene actually encourages the audience to read Lucio and his fellows as a perverse variant of the mystical body. Closer attention to the religious allusions interspersed in Lucio's comic banter shows how the fleshy economy of sexual exchange is intertwined with a state of deeper theological crisis. Lucio opens the scene with some speculation on current political events that also references a larger realm of religious controversy:

> LUCIO: If the Duke, with the other dukes, come not to composition with the King of Hungary, why then all the dukes fall upon the King.
>
> FIRST GENTLEMAN: Heaven grant us its peace, but not the King of Hungary's!
>
> SECOND GENTLEMAN: Amen.
>
> LUCIO: Thou conclud'st like the sanctimonious pirate that went to sea with the ten commandments but scraped one out of the table.
>
> FIRST GENTLEMAN: "Thou shalt not steal"?
>
> LUCIO: Ay, that he razed.
>
> FIRST GENTLEMAN: Why, 'twas a commandment to command the Captain and all the rest from their functions! They put forth to steal. There's not a soldier of us all that in the thanksgiving before meat do relish the petition well that prays for peace.
>
> SECOND GENTLEMAN: I never heard any soldier dislike it.
>
> LUCIO: I believe thee, for I think thou never wast where grace was said.
>
> SECOND GENTLEMAN: No? A dozen times at least.
>
> FIRST GENTLEMAN: What? In meter?

LUCIO: In any proportion or in any language.
FIRST GENTLEMAN: I think, or in any religion.
LUCIO: Ay, why not? Grace is grace, despite of all controversy;
    as, for example, thou thyself art a wicked villain, despite of all
    grace. (1.2.1–26)

Lucio moves from political speculation about the Duke's possible foreign
alliances and antagonisms to suggest more domestic concerns: he depicts
a conflict between the "commandment" of the law and the pirate captain's free pursuit of his economic "function" that is structurally similar
to the potential conflict between the legal and economic functions of the
Duke's sovereignty. The pirate's empty piety demands the formal semblance of a body of laws, but this "table" must be defaced, "scraped,"
counterfeited, to eliminate the appearance of contradiction between the
sanctified laws and the pirate's business ("'Thou shalt not steal'? . . .
Ay, that he razed."). This disfiguration of the Ten Commandments is
emblematic of the tensions of the historical moment of the play, as these
biblical laws were increasingly central to the moral universe of both
the Reformation and the Counter-Reformation.[35] The image of the Ten
Commandments, as defaced by the pirate captain, implicitly emphasizes
the contradictions that may arise among the various political, economic,
and religious aspirations of the early modern sovereign.

Alongside its implicit critique of divine right ideology, Lucio's comic
banter also incorporates serious questions about what kinds of spiritual
community are possible in the world of the play, and by implication,
early seventeenth-century England. Lucio and his friends clearly do not
endorse the rising prominence of Old Testament legalism as they imagine
a defacement of its "table." More subtly, but more tellingly, they trace
a version of spiritual order centered not on scripture but on the sacraments. Their dialogue moves from echoing of the liturgy of the Mass
("Heaven grant us its peace!") at the beginning,[36] through another possible Eucharistic echo in the witty banter about "thanksgiving before
meat," and ends with Lucio's affirmation of the universality of "grace."
Whatever its possible topical referents, the "King of Hungary" puns
on the idea of hunger: a hunger that may be literal for the soldiers,[37]
but also, given the passage's other references to "heaven" and "grace,"
potentially spiritual. In a context marked by myriad religious allusions,
the "composition" in Lucio's opening speculation about current events,
which envisions a violent division that is overtly international and political, also implicitly summons up the ideal of unity associated with the
corpus mysticum. Lucio's louchely phrased theological conclusion that

"grace is grace despite of all controversies" similarly moves the conversation toward higher theological ground. Lucio's line emblematizes the paradoxical rhythm of the play: first, he asserts a notion of grace that potentially transcends all difference, available to all; this idea of a freely available grace stands in accord with the medieval theology of the *corpus mysticum*. However, in the next breath, he playfully reasserts a difference between himself and the Gentleman ("thou art a villain"), although Lucio certainly shares many of his qualities, including, presumably his "grace" (or lack thereof). Lucio proffers, but immediately withdraws, a unifying ideal of grace, leaving the question of its viability in the world of the play in suspension.

In a generous sense, Lucio's argument about "grace" can appear continuous with Isabella's rhetorical gesture of recalling "all the souls that were forfeit once" in the passage cited at the beginning of this chapter. Indeed, Peter Lake suggests that, taken together, these characters articulate a strain of implicit anti-Calvinism in the play, an "alternative theology of grace" that offers "a vision of the atonement that extends the mercy of God and the prospect of salvation to all," emphasizing the "*process* of salvation, rather than . . . an exclusivist grace of election," such as that presumed in Angelo's Puritan judicial stance.[38] To expand on Lake's suggestion, Lucio and Isabella are two complementary opposites in the conceptual world of the play, where their concupiscence and chastity express the continuing dynamic of efficacious action, one which is redolent of a theology of works. However, for much of the play, they also represent two variations on this theme that never quite merge into a satisfactory, moderate, and unified argument. In the milieu of Vienna, the coin of sacramental grace is clipped and debased, as both characters also divergently resist and embrace the emergent secular conceptions of economy that encroach upon this more traditional conceptual order. Lucio's appeal to a universally available grace and the liturgical echoes of his companions are almost immediately undercut by the lewd banter conflating coins and sexually transmitted diseases, a passage in which the sacramental implications of economic metaphors are rudely overwritten by the baser rhetoric of the sex trade, which is emblematic of that other economy that reckons bodies in terms of the bare monetary value of the moment and not the prospective spiritual capital of ultimate salvation. This scene subsequently introduces a potential higher-order relationship, the quasi-sacramental union of Claudio and Juliet, which also, as argued, evokes the sacramental social order of the traditional *corpus mysticum*. Yet this union is colored as well by the burgeoning materialistic calculations of the brothel world, evident in the couple's speculation on their dowry. Together, Lucio and Claudio imperfectly open up questions about the relation between earthly economics and a higher economy of mercy and grace. As proposed earlier, Isabella must now be seen as the most obvious and eloquent advocate of a fiscal theology consistent with the ethos of the mystical body. Yet, as will be demonstrated in the next section, as she is drawn further into the complex sexual transactions of the city, her discourse and her very position in the play are ultimately compromised by the Duke's need to produce a simulacrum of the mystical body fit for the rule of a proto-secular political economy.

Comic Economies, Religious Antinomies: The Ends of *Measure for Measure*

The final act of *Measure for Measure* functions as an allegory for the ruler's reintegration of his legal and economic functions insofar as it presents, in its rapid succession of public marriages, the spectacle of the unruly sexual economy of Vienna becoming subject to the binding force of the civil marriage contract. The Duke's proposal of marriage to Isabella, however, reaches beyond the mere legal structure of the marriage contract to seek a higher means to guarantee the unity of the *corpus mysticum* and the *corpus politicum,* and thus, the social stability of the city. The Duke's proposal to Isabella can be understood as a coded act of marrying the body politic,[39] but more importantly, it illuminates how the Duke seeks to use this prospective marriage to create a quasi-sacramental simulacrum of the mystical body. With the help of the Duke and the bed trick, Isabella has maintained her status as both exceptional and anachronistic virgin—and thus her place in a more traditional scheme of spiritual or theological value. However, the marriage twist at the end reveals that the Duke, in an exercise of fiscal theology, has sought to multiply the theological capital that she represents for his own purposes, insofar as he has preserved her virginity for political "use." As in other instances in the play, a sacramental economics appears in tension with a more cynical set of calculations. As the marriage is not actually performed onstage, this tension remains unresolved. Isabella and the Duke, like Vienna as a whole, linger somewhere between contradictory notions of economy at the end of the play.

The preservation of Isabella's virtue is contingent on her replacement with Mariana in Angelo's bed, another character caught up in contradictory schemes of value. The situation of Mariana—the once and future wife at the center of the machinations of the bed trick, and the eventual

intercessor for Angelo on the model of her namesake, the Virgin Mary—
reveals the underlying crisis that Angelo's previous action creates in the
political economy of Vienna. The Duke's obscurely economic opening
remarks in act 1, as discussed earlier, may now be read—in light of the
revelations that emerge in the plotting of the bed trick—as a cryptic reference to Angelo's broken engagement to Mariana, the substitute for
Isabella that the Friar-Duke so conveniently and immediately produces
upon learning of Angelo's treacherous proposition. Like the "thrifty
goddess" Nature (1.1.41), Mariana is a woman deprived of her rightful
claim to Angelo's "property," but who will finally achieve both "thanks
and use" (1.1.43) at a favorable rate of interest. Furthermore, in the
Duke's account of Mariana's unfortunate history, there are hints that in
violating the code of good erotic and economic conduct, Angelo has also
violated the interests of the sovereign himself. The Duke identifies Mariana as "the sister of Frederick, the great soldier who miscarried at sea"
(3.1.234–35), and the loss of her dowry, the reason for Angelo's rejection, occurs when "her brother Frederick was wracked at sea, having in
that perished vessel the dowry of his sister" (3.1.241–43). Mariana is
tied to the ambiguous figure of the soldier-pirate, a major contributor of
raw material for the royal mint, a vital component in the early modern
English sovereign's *fisc*. Mariana is thus metonymically linked to the *res
nullius* of the fiscal sphere of Vienna—her dowry is imaginatively connected to the common treasury of the state, not only in the story of her
loss of the dowry and Angelo, but also in the Duke's evident concern for
her future well-being. Beyond the political and economic concerns that
the bereft Mariana represents, the broken engagement stands as another
sign of Angelo's alienation from the mystical body, as he has failed to
respect the integrity of the social bond created by his prior agreement, in
the interest of protecting himself from any monetary loss.

The case of Angelo's previous engagement illustrates how rigid adherence to the letter of the law can prove just as disruptive to the *fisc* and the
corpus mysticum as utter neglect of the law. Angelo's prompt disavowal
of Mariana is enabled by the fact that the loss of her dowry occurs during
the interim between the betrothal and the formal wedding: "She should
this Angelo have married, was affianced to her oath, and the nuptial
appointed. Between which time of the contract and limit of the solem-
nity, her brother Frederick was wracked at sea, having in that perished
vessel the dowry of his sister" (3.1.238–43). Angelo's Puritanical habit of
insisting on the absolute letter of the law, and his corresponding denial of
the validity of less formal—but also traditionally sacramental—marriage
customs, leave him free to break the preliminary contract with Mariana

once the prospect of significant financial gain from the match is gone. It is a common observation that Angelo and the man he condemns, Claudio, are involved in similarly ambiguous marital situations.[40] Through the bed trick, the Duke manages to make this similarity into a nearly perfect symmetry. However, prior to the Duke's intervention, Angelo's relationship with Mariana is the inverse image of Claudio's relationship with Juliet: Claudio privileges the customary and implicitly sacramental "handfast" or pre-contract, allowing this extralegal, traditional agreement to license his sexual activity before the formal wedding, which he delays in hopes of winning a larger dowry, while Angelo emphasizes only the formal ceremony, casting aside his pre-contract when it is clear no dowry will be forthcoming. Claudio's lack of concern for a formal wedding creates a bastard child, while Angelo's dismissal of the customary agreement creates a bereft spinster.

Both forms of abuse of the sacrament of marriage create potential economic burdens on a sovereign who appears to have taken on responsibilities that formerly belonged to the ecclesiastical sphere, specifically, charitable care of orphans and widows. This suggestion is ironically emblematized in Lucio's lascivious remark that "ere [the Duke] would have hanged a man for the getting a hundred bastards, he would have paid for the nursing a thousand. He had some feeling of the sport, he knew the service, and that instructed him to mercy" (3.2.119–22). Here again, as in the opening act, Lucio scandalously mingles an economics of the flesh with the fiscal theology of the mystical body: he recognizes the Duke's acts of "service" and "mercy" but attributes them to a sympathy stemming from lust rather than grace. The Duke as Friar vehemently denies such a motivation, but his disguise at this moment may give us pause: even if not motivated by lust, the Duke has shown himself capable of inhabiting the guise of piety for politic purposes. Lucio's remarks, coupled with the Duke's Friar disguise, imply that the state of Vienna has positioned itself as a simulacrum of the mystical body. In this context, both Angelo and Claudio embody forms of social and economic disequilibrium that threaten to impinge on the resources of such a commonwealth.

The Duke's solution to these opposing yet parallel examples of irresponsibility is to endow the customary "pre-contract" with the force of law. He thus exercises the prerogative outlined by Bodin: "custom has no force but by sufferance, and only in so far as it pleases the sovereign prince, who can make it a law by giving it his ratification."[41] The bed trick presents a clear opportunity to put this theory into practice, for it allows the Duke to set a precedent in which the pre-contract is deemed legally binding. It also foreshadows his proposal to Isabella insofar as it presents another case in which the ruler turns a concept originally rooted in sacramental tradition (the agreement to marry between two baptized partners) into a matter of arbitrary political will. He assures Mariana of the legitimacy of her impending rendezvous with Angelo: "He is your husband on a precontract. / To bring you thus together 'tis no sin, / Sith that the justice of your title to him / Doth flourish the deceit" (4.1.79–82). While the spiritual authority of the Duke's pronouncement is dubious, its legal authority, given the Duke's actual status as a sovereign with the power to convert custom to law, is unimpeachable, despite the fact that the Duke's scheme appears to blur the boundary between ruler and bawd.[42] The Duke grants Mariana the legal right, the "title," to possess Angelo on the basis of a pre-contract that previously seemed only to have the (legally) weak force of a customary agreement; at this moment, he fulfills his earlier promise to demonstrate the limits of Angelo's "property" in himself ("Thyself and thy belongings / Are not thine own so proper" [1.1.32–33]). In this act, "justice" itself is transformed; rather than functioning as the power of "mortality" (as Angelo himself defines it throughout the play), "justice"—in the Duke's legitimation of this "precontract"—becomes that which embellishes or adorns the duplicity of the bed trick, the surplus value earned from an act of counterfeiting. This form of "justice" can only emerge when the law is determined by the economics of sexual exchange, rather than the logic of retribution and "terror." The Duke's sanctioning of this scheme in the guise of a Friar implies that his edict creates a simulacrum of the older sacramental tradition of marriage, one that ultimately privileges *fiscus* over *Christus*.

The Duke's own participation in the final marriage scheme, however, shows that the ultimate significance of marriage, and the sphere of the mystical body to which it is metonymically linked, cannot be reduced to a legalistic scheme of contractual obligations and monetary transactions. If marriage becomes regularized according to economic contract in the case of Angelo and Mariana, a more traditional conception of marriage as a sacramental allegory, as the union between *corpus mysticum* and Christ or sovereign, is reinforced by the Duke's proposals to Isabella.[43] The values of fiscal theology and political economy are intimately intertwined in these proposals. The values that Isabella brings to the marriage are spiritual and allegorical, values that need to be restored in the wake of the abuses of the sacrament of marriage and Angelo's nightmarish distortion of Calvinist theocracy. Although Isabella begins the play appearing to exempt herself from the body politic as a cloistered nun, she ends up becoming assimilated to it by the series of exchanges that take place in the course of the action, especially through the bed trick and the Duke's marriage proposal. In the face of Angelo's efforts to manipulate her into a sexual transaction, Isabella's evident sanctity is held in reserve to further infuse the Duke with spiritual authority. In this sense, she provides the Duke with a spiritual dowry that extends beyond any possible monetary dowry, but that is, ironically, also conflated with the economics of more materialistic, monetary dowries by virtue of its link to the other marriages. The end of the play depicts the social order ruled by the Duke as the product of an ongoing negotiation between material conditions and spiritual ideals, between the remainders of past forms of sacramental order and aspirations for future reformation of the body politic.

This provisional negotiation with the sphere of the *corpus mysticum* emerges in the way that the Duke ultimately deviates from the hierarchical notion of marriage as a "headship" of the husband/king over the wife/body (the model derived from Ephesians and popular with James I, as we have seen) insofar as his final proposal to Isabella collapses the ideal of headship into a potentially equitable relation. This possibility appears in the two repeated yet contrasting proposals that the Duke makes to Isabella.[44] In his first proposal, the Duke speaks in the voice of hierarchical headship, in the imperative ("Give me your hand and say you will be mine" [5.1.564]). His second proposal, however, projects a horizontal scheme of relations ("if you'll a willing ear incline, / What's mine is yours, and what is yours is mine" [5.1.510–11]), raising the possibility of a mutual sharing of power and property between sovereign and subject. This second marital body presents an incipient egalitarian structure of sovereignty, predicated upon the traditional concept of the *corpus mysticum,* a body of members joined through lateral affective bonds (the Augustinian city of the "heart") which no one but Christ can claim to head. In the Duke's second proposal, as Julia Lupton claims, "marriage becom[es] the mechanism for a more lateral and contractual linkage of the Duke to the city via its institutions."[45] However, it is important to recognize that the egalitarian proto-liberal aspects of this moment also build on a substantial substructure of older concepts: sacramental marriage, fiscal theology, and, ultimately, the communitarian tradition of the *corpus mysticum.* Therefore, we must acknowledge that, as much as it looks forward to a "liberal" future, this moment in the play looks backward at an older order that included, despite the conventional notion of traditional constrictions, a more fluid relation between rulers and subjects, as ideally guaranteed by the common sacramental life that they shared in the mystical body.

The Duke requires an infusion of the sanctity that Isabella represents to renew his authority, but Isabella's anachronistic sanctity remains partially inassimilable to the authority of the Duke's hierarchical headship. Isabella's silence in the wake of the Duke's proposals—she does not speak again after her plea to pardon Angelo, "Thoughts are no subjects, / Intents but merely thoughts" (5.1.519–20)—represents her resistance to political appropriation on the part of a member of the mystical body. By remaining silent, she potentially resists assimilation to the Duke's simulacrum of the mystical body, and she hints that the social, political, and economic divisions of Vienna will not be entirely repaired by the spectacle of their marriage. This silence holds out the possibility that Isabella might maintain her status as a consecrated virgin even after she has circulated through the commonwealth of Vienna. This possibility would realize her identification with a form of fiscal theology that intermixes earthly economics and spiritual promise—without turning the full profit over to a particular political ruler.

Isabella's silence in the face of the Duke's offer of marriage is a kind of senselessness that limns the contours of a sacramental body beyond the Duke's full grasp. Isabella's silence corresponds to her persistence beyond the frame of her appointed space and time (when she steps out of the walled-off convent into the larger economy of Vienna). Her deferral of speech conveys the senselessness of a sanctity that can never be fully assimilated to the political projects of the Duke nor to the seething economy of sexual exchange—although it is also never fully divorced from either. Isabella's senseless sanctity represents the persistence of another concept of the *corpus mysticum* that survives beneath and beyond the comic ending of *Measure for Measure,* guaranteeing that the suspended union between the Duke and Isabella cannot be reduced to a simple material transaction.

"Razing the Sanctuary": Fiscal Theology and Sacramental Travesty

The Duke's final position vis-à-vis the sacramental order of the mystical body may be clarified in a comparison with the impulses of his deputy, who, in expressing his own desire for Isabella, articulates a dark vision of the implications of a more radical Reformation. The tense interviews between Angelo and Isabella in act 2 also reveal aspects of the disintegration of the fiscal theology of the mystical body that cannot be entirely rectified by the Duke's efforts to reconstruct a simulation

of the *corpus mysticum* at the end of the play. At the beginning of this
sequence, Angelo articulates his lapse into corrupt desire for Isabella in
economically tinged figures that disparage the sacraments and threaten
the integrity of the mystical body of the city he is supposed to rule. Most
notably, he conjures a vivid image of the dissolution of the monasteries
to express his sudden desire to possess Isabella sexually, outside any sacramental framework altogether:

> Having waste ground enough,
> Shall we desire to raze the sanctuary
> And pitch our evils there? O fie, fie, fie!
> What dost thou, or what art thou, Angelo?
> Dost thou desire her foully for those things
> That make her good? (2.2.206–12)

Angelo's impulse to seduce Isabella leads him to question the stability
of his identity; this desire leads him to express a potential disjunction
between his being ("what art thou") and his acts or performances
("what dost thou"). This questioning of his essential character is intimately linked to the recognition that his desire arises in complex relation
to Isabella's status as religious, which appears metonymic for an entire
sacred order. The ambivalence of Angelo's position is concentrated in the
question of his "desire to raze the sanctuary." On one hand, "raze" is
homophonic with "raise," and, until clarified by "pitch" in the next line,
it can seem to express a desire to elevate Isabella, to build up the "sanctuary" that she represents.[46] "Raze"/"raise" also may imply inflating or
expanding the value of the sanctity that Isabella represents. From this
angle, Angelo might appear to be investing enthusiastically in the economy of grace that Isabella has posited in her arguments for mercy earlier
in the scene. On the other hand, "raze" is quickly revealed to mean
instead "erase," render vacant or void, an empty space for "pitch[ing] our
evil." Angelo's identification of Isabella with a "sanctuary" threatened
with defilement relates Isabella's body more precisely to the sanctuaries
of the Catholic past converted to "waste ground" by the era of the play,
yet remembered in sixteenth-century antiquarian discourses.[47] From this
perspective, Angelo's "desire to raze the sanctuary" evokes a different
economic order. The image conjures the memory of the dissolution of the
monasteries and convents at the onset of the English Reformation in the
sixteenth century—a destruction of the infrastructure of the sacred that
directly expanded the worldly *fisc* of the English sovereign. The dissolution is emblematic of a drastic conversion of medieval fiscal theology

to a set of secular economic calculations. Cast in these terms, Angelo's desire expresses a more destructive relation to the sacramental order of the mystical body than the Duke's later proposal of marriage to Isabella, even if the two acts might be superficially compared.[48]

Angelo's disregard for the integrity of the body politic as a *corpus mysticum* culminates in his attempt to coerce Isabella by using a coinage analogy that travesties the larger pattern of fiscal theology in the play. Angelo's recourse to images of coining levels the difference between the crimes of murder, theft, illegitimacy, and counterfeiting. By implication, it also disorders the distinction between "mortality" and "mercy," the very qualitative terms he is charged with discerning and negotiating between in his role as the Duke's substitute authority. Angelo takes over the language of coinage that the Duke had introduced in "electing" him in act 1. This is the language of sovereignty (insofar as coins are "marks of sovereignty" as much as they are tokens of a fiscal theology), but Angelo's deployment of this language perverts the Duke's inclination to preserve forms of sacramental order. Angelo's fiscal theology is directed toward death and damnation, rather than charity and life, as he declares to Isabella that

> It were as good
> To pardon him that hath from nature stolen
> A man already made, as to remit
> Their saucy sweetness that do coin God's image
> In stamps that are forbid. Tis all as easy
> Falsely to take away a life true made
> As to put metal in restrainèd means
> To make a false one. (2.4.44–51)

The economic rhetoric of Angelo's analogical sequence is non-mediating and paratactic rather than hypotactic. Pardoning fornication is "as good" as pardoning an act of counterfeiting, and an act of murder is "as easy" as producing a bastard through an illicit sex act ("restrainèd means"). Angelo's argument fails to acknowledge the nuanced distinctions that one might make between varying degrees of sin and crime (for example, distinguishing a crime committed against the life of another person from a crime against property). Angelo's blunt claims posit absolute opposites that, ironically, actually become indistinguishable: life and death, reproduction and murder blur together in the "metal" or "mettle" of Angelo's speech.[49] Although Angelo's economic rhetoric in this passage superficially resembles the fiscal theology allusively employed by

other characters, his actual argument subverts the logic of the more traditional formulations that occur elsewhere in the play.

Angelo introduces the coin as a leveling principle, a general equivalent corresponding to the materialism and ethical vacuity of his newly
disclosed reprobate status. He articulates one possible outcome of an
extreme, distorted interpretation of Calvinism: the determinedly reprobate, devoid of hope of grace, lose any incentive to act toward others
in an ethical manner. Angelo's radical leveling of spiritual efficacy is
expressed in the way he symptomatically poses "mercy" as a product of
economic exchange. Angelo's recourse to figures of coinage draws upon
but also distorts the fiscal theology of Isabella's economy of salvation in
the passage discussed at the opening of this chapter. In contrast to Isabella's fiscal theology, Angelo's notion of economic exchange is devoid of
interplay between immanent and transcendent values. It instead asserts
the relentless reign of purely materialistic economy that amounts to a
darkly parodic version of the Christian economy of salvation.

Isabella's reply, "Tis set down so in heaven, but not in earth," (2.4.52),
underscores her concerted effort to temper the inversion of fiscal theology in Angelo's appeal. She implicitly accepts the disturbing equivalences
implied by Angelo's ordering of crimes, an ordering that finds no difference between murder that acts "falsely to take away a life true made"
and fornication, the "restrainèd means" that create "false" (illegitimate)
life, but she attempts to relativize the terms of judgment. Isabella insists
that while God may judge these sins as equally mortal, human judges,
burdened with less perfect insight, must take into consideration extenu-
ating circumstances.[50] Isabella attempts to reintroduce, by reference to
the discrepancy between creator and creature, some notion of mediation
into the inhuman economy of judgment that Angelo asserts.

Isabella's conception of fiscal theology, however, proves vulnerable to
distortion when it confronts an interlocutor who rejects her underlying
social and theological assumptions in favor of an immanent economic
logic. This distortion culminates in Isabella's own lapse into a usurious
attitude toward chastity later in the interview. Isabella's struggle to come
to terms with Angelo's fallen version of economics is symptomatic of a
larger disorientation of the communitarian mystical body. Her ability to
maintain the integrity of her vision of an economy of grace comes under
particular pressure when she faces Angelo's charge to "lay down the
treasures of your body" (2.4.103) to his desire. She counters this solici-
tation with a resistant projection of the "rubies" of the tortured virgin
martyr's body.[51] Isabella's reversal both escapes and assimilates itself to
the position it opposes, the violation of her chastity cast as an economic

proposition. Isabella recognizes the price (her sexual submission) that Angelo demands in return for her brother's life (which is forfeit for his own sexual transgression). This price amounts to her iconoclastic erasure as the "thing enskied and sainted" (1.4.36) who had emerged from the cloister of the "poor Clares" in act 1. She reacts to this threat by constructing a vivid, iconic image grafted from the virgin martyr tales circulated in the medieval collection of hagiographies known as the *Golden Legend:*

> . . . were I under the terms of death,
> Th' impression of keen whips I'd wear as rubies
> And strip myself to death as to a bed
> That longing have been sick for, ere I'd yield
> My body up to shame. (2.4.107–11)

The erotic implications of Isabella's speech have long been noted by critics, often in overtly psychologizing interpretations that read this speech as an eruption of Isabella's supposed repressed sexuality.[52] However, such speculation tends to obscure the allegorical substructure of the scene: other critics have described—as persuasively—how her image of martyrdom is grounded in a long tradition of virgin martyr tales.[53] To split the difference between these readings, it is possible to recognize that Isabella's imagery is sexualized by the specific context of Angelo's proposal without attributing this to hypothetical sexual repression on the part of her character.[54] As Isabella tries to apply an iconographic torque to Angelo's pornographic imagination, she ironically only becomes further mired in its grip. Her Catholic paean to the merit of bodily and spiritual integrity is overwhelmed by Angelo's hypocritical travesty of fiscal theology and reduced to a merely titillating sexual scenario. In this context, her image of martyrdom becomes a mere play of bodily surfaces without a redeeming horizon. The retrospective turn in her language, however, preserves a certain theological depth beneath this circulatory surface, if only in the fossilized form of a martyr's lapidary body.

Isabella's attempted retreat into the medieval Christian tradition of virgin martyrdom participates in the economic tropes woven throughout this scene and the play as a whole. In a repetition and attempted reversal of Angelo's demand to "lay down the treasures of your body" (2.4.104), Isabella imagines the marks or "impressions" of the lashes of the whips that she "longs" for as "rubies." She thus constructs her potentially martyred body as a lapidary body, metonymically linked to the predominant imagery of coinage.[55] Julia Lupton observes that "the word 'impression' keys into the play's network of words concerning stamping, pressing, and minting . . . the perforating marks projected onto the displayed screen of the mortified body imagine a hagiographics visibly attesting to chastity preserved."[56] This virtually cinematic image nonetheless represents an ironic rhetorical turn for Isabella: in an effort to exempt herself from the commodification of bodies implied by Angelo's sexual proposal, she indulges in a kind of spiritual usury, comparable to her brother's erotic usury, projecting herself into a lapsed time in which the archaic codes of virgin martyrdom remain in effect, allowing her to inhabit a body congealed into the impenetrable hardness of a jewel. Like other examples of fiscal theology in the play, this religious metaphor relies on a concrete economic analogy. Here, however, in responding to the pressure of Angelo's proposal, Isabella's economic articulation of a spiritual aspiration becomes deformed, weighed down by the need to defend against a different set of economic calculations. Isabella's identification with the image of the lapidary martyr's body expresses at once a desire for escape from the realm of sexualized economy, the sphere in which the Eucharistic *corpus mysticum* has collapsed into the corporate political body of a city bound together by the circulation of the coin—mediated by the sovereign's coin, rather than by any ritual of communion—and the impossibility of achieving such an escape, rhetorically and conceptually. Isabella's desire for martyrdom is illegible except in economic terms; its spiritual value persistently exceeds the crisis that she faces in this instant of the play.

In such moments, *Measure for Measure* appears closer to the late sixteenth-century tragedy of *Titus Andronicus,* where, as we have seen, tensions about the sacramental forms of life that constitute the mystical body emerge in acts of sacramental travesty and pseudo-martyrological violence. In *Measure for Measure,* similar tensions appear more allusively in the comedy's ubiquitous economic rhetoric. Despite a less graphic dramatization, tracing the logic of fiscal theology throughout the play reveals a work no less urgently concerned with the integrity of the mystical body. Indeed, as Isabella demonstrates with her provocative discourse of "terms of death" and "keen whips," the martyrological imagination foregrounded in *Titus* remains a significant backdrop in the later comedy. The liturgy of the martyr will return, with a vengeance, to center stage in the Civil Wars of the mid-seventeenth century, as all factions of a religiously fractured nation struggle to lay claim to its cohesive force. Fantasies of mystical marriage will not suffice to rebind imaginatively the *corpus mysticum* of the English nation at this later point of crisis; instead, the ruler himself must occupy the martyrological position to reconfigure the mystical body. The socio-sacramental dynamism that Foxe's work bequeaths to the figure of the martyr (the inheritance of medieval communitarian tradition of the mystical body), and that Shakespeare interrogates in significant ways throughout the late sixteenth and early seventeenth centuries, ironically culminates not only in kingly decapitation and interregnum, but also in a longer-term recovery of sovereign sanctity. The complex legacy of sacramental martyrdom is a persistent feature of the literature that emerges from the conflicts of the mid-seventeenth century, providing a common set of tropes upon which writers as divergent as John Milton and Charles Stuart draw to make their arguments to a divided body politic.

CHAPTER FIVE

"Their Martyr'd Blood and Ashes Sow"

Martyrology, the English Mystical Body,
and the Seventeenth-Century Civil Wars

The first chapter of *The King's Two Bodies* surveys how the history of
the English concept of the king's two bodies is articulated in a series of
Tudor legal cases. The final "proof" that the king's two bodies was a viable early modern English construct arises not in sixteenth-century court
cases, however, but in the premier moment of sovereign crisis in the next
century: the split between a "body politic" inflected with the medieval
inheritance of the *corpus mysticum* and the natural body of the king.
This division became evident in the rising conflict between Charles I and
Parliament in the early 1640s. Kantorowicz observes:

> Without those clarifying, if sometimes confusing, distinctions between
> the *King's* sempiternity and the *king's* temporariness, between his
> immaterial and immortal body politic and his material and mortal
> body natural, it would have been next to impossible for Parliament
> to resort to a similar fiction and summon, in the name and by the
> authority of Charles I, King body politic, the armies which were to
> fight the same Charles I, king body natural. By the Declaration of the
> Lords and Commons of May 27, 1642, the King body politic was
> retained in and by Parliament whereas the king body natural was, so
> to say, frozen out. (Kantorowicz, *King's Two Bodies,* 20–21)

The condition of possibility for this constitutional crisis was the persistence of the "crypto-theological idiom" of the king's two bodies,
according to Kantorowicz (19). The Reform-minded Parliament claimed
the capacity of both a *corpus mysticum* and a *corpus politicum*. Ironically, insofar as this move relies conceptually upon a medieval doctrine

of corporateness, it appears to contradict this same Parliament's drive to complete the Reformation of the English church and society. Of course, this Parliament would eschew understanding its actions in terms of the Mass, as the fifteenth-century Parliament discussed in chapter 1 once did. Yet, as is well known, the spiritual integrity and ritual life of Britain would be a constant preoccupation of this Parliament. Indeed, the regicide itself—dispensing with the *corpus naturale* of the king altogether—finally came to appear integral to the effort to reform the mystical body of the realm.

Although Kantorowicz does not dwell particularly on the religious aspects of the crisis (it is in this same section of the book that he marginalizes the impact of the "religiously-excited" era of the Reformation on the development of the two bodies doctrine [19]), his account sheds some light on the central importance of Parliament's concern with the collective spiritual integrity of the realm to this political and social breakdown. Religious conflict is directly inscribed on the medallions through which Kantorowicz traces the development of the crisis. The 1642 Declaration encapsulated in the legend on one of these medallions admonishes the "natural" body of Charles, who "SHOULD HEAR BOTH HOUSES OF PARLIAMENT FOR TRUE RELIGION AND SUBJECTS FREDOM STANDS" (qtd. in Kantorowicz, *King's Two Bodies*, 22). In this admonition, a political condition—"Subjects Fredom"—is symmetrically balanced with a spiritual condition—"True Religion." Parliamentary forces laid claim to defining both conditions in contradistinction to the king's religious and political settlement, in the name of the integrity of *corpus mysticum* and *politicum*. The medallions testify that this "constitutional" struggle remained far from purely secular; indeed, it constituted a struggle over how to define the *corpus mysticum* of England in terms of religious ritual and doctrine as much as legal and political rights.

This conflict about the meaning and essence of the English nation as a mystical body is also a crucial subtext for John Milton's polemical and literary work in the 1640s and 1650s. Milton was, of course, an important player in the debates that shaped Parliamentary politics. His views evolved throughout these years, however, as did those of his political rivals and interlocutors.

In his 1641 prose treatise *Of Reformation*, Milton transforms "conventional formulations" of the body politic and the mystical body of the church, according to Janel Mueller.[1] Milton sketches a "dynamic" notion of the corporate body beyond that of his predecessors; as Milton "recast[s] native apocalypticism as a unitary framework where a divine design finds realization in and through the struggles of the English people,"[2] he also interrogates some of the assumptions of earlier English Protestants. He eschews the "imperial" emphasis of Foxe (the placing of responsibility for Reformation in the hands of the secular ruler) and questions the value of the martyrdom of some of Foxe's "preletical" heroes (such as Cranmer and Ridley).[3] This interrogation is part of a larger project that Mueller describes as "nothing less than refounding and politicizing the concept of the Church as Christ's body."[4] Mueller claims that this "refounding and politicizing" consists, for Milton, in greatly enhancing the role of popular consent (in effect democratizing the government and discipline of the church, along roughly Presbyterian lines), which Milton assumes will entail dissolving inherited ceremonies and set forms of worship as well as episcopacy itself. Mueller shows that concern for the integrity of a *corpus mysticum,* which is being understood in modified Calvinist terms, animates Milton's political activism in the early 1640s. Indeed, part of his boldness lies in pushing the analogy between political and mystical bodies further than his predecessors. However, Milton displays little patience for notions of the mystical body or its reformation that deviate from his militant reformulations. Accretions of church tradition are imagined as diseased growths to be cut off: church corruption extends not just to the bishops, but also to the forms of worship they practice. Paradoxically, Milton celebrates popular sovereignty in religion and politics, unless the populace deviates from what he considers truly holy and free. The long struggle of the mid-seventeenth century, however, reveals that principles of kingship as well as habits of religious ceremony (in the form of the Book of Common Prayer) turn out to have a more abiding popularity than Milton grants in the overheated moment of the early 1640s.

The dynamism of Milton's sense of the "mystical body" is further elaborated by Joanna Picciotto, who argues that, contrary to secularizing accounts of the rise of an English "public sphere," older sacramental notions of the *corpus mysticum* continued to shape ideas about the commonwealth up to the Restoration.[5] Picciotto does claim, however, that the nature of this "sacramental" corporate identity had profoundly changed by the mid-seventeenth century: for radical figures such as Milton and the "Digger" leader Gerrard Winstanley, the "sacrament" had become something "productive"—"identified with the progressive production of Adam rather than the ritual consumption of Christ."[6] What was to be "produced" was "truth" and "knowledge" about the natural world through a regime of intellectual work and experiment, shared out among an "Adamic spectatorial body."[7] A significant crux of Picciotto's argument is a reading of Milton's *Areopagitica* against Augustine's exposition of psalms:

Augustine figures the Fall as a breaking of Adam's body, whose
pieces were scattered to the four corners of the earth; Christ gathered these fragments together and "forged them by the fire of love,
and made one what was broken." Thrusting the unity of Corpus
Christi out of the ritual present and into the historical past, Milton
presents it as a goal to be reattained through human effort. Even
more boldly, he converts Adam's body into the body of truth, transforming the topos of a broken and scattered humanity into a figure
for the state of human knowledge: humanity's postlapsarian fragmentation becomes a specifically epistemological problem.[8]

In this understanding, an affective experience of social and sacramental bonding in Augustine becomes, for Milton, a primarily intellectual
process. The unity of Corpus Christi is replaced and recovered by the
"knowledge" of the body of Adam. The body of Christ is not, for Milton,
something lived in and through socially cohesive sacramental rituals, but
rather is constituted through collaborative intellectual inquiry.

While Milton and similarly minded radicals may have hoped to
reconstitute the mystical body in an intellectual understanding, it is far
from clear that the "mystical body" was—at least in the turmoil of the
mid-seventeenth century—truly reconfigured and experienced in this
experimental, intellectual manner by the masses of the English people.
This period is celebrated for its religious and political ferment. Myriad
sects (Quakers, Fifth Monarchists, Diggers, Ranters, and so on) arose
in the vacuum created by Parliament's abolition of the authority and
structure of the Church of England, as is well known.[9] However, a focus
on the fascinating extremes can also distort perspectives; there were a
number—a majority, in John Morrill's account—who eschewed joining
radical sects in the seventeenth century and maintained an allegiance to
the disestablished church. Morrill's observation about the Parliament's
lack of success in establishing a reformed Church of England is pertinent
in this context: "Successful religious revolutions adapt themselves to popular culture just as much as they change it. But the official reformation
of the 1640s and 1650s was negative, sterile . . . the more the Puritans
tried to abolish Christmas, the more certain their downfall became."[10]
The affective resonance of older forms of sacramental and spiritual experience maintained a powerful appeal for many even—or especially—in
the official proscription of these forms during the Interregnum.

While the English Book of Common Prayer was considered virtually a
"popish" liturgy by more radical Parliamentarians, insufficiently Reformed
and thus ultimately banned by Parliament in 1645, it maintained its status

as an authoritative source of religious and social order for many of a more moderate temper. In the breakdown of English social and religious life in the seventeenth century, the rhythms of aggression and resistance of the sixteenth-century Reformation were repeated in an effort to continue religious reform. This process was driven in equal parts by a fear of the specter of papistry and a desire to complete a Reformation only half finished by Elizabeth and James. Thus, iconoclasm returns with a vengeance, liturgy and holy days are abolished, and the structure of the church is again reorganized by the political realm as Parliament eliminates the office of bishop. Resisting these changes, recalcitrant parishes maintain their images and the liturgy of the prohibited prayer book, showing an affective loyalty to the older order of the Church of England despite its unsatisfactorily Reformed status.[11]

These patterns appear as an eerie replay of the events from the 1530s to the 1550s, even as the main actors have changed. All of these repetitions suggest how important the sacraments continued to be as the symbols and instruments of an integral social existence in early modern England. The events of the Civil Wars may be so perplexing from a modern, secular viewpoint because they require an understanding of the interconnection between social, political, and sacramental orders: when the sacramental order unraveled, the social soon followed, and the reverse current was also evident. Despite innovative interpretations by Milton and his fellow travelers, the idea of the mystical body as an organism that was simultaneously social and sacramental continued to be articulated and experienced in strikingly traditional terms.

The most significant repetition in this era is the return of the sacramentalized martyr, which is visible in the struggle over the martyrological legacy that had been catalyzed by Foxe's *Book of Martyrs*. In one sense, this return is related to the seeds of resistance to monarchical control over church government, which were implicit in some of Foxe's mid-sixteenth-century martyr narratives. In spite of his sometimes critical, revisionary view of Foxe's martyrology (or at least those martyrs who were also bishops, such as Cranmer), by the 1650s Milton embraces and further reconceptualizes a martyrological concept of the mystical body of the Reformed nation: this revision of the martyrological mystical body is evident in Milton's Sonnet 18 ("On the Late Massacre in Piemont"), composed in 1655. However, the martyr as mystical body proves to be an adaptable category. Before Milton appropriates Foxean martyrological tropes to imagine a new godly nation, he confronts an effort to marshal the legacy of Foxe for Royalist interests in the *Eikon Basilike* (1649)—a work which defends not only the executed king as a martyr, but also the whole abolished liturgical system of the Church of England. In its defense of both king and church, *Eikon Basilike* also invites its audience to participate in imitating and adding to the text, drawing its readers into an imaginative, affective participation in the king's martyrdom that builds upon, but also goes beyond, the reader responses invited by Foxe's earlier work. Milton's *Eikonoklastes* represents an effort to reverse the argument of the earlier work: the true persecuting agent in seventeenth-century England is, ironically, the very group that had been inspired to anti-popish paranoia and Reforming zeal by Foxe's martyrology. Historically, Milton's effort to intervene in this polemic has been judged less than successful. I will examine some factors accounting for this lack of success in the final section of this chapter by focusing on Milton's reaction to one element in the text of *Eikon Basilike*: its alleged plagiarism of a prayer from Sidney's *Arcadia*. This prayer exemplifies the liturgical dynamic implicit in martyrological spectacle, a dynamic which *Eikon Basilike* overall activates in an innovative and effective way. Milton's failure to grasp fully the affective power of the prayer demonstrates the limits of the ultimate effect of his anti-Royalist rhetoric. It also reveals the reasons underlying the failure of his effort to shape an alternative national identity from the materials of Foxean martyrology, which is the longer story of English political and cultural history as well as his own career.

Corpus Mysticum, Corpus Politicum: The Anti-Monarchical Legacy of Foxe's *Book of Martyrs* and the "Martyr'd" Nation of Milton's Sonnet 18

Before turning to these seventeenth-century efforts to appropriate the legacy of Foxe's martyrology, it is instructive to return briefly to Foxe's text to examine an episode that exemplifies the contradictory strains in this legacy. As illustrated in chapter 2, in the sixteenth century, John Foxe had made available to the burgeoning Elizabethan Protestant order a powerful rearticulation of the *corpus mysticum* grounded in martyrdom. That this reorientation initially benefits the Protestant political structure is made clear by the Elizabethan regime's well-known promotion of the volume. The dismantling of the sacramental system of the Middle Ages and the rechanneling of its investments into the narrative of martyrdom presented a volatile tactic, however. Unmoored from the Mass, the concept of the *corpus mysticum* can also cut against the sovereign, as Foxe illustrates in recounting the martyrdom of John Lambert in 1538, late in the reign of Henry VIII: this is a narrative in which he "speaks more bitterly against Henry . . . than anywhere else in the *Book of Martyrs*."[12] If Elizabeth could be imagined as both sovereign and quasi-martyr, her father represents an obverse example in the Lambert episode: the sovereign as the maker of martyrs, a threat more immediate even than the pope. In this episode, the monarch is directly involved in the trial of the martyr, an unusual situation which makes this confrontation between two conceptions of the *corpus mysticum* particularly politically charged. The episode warrants close attention in this context because it illustrates a tension within Foxe's work, one which anticipates the later seventeenth-century struggle between Royalists and Parliamentarians to claim the peculiar authority associated with the sacramental martyr. It shows how closely bound the social imagination was to the sacrament of the Eucharist, but it also demonstrates how the martyrological narrative, which attacks Eucharistic tradition, may usurp the sacramental sociality of the mystical body from sovereign control.

Like other martyrs, Lambert becomes notorious for his controversial arguments "concerning the sacrament of the body and bloud of Christ" (*Actes and Monuments* [1583], 1121). The sense that this theological debate pertains to the social cohesion of the kingdom is emphasized by the fact that Henry calls representatives from "all partes of the realm"—"all states, degrees, Byshops and all other" of the body politic of England—to witness the trial (1122). Foxe portrays Henry's insistence on a show trial for Lambert as a concerted effort to wrest back the claim to defend both traditional religion and the integrity of the larger community after the break with Rome and the dissolution of the monasteries (and shortly after he has dealt with the backlash that these actions provoked, the Pilgrimage of Grace rebellion of 1536–37). The king thus frames the session as a theater of sovereignty in which he will act the chief role as judge and upholder of social order by defending the integrity of the sacrament of unity.

Henry's costume as judge of Lambert's trial reinforces his role as the defender of sacramental integrity by inviting the audience to identify him with Christ. Foxe recounts how "the king himselfe did come as iudge of that great controuersie, with a great garde, clothed all in white, as couering by that colour and dissimuling seueritie of all bloudy iudgement" (1122). But Foxe's narrative strives to undermine the king's self-ascribed sanctity. He emphasizes the color scheme of the King's wardrobe to draw attention to an underlying conflict between martyrological lamb and animalistic predator. The king is dressed "all in white," like the "Lamb of God."[13] However, Henry is really only a false, "dissimuling" image of this

spiritual truth. The true "lamb" is Lamb-ert, whose martyr status is pro-
leptically inscribed in his very name, and the king, who intends "severitie
of all bloody judgement," actually occupies the role of wolfish prelate so
vividly imagined in *The Lambe Speaketh*. Foxe underscores this contrast
by remarking, right before the king's entrance, that Lambert arrives "euen
as a Lambe to fight with many Lyons" (1122). This moniker implicitly
blames the sovereign for Lambert's incipient martyrdom, as the Lion is a
royal animal, the "King of Beasts," as well as a notable predator akin to
the wolf. As the king prepares to defend the traditional sacramental form
of the *corpus mysticum*, Foxe constructs a counter-sacramental order.
He rearranges the traditional sacrificial elements, which the king himself
introduces to the scene, to cast Lambert, the martyred "heretick," as the
representative of the true English mystical body.

This reorientation enables Foxe to undermine Henry's moment of triumph in the trial: when Henry seizes the role as the consecrator of both
political and theological order, Lambert is ironically positioned as the
true sacrifice, who will ultimately consecrate a different form of the *corpus mysticum*. At the heart of the trial, before all of the representatives
of the political nation, the King refutes Lambert in Latin:

> LAMBERT: I answere with S. Augustine, that it is the bodie of
> Christ, after a certaine maner.
> THE KING: Answer me neither out of S. Augustine, neither by the
> authoritie of anie other, but tell me plainelie, whether thou
> saiest it is the bodie of Christ, or no? These words the king
> spake againe in Latin.
> LAMBERT: Then I denie it to be the bodie of Christ.
> THE KING: Marke well, for now thou shalt be condemned euen by
> Christes owne words: *Hoc est corpus meum.* (1122)

Henry, repeating the words of Christ as the key words of Eucharistic consecration, occupies the place of the priest in the Mass. He cites
these words not simply to refute the heretic, but also to reinforce his
dual political and theological role as the decider of what constitutes treason and heresy. The sovereign conflates these transgressions in a single
performative gesture that allows him to inhabit momentarily the role
of Christ—Christ as judge rather than holy and redeeming victim, however. In contrast to the king's ritualized rage, Foxe portrays Lambert as
"so humble and obedient a subject" (1122) throughout. Henry's mock
"Mass" has the inadvertent effect of revealing Lambert, the contester
of this sacramental order, to be the truly Christ-like figure. This scene

virtually enacts the same logic as *The Lambe Speaketh* and Foxe's title page: the Protestant martyr, subject to persecution for contesting the sacrificial Mass, is styled as the true sacrifice and thus the authentic (to Foxe) embodiment of the *corpus mysticum*.

If the king invests himself with a pseudo-priestly authority in the midst of Lambert's trial, then Lambert himself wrests some of that priestly, sacrificial aura for himself in the sequence of his martyrdom. Like other martyrs, Lambert engages in a performance of elevation at the stake, one heightened by the way he is doubly pierced in the side in a manner reminiscent of medieval representations of the crucifixion of Christ:

> For after that his legges were consumed and burned vp to the stumpes, and that the wretched tormentours and enemies of God had withdrawne the fire from him, so that but a small fire and coales were left vnder hym, then two that stoode on eche side of him, with their Hallebardes pitched him vpon their pikes, as farre as the chaine wolde reache . . . Then hee lifting vp such handes as hee had, and his fingers endes, flaming with fire, cried vnto the people in these wordes: None but Christ, none but Christ, and so being let downe againe from their Hallebardes, fell into the fire, and there gaue vp his life. (1124)

The accompanying illustration (figure 7) reinforces Lambert's resemblance to traditional images of the crucifixion; the officials who pierce him and lift him up unwittingly cooperate with the miraculous elevation of his flaming limbs to create an image of Lambert that reduplicates familiar images of Christ outstretched on the cross. The elevation of hands adds a liturgical resonance: Lambert performs Christ in actuality at the stake, while he dies for denying that Christ is really present in the Mass. A community surrounds Lambert to bear amazed witness to his perseverance in these final moments, with those in the foreground most visibly affected by the performance.

Lambert's performance as a martyr demonstrates that, while the king's "flesh" may have absorbed the sacramental residue of medieval socio-religious forms in early modernity, the same process was also already happening to "the people."[14] Foxe's text translates the sacramental order of the late Middle Ages into a newly compelling discourse of martyrdom that also provides the basis for a new form of national identity. The socio-sacramental imagination that generates the martyr narrative, as evidenced in the particular tensions of the Lambert episode, fed conflict over the order of the national Christian community. Insofar

Figure 7. "The order and maner of the burning of the constant Martyr in Christ, John Lambert." *Actes and Monuments of matters most speciall and memorable* (London, 1583), 1124. Reproduced by permission of the Folger Shakespeare Library.

as Lambert and his fellow martyrs preserved resonances of sacramental tradition, their stories conveyed an imaginative force antagonistic to royal authority and the legitimating institutions of the state church. These tensions forecast the deadly civil conflict that consumed England in the seventeenth century. Radical Protestants, who had absorbed the martyrological narratives popularized by Foxe, lashed out against a religiously retrograde monarch, culminating in the decapitation of the king and the Interregnum.[15] Doubtless, Foxe dedicates his work to reinforcing the Protestant settlement of Henry's daughter Elizabeth (although, even here, not entirely without critique).[16] Moments such as these in Foxe's work, however, show this revolutionary violence to be, in part, the ironic but inevitable legacy of reforming the sacramental mystical body in martyrological terms.

The Lambert episode again provides a way to track a critique which, in one register, will be translated into a rationale for regicide in the seventeenth century. In the earliest edition of *Actes and Monuments* in 1563, Foxe tempers his judgment of Henry by shifting to second person and directly addressing the king. In "an Apostrophe to king Henry" (included in the first edition, but omitted from later ones), Foxe imaginatively appeals to the king to reconsider his actions against Lambert, invoking the state of the Last Judgment to sharpen his point:

> But howe muche more commendable had it beene for thee, O kynge Henry (if that I maye a little talcke with thee where so euer thou arte) if thou haddest ayded and holpen the poore litle sheape, beinge in so great pearils and daungers, requiringe thy aide and healpe againste so manye Vultures and Libardes, and haddest graunted hym rather thy autoritye to vse the same for his sauegarde, rather then vnto the other to abuse it vnto slaughter . . . But O kynge Henrye, I knowe you did not follow your owne nature there in, but the pernitious councels of the bishoppe of Wynchester, notwithstandinge your wisdome shoulde not haue bene ignoraunt of this, whiche all other kinges also oughte to consider, whyche at this present through the wicked instinctions of the Bishops and Cardynals doo so rage against the simple seruaunts of Christ: that the time shall once come, when as ye shall geue accompt of all the offences whiche ye haue eyther committed by your owne fault, or by the Councell or aduise of others, what shall then happen (if these miserable heretickes whyche you here in this world doo so afflicte and tormente, shall come with Christe and hys Apostles and martirs to iudge the xii. tribes of Israel, sitting vpon their seates, if they with like seuerity shall execute their power vppon you) what then I saye, shall become of you? Wyth what face wil ye behold their maiesty whyche here in this world haue shewed no countenās of pity vpon them? With what hart wil ye implore their mercy, which so vnmercifully reiected and cast them of, whē they fled vnto your pity and mercy? . . . nowe ye kynges, vnderstand, and ye whiche iudge the earth, be wise and learned, serue the Lorde in feare, and reioyse in him with trembling, embrace his sonne, least that ye erre and pearysh from the iust way, for when his wrathe shall sodenly kindle, blessed are all they which trust in him. (*Actes and Monuments* [1563], 533–43)

In this passage, Foxe summons the specter of the Apocalypse, the eventual judgment of "Christe and hys Apostles and martirs," to authorize his admonition of the king. Far from addressing the king as a divinely appointed authority, he expresses some uncertainty about the precise metaphysical realm the king currently inhabits: "whereso ever thou arte." Even in so doing, he assumes a curious intimacy with the king, as if he were speaking to a peer, as he retrospectively urges the king to act with "pity and mercy" toward the martyr Lambert and to refuse the "wicked" advice of counselors such as Winchester. Lambert's martyrdom has, in 1563, thus become an occasion to question the integrity of the royal judgment, in the name of a mystical body of martyrs, projected into a future heavenly tribunal.

In this representation, it is essential to realize that the king himself is potentially one of the predatory animals ("Vultures and Libards [leopards]") that feed upon the "poor litle sheape" that is the Protestant martyr. Wittingly or not, Henry participates in the ghastly Mass figured in *The Lambe Speaketh*. In the 1583 edition, this address to the king is reworded and compressed.[17] Nonetheless, the apocalyptic context remains; indeed it appears more starkly stated as the intimacy of apostrophic address is eliminated: "But thus was Iohn Lambert, in this bloudy Session, by the king judged and condemned to death, whose judgement now remaineth with the Lord against that day, when as before the tribunall seate of that great iudge, both princes and subjects shall stande and appeare, not to judge, but to be judged, according as they haue done and deserued" (*Actes and Monuments* [1583], 1284). Foxe's summation here is less expansive, but, ominously, it also appears less anxious, more settled: the king is not the final arbiter of truth in religion; there is a higher judge to whom he must answer, just as his subjects must. Given his political commitments, Foxe, of course, does not himself specifically extrapolate the earthly consequences for adopting this attitude in *Actes and Monuments*. It is not hard to see, however, how more extreme antiroyal sentiments could be logically drawn from this conclusion, particularly among a population attuned to the Foxean rhetoric of sacramentalized martyrdom. This is an audience trained to locate the mystical body of the nation in precisely those figures, such as Lambert, who defy what they perceive as hierarchical subversion of right religion.

This is the kind of reading of Foxe's martyrological narratives that Milton and his allies came to privilege in the mid-seventeenth century. It came at the expense of the more "imperial" strands also visible in the celebrations of monarchs and bishops in the Tudor martyrology.[18] A spirit akin to this moment in *Actes and Monuments*, I am arguing, will animate the court proceedings against Charles I over sixty years later, when the zealous understood the court convened to judge the king as a typological anticipation of the Last Judgment. To the lawyer John Cook, indeed, this trial was "a resemblance and representation of the great Day of Judgement, when all the saints shall judge all worldly powers, and where this judgement will be confirmed and admired; for it was not only *bonum* but *bene;* good for the matter, but in the manner of proceeding."[19] Cook's "saints" are the near cousins of Foxe's judging "martirs"—they represent the same "mystical" constituency, having suffered alike under a temporal ruler's misguided sway. Rather than reserving judgment for some later date on the eschatological horizon, however, the "saints" of Charles's trial have managed to turn the tables already in this world.

The Reformation *corpus mysticum* that Parliament purported to represent in the mid-seventeenth century sustained itself on the protocols of Foxean martyrology in which sacramental life is expressed in terms of the actual tormented bodies of the martyrs. With the dismantling of the sacramental Mass, however, the mediatory and tempering capacity of ceremonial ritual was also partially disabled. This unstable and volatile situation remained into the seventeenth century. Laudian efforts to enhance the ceremonialism of Church of England rites in the 1630s were met with a counterattack in the 1640s. This reverse current grew in intensity and drew sustenance from martyrological precedent. Of course, Laud's punitive measures against dissenters, including branding and mutilation, only further encouraged identification with the Foxean paradigm.[20] Particularly for those Protestants who rejected the liturgy of the Church of England as insufficiently reformed, the martyrological narrative became crucial for forming an alternative set of social and spiritual bonds. Ironically, the dismissal or rejection of ceremonial reenactments of Christ's sacrifice makes the real presence of corporeal violence ever more crucial to the construction of the *corpus mysticum.* Such corporeal violence becomes the occasion through which the martyrs (and those who identify with them) become incorporate in Christ, by literally reenacting Christ's torture and death in the name of denouncing or refusing the ritual means through which this sacrifice had previously been understood to be reenacted and realized. Thus, the binding social force of the Mass has been replaced by the martyrological narrative, which engenders a peculiar instability in the incipient nation: it requires events of victimization to coalesce, even if such events prove to be exaggerated or fantasized. In this revised notion of the mystical body, the social unity formerly located in the Mass is replaced by a generalized logic of victimization as a principle of social cohesion.

The Irish rebellion of 1641 was an especially momentous occasion on which this logic played out on a mass scale. The event was a major precipitant of the English Civil Wars and one of the crimes for which

Charles was tried, as his responsibility for these events became an article of faith for powerful factions within Parliament. Richard Baxter's recollections of the atmosphere in which news of the Irish Rebellion was received on the eve of the English Civil War provide a vivid example of how perfervid accounts of the Irish rebellion affected a population accustomed to understanding its collective identity in martyrological terms. William Lamont cites Baxter's personal recollections of the impact of the Irish Rebellion in late 1641:

> When in time of peace they [the Irish rebels] suddenly Murdered two hundred thousand, and told men that they had the King's Commission to rise as for him that was wronged by his Parliament, the very fame of the horrid murder, and the words of the many fugitives that escaped in Beggary into England (assisted by the Charity of the Dutchess of Ormond and others) and the English Papists going in to the King was the main cause that filled the Parliaments Armies: I well remember it cast people into such a fear that England would be used like Ireland, that all over the Countrey, the people oft sate up, and durst not go to bed, for fear lest the Papists should rise and Murder them.[21]

The sense of dread conveyed here is strikingly immediate. The Irish "Papists" are understood to threaten the physical well-being of English Protestants imminently, yet they are also imagined in curiously spectral terms, as a ghostly force that might overtake the English in the middle of the night in their very beds, defying the limitations of time and space. The sense of immediate danger was enhanced by the belief that the "King was the main cause" of the violence, an especially uncanny prospect as the defender of the English body of church and state seemed to become its violator, the enemy within. Such a possibility was supported by long-standing concerns about a "popish plot" in the English court (made more or less plausible by international politics and Catholic intrigants around Henrietta Maria).[22] It was further reinforced and exaggerated by an active popular press, which conveyed "lurid accounts of atrocities and confrontations in an attempt to earn support for beleaguered Irish Protestants." This influence is seen in Baxter's figure of "two hundred thousand" Protestants slain in Ireland, a figure which, while obviously hyperbolic, was common in contemporary press accounts.[23]

While a concatenation of factors made such accounts—and the broader notion of "an international conspiracy to enslave England in popish chains"[24]—plausible to English Protestants, the role of Foxe's

martyrology in fostering a sense of collective identification with the victims of "Papist" cruelty should not be underestimated. A martyrological
interpretation of such events was telegraphed in advance by moments, like
the case of Lambert, in Foxe's *Actes and Monuments*. Insofar as Charles I
was understood to be complicit in this atrocity, he became, imaginatively,
the heir to the tyrannical Henry VIII of Foxe's Lambert narrative. A population inculcated in the codes of Foxe's martyrology could easily project
itself into Lambert's position: lambs set to be slaughtered anew for their
adherence to Protestant doctrine. The liturgy of martyrdom outlined by
Foxe constitutes the imaginative paradigm in which notions of popish
conspiracy, royal betrayal, and the potential for a Reformed mystical
body arising from these persecutions flourished. It is not too much to say
that the religious and political violence could not proceed otherwise than
in these disastrous cycles, since the Reformers were embodying the very
concepts to which they had joined in opposition.

Milton's Sonnet 18 ("On the Late Massacre in Piemont") from the
mid-1650s illustrates the legacy of Foxe's sacramentalized martyrology insofar as it argues for a sense of the English Protestant mystical
body derived from a literary interpretation of events in Ireland and
on the Continent. The subject matter of the poem, based on reports of
the plight of the Waldensian sect in the Alps in the mid-1650s (reports
with which Milton would be familiar as Cromwell's Latin secretary),
is clearly in the spirit of Foxe insofar as it documents the atrocities of
the false church and recovers an alternative tradition of the true primi-
tive Church. In this sonnet, the Piemontese proto-Protestant Waldensian
community is implicitly continuous with the English community of Parliamentarian "saints," a link significantly enhanced by the belief that the
Waldensians were slaughtered by Irish Catholic mercenaries, the near kin
of those accused of massacring scores of English Protestants in Ireland
in 1641.

As John Knott has shown, this sonnet is linked to a broader tradition of Protestant martyrology that includes Foxe's work.[25] Like the title
page of *Actes and Monuments,* Milton's sonnet envisions a community
of martyrs forged in the crucible of earthly suffering, looking ahead to
their full vindication in an apocalyptic future. This suffering for the sake
of spiritual integrity also has a political dimension: Milton's speaker
transmutes martyrs into seeds that will germinate into a militant nation.
Elizabeth Sauer emphasizes that the martyrological imagination of Sonnet 18 works to "suture" the construct of the "nation" as a collective
socio-political and religious destiny.[26] In turn, I want to emphasize that
this martyrological "suturing" participates in the larger tradition of the

mystical body, as translated into martyrological terms by Foxe, in this imaginative polemic "On the Late Massacre in Piemont":

> Avenge, O Lord, thy slaughter'd Saints, whose bones
>   Lie scatter'd on the Alpine mountains cold,
>   Ev'n them who kept thy truth so pure of old
>   When all our Fathers worship't Stocks and Stones,
> Forget not: in thy book record their groans
>   Who were thy Sheep and in their ancient Fold
>   Slain by the bloody *Piemontese* that roll'd
>   Mother with Infant down the Rocks. Their moans
> The Vales redoubl'd to the Hills, and they
>   To Heav'n. Their martyr'd blood and ashes sow
>   O'er all th' *Italian* fields where still doth sway
> The triple Tyrant: that from these may grow
>   A hundredfold, who having learnt thy way
>   Early may fly the *Babylonian* woe.[27]

The sonnet is famous for its radical shifts in temporality and mood. Yet it is the imperative mood that insistently returns in the poem, forming a refrain that echoes throughout the fourteen lines, a series of disruptive assertions. The imperatives that the speaker addresses to his "Lord" are "Avenge," "record" ("Forget not"), and "sow." The final imperative, to "sow," is, however, embedded in an ambiguous conditional voice that hovers somewhere between the subjunctive mood and the future tense. The identification of the Waldensian martyrs with "thy Sheep" in "their ancient Fold" obviously alludes to the tradition (derived from the psalms and vividly illustrated in *The Lambe Speaketh* and Foxe's later martyrology) of identifying martyrs with sheep (and ultimately with Christ as the sacrificial Lamb of God). The lamb imagery at the heart of the sonnet thus conveys the sacrificial, sacramental dimension of the martyrological narrative: as "thy sheep," the Waldensians are a community imaginatively consecrated in a way analogous to the way the Host is consecrated as the "Lamb of God" in the Mass.

The casting of the Waldensians as "sheep" follows closely upon the imperative to "record," which conjures precisely the image of a written and bound martyrology such as *Actes and Monuments*. This "record" is displaced, however, to the realm of heavenly omniscience. "Record[ing]" (line 5) is the necessary prerequisite, in the logic of the sonnet, to "sow[ing]" (line 10), as if the inscribing of such a volume is itself an act of consecration that will enable the transubstantive shift of the sestet of the sonnet. The sowing of "blood and ashes" merges classical and Christian allusions ranging from Cadmus's autochthonous Theban army to Tertullian's adage that the "blood of the martyrs is the seed of the Church" to the parable of the sower from Matthew 13:3.[28] The specific detail of "ashes" is particularly evocative of Foxe, whose martyrs are conspicuously burned, rather than slaughtered in cold blood, as was evidently the case in the Waldensian massacre. In this passage from "recording" to "sowing," the sonnet represents a mystical body conceived in martyrological terms and reborn as a militant body politic. This is not an individual but a collective passage, and imminent as much as transcendent. It is also a transubstantive passage that both counters and displaces the Real Presence enacted in the "Babylonian" Mass. For the sonnet celebrates the memory of the martyrs and conjures the idea of a purer national *corpus mysticum,* and it does so by imagining a conversion in which the blood of the martyrs must be textually mediated in the "record" and thereby be realized—made real—as the militant nation that eschews the "Babylonian woe"—entrancement by popish and civil idolatry.

In drawing upon the martyrological reportage of the Irish massacres of the early 1640s, Milton's sonnet illuminates the mechanism by which a radicalized faction of the English Protestant nation discovers itself as a mystical body and an incipient colonial power. This sense of embattled Protestantism also of course fed the violence and upheaval of the Civil Wars in Britain and the rise of Milton's patron Oliver Cromwell. The traumatic specter of Irish Catholic revolt is displaced onto the landscape of the Piemontese massacre (which was purportedly carried out, in part, by Irish Catholic mercenaries), and in Elizabeth Sauer's formulation, the psycho-social trauma of that rebellion provides the basis of a developing national and imperial identity for England in the sonnet:

> The Miltonic voice in the sonnet merges with those of the martyrs and those of the nation, as the verses resonate with Hebraic, Christian, journalistic, homely, nationalistic and apocalyptic imagery. At the same time, the outrage that characterized the historical and literary reactions to the Piedmont massacre provokes the cry for divine retribution in the sonnet and offers a pretext for the reinforcement of an imperialist ideology that materialized in the colonization of Ireland and proposed transplantation of Irish Catholics.[29]

The martyrological thread is woven into a complex fabric of imagery in the sonnet, but particularly insofar as it "merges" with the perspective of the Miltonic speaker, it is crucial for defining the specific kind of Protestant national identity that the poem seeks to instill. This is the notion of a mystical body promulgated by Foxe, and although Sauer does not refer to this concept, she does note that English Protestants of the seventeenth century find in Foxe a ground for "their own consensual unity": *Actes and Monuments* supplies "some of the stitches for the sutures for the elect nation."[30] Thus, "'the blood of the martyrs becomes the seed of colonialism,'" conveying "the imperial potential implicit in the acts and expressions of reformation/regeneration."[31] Again, it is crucial to recognize how the paradigm of a martyrological *corpus mysticum* informs the development of imperialistic political ideals that were to have immense consequences for the modern era.

The ideological moves that Sauer identifies in Sonnet 18 are also visible in various other polemical contexts, for Milton deploys the affective rhetoric of martyrdom to argue for an assertive English Protestant nationalism in Ireland in prose works as well. In *The Reason of Church Government* (1645), for example, he emphasizes the "long work" of the Reformation by evoking the plight of "the poor afflicted remnant of our martyred countrymen [in Ireland], . . . counting . . . the minutes with their falling tears, perhaps with the distilling of their bloody wounds." Besides a reproach of Charles for failing to protect them, the image of "our martyred countrymen" also establishes the Irish Protestant martyrs as a collective: they demonstrate the potential to regenerate and more fully reform the English nation insofar as successfully "quell[ing]" the Irish rebellion, Milton claims, would be tantamount to "beginning at the reformation of our church."[32] These prose polemics about the Irish situation clarify the affective appeal of the link between martyrology and Protestant nationalism poetically developed in the later sonnet.

If we read Sonnet 18 as a provocative call to found a nation—a new mystical body—in martyrological terms, Milton's evocation of the autochthonous origin of Thebes is particularly striking. The story of Cadmus sowing the dragon's teeth to produce the citizens of Thebes (the *Spartoi* or "sown") is a myth of origin and foundation that, on one hand, circumvents the contribution of the female, the human mother, as soldier-citizens spring directly from the earth (Ge or Gaia, the divine personification of mother Earth). This fantasy of spontaneous civic generation may be compared to the foundation myth of Athens, which also located its origins autochthonously in the myth of Erechtheus (born also of Ge, who was fertilized with the semen of the god Hephaestus spilled in pursuit of the virgin patron goddess Athena).[33] While for Athens, this autochthonous foundation myth was a way of guaranteeing civic purity, the Theban myth of foundational autochthony, on the other hand, offered a darker vision of civic origins. The Dragon and the site on which Thebes was founded were sacred to Ares, the god of war; when Cadmus offends Ares by killing the Dragon, he earns a lasting curse for the city.[34] The *Spartoi* set upon each other in battle almost as soon as they are formed; only five survive this spontaneous civil war to become the first citizens of Thebes. This legacy of impurity and violence recurs through the famous Theban tragedies of Oedipus: contaminating, self-consuming violence defines the Theban nation from its beginnings, and perhaps even before.[35]

In conflating the Cadmus myth of autochthonous foundation with resonant strains of Christian scripture and tradition, Milton creates a jarring literary admixture consistent with the generically and formally disruptive character of Sonnet 18. The allusion to Cadmus sowing the dragon's teeth underscores the sense that this sonnet is preoccupied with envisioning a form of national foundation. Autochthony may appear an attractive trope for this new national myth of origins insofar as it appears at first glance to allow Milton to envision a national religious identity untroubled by historical involvement with the Roman Catholic Church as a "mother Church." It is this maternal church that the sonnet implicitly refers to as "Babylonian"—evoking also the Roman church as the Great Babylonian Whore, the obverse image of the great mother church.[36] The "hundredfold," who grow autochthonously from the "blood and ashes" of the martyrs, are supposedly free, like their ancient Greek predecessors, from the contamination of this particular maternal bond.

However, by emphasizing a national origin in "blood and ashes," the sonnet actually insists on the impurity of a foundational violence: in the original myth, the autochthonous Theban citizens are also soldiers, and their first defining war is against themselves. This aspect of the myth is particularly resonant in Milton's historical context, defined by long years of civil conflict. Milton may also be drawn to allude specifically to Thebes because the Theban Dragon could be taken to refer to the Roman Catholic Church, frequently allegorized as a "red Dragon."[37] This potential genealogy reinforces a countercurrent of self-contaminating autochthony in the sonnet insofar as (perhaps inadvertently) it implies the impossibility of locating a space or a history uncontaminated by foundational violence. The doubleness of the allusion, which of course includes a reference to Christ's parable of sowing the word, is perhaps intended to overwrite the pagan legacy of violence conveyed by the Theban Cadmus myth. Nonetheless, the sonnet also clearly seeks to "sow" a more militant brand of Christian identity. The sonnet suggests that an infusion of the warrior ethos of the Cadmus legend is essential for the generation born to "fly the Babylonian woe." Indeed, in *Eikonoklastes,* the "Waldenses" are celebrated—and contrasted to more traditionally minded Englishmen— for their supposed ancient purity of faith, precisely in the section where Milton attempts to refute the king's defense of the Book of Common Prayer (discussed at greater length later). Milton claims: "those Churches in *Piemont* have held the same Doctrine and Government, since the time that *Constantine* with his mischeivous donations poyson'd *Silvester* and the whole Church. Others affirme they have so continu'd there since the Apostles."[38] The Waldensians thus represent the fantasy of a pure, origi- nal source, with a legitimate claim to Apostolic origins—uncontaminated, as the English are, by centuries of "popish" practice. The poem deplores their destruction, yet in transforming it into an autochthonous generation of a new people, it also imagines that their martyrdom will disseminate their purported originary purity to other locations—such as Britain— which lack such an untainted religious history.

While Sonnet 18 demonstrates how Milton seeks to fashion a martyr- ological national identity from a poetics of collective suffering, so as to produce a purer mystical body, Royalist propagandists discover, in the very midst of their greatest defeat, the opportunity to resanctify the royal body as the incarnation of that national mystical body. Once the king has lost his natural body altogether, he turns out to be quite adept at reoccupying the mystical body politic. This reoccupation occurs precisely insofar as he is able to take on the guise of a martyr to Parliamentary violence, a violence that Milton's rhetorical violence in *Eikonoklastes* and Sonnet 18 redoubles. Before turning to Milton's attempt to dis- mantle the king's martyrdom, however, it is necessary to analyze how the king as martyr and avatar of the national mystical body is power- fully constructed in the celebrated posthumous apologia, *Eikon Basilike.* This is a work that presents an alternative experience of social and sacramental bonding, one which draws not only on the martyrological imagination but also on the liturgical tradition supposedly banished in Milton's autochthonous nation.

The Liturgy of Martyrdom and the English Mystical Body in *Eikon Basilike*

If the English Civil War is understood primarily as a war of religion, as the preceding section illustrates, the institution of English monar- chical sovereignty is torn apart precisely by that which it had tried to assimilate, the church.[39] The English body politic was shattered precisely because the phantasmic Catholic threat turned out to reside uncannily within the most familiar structures of the English communal body.[40] In the eyes of supporters of Parliamentary revolt such as Milton, the English people became the martyrological victims of a crypto-Catholic tyrant. Nonetheless, Charles passed through the crucible of trial and execution into a literary afterlife as a martyr. With an irony that goes to the major point in my own narrative of historical explanation, the executed king is established as a martyr by a text which depends upon the same protocols that had been derived from Foxe and used by his enemies to define a militantly Protestant English mystical body and that point to the underlying continuity of the late medieval Catholic paradigm of the *corpus mysticum*.

Eikon Basilike—first published immediately after the king's execution in January 1649—represents a significant intervention in an environment in which a rapidly developing print news media profoundly shaped events charged with political and religious controversy on a mass scale.[41] In its immediate moment, the *Eikon Basilike* appeared to many to convey the king's personal perspective on the events that had roiled the nation, although the current scholarly consensus is that the volume is actually a composite work: a "heteroglossic, collaborative royalist effort" compiled by John Gauden, a Church of England clergyman (later bishop of Exeter) working with diverse manuscripts—"loose papers"—authored by Charles himself.[42] From one perspective, *Eikon Basilike* represents the culmination of the representational strategies of Charles's immediate Tudor-Stuart predecessors: the textual absolutism of King James and the "iconic performativity" of Elizabeth.[43] Richard Helgerson notes that this recapitulation of royal modes of representation betrays a certain affinity between the textual aesthetics of the "King's Book" and those of the Counter-Reformation: "*Eikon Basilike* drew on a set of culturally conditioned responses against which the new culture of print was defining itself, responses that had previously served Elizabeth and Shakespeare and that even then were serving Counter-Reformation Catholicism. This unbookish—indeed anti-bookish—book thus turned print against itself."[44] Helgerson's larger point, that the *Eikon Basilike* draws upon devotional impulses that predate the apparent dominance of a print-obsessed scripturalism that appears at its height at the moment of Charles's execution by a Parliamentary faction, is well taken, but he underestimates the extent to which such impulses were always deeply intertwined with Protestant print propaganda, most notably in the form of the martyr narrative.

Indeed, it is hard to imagine that *Eikon Basilike* would have made such a stunning impact on the English public if the path for its reception had not been laid by Foxe's *Actes and Monuments*. In the introduction to their edition of *Eikon Basilike,* Jim Daems and Holly Faith Nelson explore the connections between Foxe's martyr book and the "King's Book": "[Charles] is presented as a Protestant martyr, not unlike those described by John Foxe in his *Acts and Monuments,* a book read by the king during his imprisonment."[45] The editors are insightful about the polysemic, hybrid nature of the royal martyrology, and the debt that they discern to Foxe is crucial. However, it is important to revise their understanding of Foxe's original achievement, which presents Foxe's martyrology in primarily individualistic terms: martyrology (like spiritual autobiography) was "effective in justifying the individual conscience, the inner light of the believer, in the face of established religious forms." In this regard, they claim, the "King's Book" departs from the tradition: "it asserts the fixity of the king's conscience through his defence of the established duties and obligations against over-zealous innovations." They continue: "Whereas the genres normally recounted an individual's successive confrontations with a corrupt worldly regime in order to bring about the spiritual regeneration of Protestantism, *Eikon Basilike* presents the king as the fixed rock of established authority, a still point buffeted by various forms of social chaos that threaten order."[46] While there is no doubt that the king's book reverses the current of certain generic expectations, as he is obviously the very embodiment of a "worldly regime," the individualism attributed to the genre of martyrology is overstated. As I have argued, the Foxean martyr is suffused with social-sacramental significance: the liturgy of Foxe's martyrs perpetuates a version of the *corpus mysticum* for the Protestant nation, a corporate body for the English nation that is dependent on the experience or threat of persecution. Persecutory violence constitutes the sacrificial mechanism that transubstantiates the corporate mystical body in the cultural imagination of early modern England. As we have seen, Milton's Sonnet 18 testifies to the power of such accounts for formulating an ideal of the mystical political nation. And as Foxe's narrative of the Lambert episode shows, the king (as much as his supposed Papist Irish allies) can easily occupy the place of the persecuting power needed to sanctify and perpetuate the national *corpus mysticum* conceived in this manner.

Yet, as forecast by Foxe's treatment of Elizabeth as quasi-martyr, and as fully demonstrated by the *Eikon Basilike* phenomenon, the royal figure can also occupy the place of the martyr. In this reversal, divine right ideology amplifies the mystical corporational effect. When the tradition of Foxe's martyrology is understood as conveying this wider sense of a mystical body, a collective identity fused in vicarious sacrificial experience, *Eikon Basilike*'s revision of this tradition is less radical than it might at first seem. Martyrs, after all, are (in Foxe's formulation) also the embodiments of a mystical body, a socio-sacramental order. And if the king can successfully represent himself as undergoing martyrological persecution and death, he can graft this peculiar form of corporate mystical order onto his more worldly claims to authority. Such grafting results in a politically potent imaginative effect. While Charles may illustrate, for Kantorowicz, the splitting apart of the bodies mystical and natural while he lives, he fuses them in a newly powerful form in his manner of death and in his textual afterlife, one which ultimately revives the fortunes of the office of the English monarchy.

In its deployment of tropes of martyrdom, *Eikon Basilike* actualizes a fantasy that had already been actively promoted by Royalist writers throughout the turmoil of the 1640s. Lois Potter observes that in Royalist tracts published prior to the king's execution "it sometimes seems as if his own party was unconsciously *willing* the king to die. Writers had created a fictitious saintly Charles I, and then fallen in love with their own creation."[47] While his supporters may have lain the ground for Charles's martyrdom in the years prior to his actual execution, *Eikon Basilike* directly seeks to capitalize on and extend this martyrological status. In the chapter addressed to the Prince of Wales, the future Charles II, the persona of Charles I identifies himself as a particular kind of martyr:

> I may (without vanity) turn the reproach of My sufferings, as to the world's censure, into the honour of a kind of Martyrdom, as to the testimony of My own Conscience; The Troublers of My Kingdom having nothing else to object against Me but this, That I prefer Religion, and Laws established before those alterations they propounded. (*Eikon Basilike*, 188)

The Charles persona of *Eikon Basilike* claims to find within himself, in his "Conscience," a valid affirmation of his own "Martyrdom." Yet he seeks to secure this claim to martyrdom not only through the pure "testimony" of "Conscience" but also through an appeal to civic tradition, to his public role as the keeper of "Religion, and Laws established." His voice appeals to a concern with the body politic merged with the mystical body. He thus constructs a martyrdom that is simultaneously personal and transpersonal, anchored in his historical status as the bearer of two bodies—political and theological.

Eikon Basilike capitalizes on the legacy of Foxe from its opening page. The famous frontispiece by William Marshall, which depicts the three crowns of Charles' martyrdom (figure 8), subtly recapitulates the three levels of the *Actes and Monuments* title page analyzed in chapter 2 (figures 4 and 5). In the *Eikon Basilike* frontispiece, we again encounter a visual narrative that takes place across three interrelated yet hierarchically arranged levels: the heavenly top, the sacramental middle, and the earthly bottom. As on Foxe's title page, the *Eikon Basilike* frontispiece represents the middle, sacramental level as the realm of martyrdom, mediating between heaven and earth. As opposed to Foxe's ranks of martyrs, here the single figure of the king occupies the mediatory space as he reaches for the thorned crown of martyrdom. The sense that his body enacts a mediation between divine and human realms is further reinforced by the beams that penetrate his head. The scriptural texts next to the martyrological crown also align this scene with a tradition of Protestant martyrology, implying that Charles is martyred for the cause of upholding a true interpretation of scripture, one implicitly opposed to the false conceptions of his persecutors.

While the frontispiece aligns *Eikon Basilike* with a larger English Protestant martyrological tradition, the prayers that are attached to the end of each chapter of *Eikon Basilike* merge the nationalist martyr mythology of Foxe with a fashioning of internal spiritual experience that also effectively re-creates the sense of a larger mystical body. These meditative prayers, which seem akin to the Counter-Reformation spirituality of Jesuit founder Ignatius Loyola's *Spiritual Exercises,* work to sanctify the singular monarch by inviting the reader to pray along with the king. The prayers present a "model for devotion" that readers might practice for themselves, deepening their imaginative connection to the king by imitating and internalizing prayers associated with his trial in the manner of "the Prayer Book and prayer manuals."[48] At the same time, insofar as they engage a wide audience in repeating the king's prayers, they invite collective participation in this process of sanctification. This dynamic relationship between individual and communal responses reconfigures the English mystical body in the performance of prayerful mediations on the martyred king's lost political and natural body. Later editions of *Eikon Basilike* added further prayers from diverse sources (including, controversially, Sidney's *Arcadia,* a supplement discussed in detail in the final section of this chapter). The incorporation of these additional prayers into the *Eikon Basilike* exemplifies one of the most politically threatening aspects of the Royalist tract for Parliamentarians: its capacity for inclusion and pluralism, an openness that it shares with

Figure 8. William Marshall, frontispiece of *Eikon Basilike: The pourtraicture of His Sacred Majestie in his solitudes and sufferings* (London, 1648). Courtesy of Saint Louis University Libraries Special Collections.

the genre of romance, specifically its tendency to break off, as well as begin, in medias res.[49] According to Elizabeth Skerpan-Wheeler, the supplementary prayers added to the text after the first edition illustrate the "collaborative" nature of royal "self-representation" in *Eikon Basilike*.[50] Wheeler notes that the prayers are not explicitly identified as written by Charles, despite Milton's charge of deliberate plagiarism on the king's part (examined in greater detail later).[51] The addition of these prayers is a reminder that "there is no single, unified, 'official' version of the text. From the start, the image was democratized. The king's subjects bought the image, created new illustrations and poems, and added them to the king's book."[52] The *Eikon Basilike* encouraged a collaborative dynamic that created a religious and political understanding shared by diverse members of the commonwealth, who became a new mystical body by virtue of their participation in the memorial to the royal martyr.

The open-ended character of *Eikon Basilike* is also reminiscent of the martyrology on which it is modeled, Foxe's *Actes and Monuments,* another volume that underwent continual revision and expansion throughout the sixteenth and seventeenth centuries. Wheeler observes: "like *Acts and Monuments, Eikon Basilike* became an open invitation for supplementation, encouraging readers to make the king's experiences their own by bringing their own sensibilities—and compositions—to each new edition."[53] This open structure enhanced the ability of *Actes and Monuments* to produce a Reformed notion of the mystical body among its audiences; thus, *Eikon Basilike* followed a successful formula to reknit a significant section of the English people into a new consensus, centered now on a cult of royal martyrdom that included and transformed the forces that had brought about the martyrdom itself. *Eikon Basilike* functioned as a kind of seventeenth-century wiki-text, which approximated democratic participation in the service of mourning the king even as it reconstituted dissolved political forms and religious traditions.

Most importantly, as I have suggested, this imagined participation in the king's martyrdom also represents a recollection of a liturgically constructed mystical body. As Isabel Rivers observes, "the fate of the king and the Prayer Book [the English Book of Common Prayer]" became "inevitably intertwined" in the struggles of the 1640s.[54] This interrelation is highly visible in *Eikon Basilike,* which includes a full chapter—chapter 16—defending the integrity of the prohibited liturgy: "Upon the Ordinance Against the Common-Prayer-Book" (*Eikon Basilike,* 130–35). In this chapter, we can trace how liturgy is fused with martyrology, as a form pioneered by Foxe is endowed with a new rhetorical and political force underwritten by the actual sacrifice of the king.[55]

In the chapter on the "Common-Prayer-Book," the persona of the king presents himself as the defender of "our public Liturgy" against the "Innovations" and "Novelties" of his Parliamentary foes (130–31). The prayer book itself takes on a quasi-martyrological body—it is "crucified" by the "Ordinance" of Parliament, a phrasing that insists upon a metonymic relationship between king, book, and Christ (131). The king's persona offers a stout defense of the "Set and prescribed Forms" so detested by Milton and his allies; the king appeals to the need to maintain a cohesive community in worship by following rites "which are common to the whole Church" (131–32). This defense evokes a collective experience of worship rather than an appeal to a top-down authority structure. Such arguments in defense of the previously established liturgy perpetuate the performative structure of the whole *Eikon Basilike* project, which invites continual participation in prayers, such as the one concluding this particular chapter: "*Let us not want the benefit of thy Church's united and well-advised Devotions*" (135). The emphasis throughout falls on the social and spiritual unity supposedly achieved by maintaining a "common" liturgy: "*our daily bread,*" the "joint abilities and concurrent gifts" of the "Composers of the Service-Book," who devise prayers that "best fit the Church's common wants" (132). The voice of the king predicts that the loss of "constant Liturgies of Public composure" (133)—which he, in the classic rhetorical twist favored in Reformation debates, links directly to the "Ancient Churches"—will lead to wider social dislocation. Such arguments illustrate how the connection between the social and the sacramental remains current even through the crisis of the mid-seventeenth century: the "want" of the common set liturgy will be felt, "Charles" prophesies, "in more errors, schisms, disorders and uncharitable distractions in Religion" than even previously witnessed in the realm (133).[56] The desire to use the liturgy of the Prayer Book is affiliated with not only "a duty of Piety to God" but also "Obedience to the Laws" (134). The *Eikon Basilike*'s defense of the liturgy thus merges political and religious arguments—both forms of duty necessarily reinforce each other, and a breakdown of one order will inevitably cause the collapse of the other.

The king's voice concludes by attributing a base political motive to those who have dismantled the Book of Common Prayer; this attribution also conveniently reinforces the king's sacral status as the head of the church. The king's persona proposes that one of the biggest problems with the Book of Common Prayer, according to his detractors, was that "it taught them to pray so oft for Me" (134). The king essentially claims that Puritan piety masks a basic will to political discord and disorder. Again, the conflation of political and holy office is forceful, particularly since it is underwritten here by the king's evident status as a martyred victim of these same persecutors. Like the martyrs in Foxe's earlier book, his martyred flesh is the Real Presence (simultaneously political and theological) that guarantees the efficacy and coherence of socially significant rites and prayers.

In *Eikonoklastes,* the polemical response to the king's book written at the urging of the Parliamentary government and also first published in 1649,[57] Milton attacks this chapter of *Eikon Basilike* precisely by associating the Book of Common Prayer with the Roman Catholic Mass. He refers to an incident in the early sixteenth-century history of the Book of Common Prayer to reinforce his claim: "*For the matter contain'd in that*

Book we need no better witness than King *Edward* the Sixth, who to the Cornish Rebels confesses it was no other then the old Mass-Book don into English, all but some few words that were expung'd" (*Eikonoklastes* [second edition], 143).[58] Milton is in fact citing an argument that was used to calm a sixteenth-century uprising—which he calls an "irreligious Rabble" (143)—to discredit the Prayer Book altogether. The imposition of the same Prayer Book that seems oppressively conservative to Milton in the mid-seventeenth century was a radical, socially disorienting break with the past to the Cornish men and others in the sixteenth century. Paradoxically, Milton's reference to this uprising is a reminder of the social significance of the Mass, of the popular attachment to traditional "set forms" of liturgy, and of the volatile reactions provoked in early modern culture by the dissolution or alteration of such forms. The residue of that struggle in Milton's own words continues as proof of the power of these older forms as means of articulating an English *corpus mysticum.*

This moment is symptomatic of Milton's larger struggle to counteract the popular image of the king as martyr in *Eikonoklastes:* Milton seeks to preserve the general category of martyrdom as politically and religiously meaningful—as demonstrated, it is essential to his own imagining of the English Protestant nation—while attacking the particular martyrdom of the king and, by extension, the value of the social and religious order which the king purports to defend in his martyrological death. As should be clear from the preceding argument, however, these positions cannot be cleanly differentiated or fully opposed to each other, a problem which leaves Milton unable to counteract the substantial popular appeal of the royal martyrology in his polemical tract.

The *Eikon* Under Erasure: Milton's *Eikonoklastes* and the Romance of the Royal Martyr

Milton's arguments about the flaws of the liturgy of the Book of Common Prayer equally apply to the whole project of the *Eikon Basilike:* the king's martyrology repackages the image of Charles Stuart to lure the English people into a regressive state, to captivate them with a constructed illusion of the past, one which inevitably distracts them from the potential future benefits of a properly reformed religion and a republican government. Since this image of the king is, in Marshall Grossman's words, essentially the "image of his book,"[59] Milton pursues a deliberate strategy of textual disruption throughout *Eikonoklastes.* As he methodically dissects each chapter of *Eikon Basilike,* he attempts to show the seams and gaps in the final propagandistic coup of a regime that, like the pope and his plots in the radical Reformist imagination, was ever skillful at fashioning "Tyranny into an Art" (*Eikonoklastes* [second edition], "Preface," B1r). To shatter the magical "Art" of *Eikon Basilike,* then, Milton's strategy is "to dismember the king's text by inserting hostile commentary into a string of always fragmentary quotations" to expose the mechanisms of forgery, the network of "falsehoods, distortions and thefts" that project the captivating image of an unjustly martyred king.[60] With these tactics, Milton attempts to diminish the affective appeal of the book: according to Lana Cable, in *Eikonoklastes,* "Milton's real target" is "not the royalists' propagandistic document itself, but the icon-loving affective imagination of each of its readers."[61]

The martyr narrative, including its liturgical and participatory elements, is a key component of the affective charge of *Eikon Basilike,* and insofar as *Eikonoklastes* attacks the king's martyrological status, it challenges *Eikon Basilike*'s inheritance of the political and religious legacy of Foxe's martyrological mystical body. The very fact that Milton must mount such a challenge testifies to the particular force of this martyrological legacy in the seventeenth-century English political and religious imagination. The legacy of Foxe's martyrs is also essential to Milton's conception of the ideal English nation, a nation that he seeks to summon into being with his disruptive rhetoric. As we have seen, Sonnet 18 "On the Late Massacre in Piemont" presents a vision of such a nation, which arises differently from the martyrological mystical body: the autochthonously generated polity sprung from martyrs' "blood and ashes," infused with a pure faith, would not be in danger of captivation by spectacles such as the "King's Book" or "popish" liturgies such as those of the Book of Common Prayer. Unfortunately for Milton, the population to which *Eikon Basilike* appeals seems closer to those sixteenth-century Cornish men who cling to their old rites rather than embracing liberation from the "Tyranny" of set forms. In other words, the liturgical dimension of the martyrological narrative continues to possess an affective force that is not so easily exorcised, particularly when it is reinforced by a long tradition of conceiving of the monarch as quasi-divine. Nonetheless, Milton strives to summon his ideal audience into being through a sustained act of rhetorical iconoclasm. He attempts at every turn not simply to observe the contradictions between the king's words and his actions, but to read the style of the book as foreign, feminized, and quintessentially "papist."

Much of Milton's effort goes into demonstrating the superficial and manipulative aspects of the king's performance of martyrdom, which implicate also, of course, his claims to transcendent authority and sovereignty. In the section of *Eikonoklastes* where he rebuts the king's address to the Prince of Wales, Milton argues that the king's transcendent authority is constituted only by the negativity of his veto power over the Parliament's actions. Despite this authority derived from sheer negativity, Charles "reck'ns to himself more than a negative *Martyrdom*" (205). The positivity of the image of martyrdom masks the reality of Charles's merely negative sovereignty. Milton attacks the positivity of this image by drawing attention to the calculations behind Charles's effort to fashion himself as a martyr, a calculated self-fashioning which he opposes to an authentic divinely ordained martyrdom: "He who writes himself *Martyr* by his own inscription, is like an ill Painter, who, by writing on the shapeless Picture which he hath drawn, is fain to tell passengers what shape it is" (*Eikonoklastes* [second edition], 205). In this comparison of the Charles who would "write himself *Martyr* by his own inscription" to an "ill Painter," Milton damns the king's tyrannical self-aggrandizement and aesthetic sensibility in one analogy.[62] He casts the king's effort to inhabit the role of martyr as a pathetic attempt to construct an artificial spectacle devoid of actual spiritual value. Furthermore, Milton's rhetoric is an attempt to diminish the king's claim to martyrdom by casting it as a self-creative act in a performative, theatrical sense: it is an aestheticized tragic gesture, rather than an act embedded in a larger religious culture in which the figure of the martyr is invested with sacramental value.

Milton further attempts to deny Charles the status of martyr on the grounds that it is impossible to undergo martyrdom in the name of any "establisht" religion. If Charles can be called a martyr for defending the established Church of England, then so can the Jesuits who uphold the Roman church: "And if to die for an establishment of Religion be Martyrdom, then Romish Priests executed for that, which had so many hundred years bin establisht in this Land, are no wors Martyrs then he" (*Eikonoklastes* [second edition], 205). Milton associates the brand of martyrdom sought by the Charles of *Eikon Basilike* with the most prominent examples of Catholic martyrdom visible in early modern England, the public executions of Jesuit missionaries. These stand as models and are curiously dignified over Charles as having, at the least, the more viable historical claim, spanning "so many hundred years." Nonetheless, from Milton's perspective, it is because of this proximity to a specifically Catholic claim to martyrdom that Charles forfeits his right to claim martyrdom on the basis of "conscience": "Lastly if to die for *the testimony of his own conscience,* be anough to make him Martyr, what Heretic dying for direct blasphemie, as som have don constantly, may not boast a Martyrdom" (*Eikonoklastes* [second edition], 205–6). Immediately after denying the validity of Charles's martyrdom for its imitation Catholicism, Milton rehearses a commonplace argument against conscience as a criterion for martyrdom, an argument itself frequently deployed against Protestants themselves (for example, by Henry VIII against Lambert in the episode recounted by Foxe). An ideological incoherence afflicts Milton's argument against Charles's martyrdom: the more he enumerates the grounds under which the king's claim to martyrdom may be illegitimate (as an empty aesthetic performance, the product of an imperfect individual conscience, or an over-"establisht" cause), the more he risks undermining the general principle of martyrdom itself, a principle that, as his other works show, he continues to regard as essential to the cohesiveness of English Protestant nationalism.

Milton's strained effort to nullify Charles's status as martyr reflects the difficulty he finds in addressing the multifaceted construction of martyrdom in *Eikon Basilike,* a martyrdom that is simultaneously intensely personal and expansively transpersonal. Charles can "write himself *Martyr*" because his book is adept at tapping into a complex discourse of martyrdom as a source of sacral power, social order, and political legitimacy, a discourse that Milton himself appropriates, and therefore cannot dismantle entirely, even when it works against his political purpose. Both *Eikonoklastes* and *Eikon Basilike* frame their arguments within the sacramental paradigm of a martyrological *corpus mysticum. Eikon Basilike*'s argument thrives on its ability to draw diverse cultural materials into this paradigm, its capacity to incorporate an ever-wider array of texts into the liturgy of the royal martyr. While Milton elsewhere shows the capacity to create a dynamic vision of a martyrological collective (as the allusive range of Sonnet 18 demonstrates), his argument in *Eikonoklastes* tends to insist on an austere delimitation of martyrdom, and by extension, the Reformed mystical body; he strives to show that the king was an ill-fitting head of such a body, and therefore was rightfully cut off. Such arguments, however, fail to address those aspects of *Eikon Basilike* that are truly threatening to the regicidal Parliamentarian position. Milton's attack on the most celebrated example of the incorporative character of *Eikon Basilike*'s martyrology will fully illuminate the dilemma.

In the first chapter of *Eikonoklastes,* Milton announces the discovery of an act of literary bad faith that should prove damaging to the whole project of the royal martyrology: the first prayer in the king's supposed final devotional sequence (part of a supplement to the original text which first appeared in William Dugard's edition of *Eikon Basilike,* published in March 1649) has been lifted wholesale from the third book of Sir

Philip Sidney's *Arcadia*.[63] A foreign textual object embedded in the body of the *Eikon Basilike*, "plagiarized from another author, an inappropriate genre, and a female speaker"[64] (the imprisoned princess Pamela), the prayer represents a rich target for Milton's polemical assault. He will seek to argue that the contamination evinced by the supplementary prayer is not simply isolated and local, but endemic to the book as a whole. However, if the prayer is considered more carefully, both in its original, fictional context and as a meaningful supplement to the "King's Book," the plagiarized text that at first appears to be the Achilles' heel of the royal martyrology actually exemplifies the assimilative strengths of the work that enable it to reconstruct a version of the mystical body. From this perspective, Milton's critiques will appear quite beside the point.

In an early modern literary culture with freer standards for imitation and originality, the fact of the "borrowing" is less dire than the source of the borrowing itself. However, according to Milton, the *Arcadia* prayer is offensive not only because it is "stol'n" from an inappropriate source, but also because it has the character of a Roman Catholic form of worship: it stands out as a "special Relique of his saintly exercises" (*Eikonoklastes* [second edition], 11). In this regard, it is of a piece with all of the other superstitious trappings adopted by the royal cult, including "this his Idoliz'd Book, and the whole rosarie of his Prayers" (*Eikonoklastes* [second edition], 13). Milton neatly subsumes Pamela's prayer into the category of idolatrous Catholic object; it becomes one particularly glittering, if false, bead on the supposed "rosarie" at the end of the book. The offense of the prayer is so great that it is actually God (rather than Milton) who has revealed the fraud of Pamela's prayer,

> thereby testifying how little he accepted them from those who thought no better of the living God then of a buzzard Idol, fitt to be so servd and worshipt in reversion, with the polluted orts and refuse of *Arcadia's* and *Romances,* without being able to discern the affront rather then the worship of such an ethnic Prayer. (13)

Eikon Basilike's reduction of the spirit of the "living God" to a purely formal "buzzard Idol" is an outrage with which the *Arcadia* is complicit insofar as it provides the "polluted" material enabling a religion and a politics perpetually "in reversion." Merritt Hughes glosses "reversion" as a legal term for "the right of succeeding to property or office after its occupant has died or for any reason surrendered possession,"[65] but the term carries a series of additional resonances. "Reversion" stems from the Latin *reversio,* an act of returning, and its more precise legal sense applies to a right of succession that remains in the possession of an earlier owner or an unbroken chain of inheritance, only transferable to another party on the basis of the will of the original owner. Beyond this strictly legalistic sense in which a future state of affairs is determined by the authority of the past, "reversion" suggests the act of returning to an earlier state or place. "Reversion" can also signify the resumption of abandoned rituals, a swerve into the ancestral or the atavistic. Along these lines, "reversion" can also imply a general state of being turned oppositely, always pointing in the reverse direction. Both of these senses are active as Milton subsumes the prayer into his generally negative view of traditional religious ritual. Milton's objections to Pamela's prayer echo his objections to the Book of Common Prayer, which he also understands as reversionary insofar as it perpetuates the medieval Mass, a rite that is not only archaic but also opposed to what Milton considers appropriate forms of Christian worship.

This liturgical dimension of "reversion" is heightened by a more concrete sense of the word: "reversion" can also refer to the "rest, residue, or remainder of something," even more specifically, the remains of a meal.[66] Milton explicitly plays on this final sense in his reference to the "polluted orts and refuse of *Arcadia's* and *Romances,*" likening the Arcadian romance tradition to the crumbs and leavings of a banquet, a comparison that, enhancing his critique with Eucharistic mockery, suggests that Pamela's prayer is closer to a "Mass-Book" like the Book of Common Prayer than might appear at first glance. Immediately before this passage, Milton alludes to Paul's prohibitions on eating food consecrated to idols: "if only but to tast wittingly of meat or drink offerd to an Idol be in the doctrin of St. *Paul* judg'd a pollution, much more must be his sin who takes a prayer, so dedicated, into his mouth, and offers it to God" (*Eikonoklastes* [second edition], 12). Milton somewhat overstates Paul's case against "idol meat" in 1 Cor. 8 (since, after all, it is also here that Paul affirms that "an idol is nothing," indifferent to those in Christ). However, the communal context of 1 Cor. 8 may be the more pertinent frame of reference. In 1 Cor. 8, Paul focuses most explicitly on avoiding idol meals to set a good example for the weaker members of the Christian community. Idolatrous prayers, like idolatrous food, are ingested, internalized; they both put their consumers in danger of "pollution" from the inside out, corruption afflicting the inner man before the outer. This corruption also potentially extends to the community as a body of Christ in Paul's logic, and Milton appears to be playing upon this threat of collective contamination in citing the passage, particularly given his aversion to set forms of prayer and liturgy. The prayer, repeated as a set form of Royalist liturgy, functioning as an oblique version of the Catholic Mass, may bind its audience into precisely the kind of social mystical body that Milton wants to eliminate. Milton attempts to limit this threat even further by reducing the "meat and drink" from the Pauline text to "orts and refuse" used to worship "in reversion," marking the *Arcadia* not only as the expression of an obsolete religious practice, but also as ultimately negligible, possessing the minimal value of almost nothing, an "ort" or crumb.[67]

Thus, according to Milton's argument, the "civil kinde of Idolatry" (*Eikonoklastes* [second edition] "Preface," B1r) promoted by *Eikon Basilike* is on the same continuum with the ossified traditions maintained by the prelates of the English church, who insist, he asserts in an earlier tract, *The Reason of Church Government,* on a religious practice that is "confined and cloyed with repetition of that which is prescribed,"[68] a critique also echoed in his attack on the Book of Common Prayer elsewhere in *Eikonoklastes.* By appropriating the romantic trappings of the *Arcadia,* the king's book recalls the "cloy[ing]" ritual of the English church, which similarly evokes a sense of archaic enchantment. The new cult of the martyred king is most efficacious insofar as it feeds a system of religious devotion that Milton seeks to discard; it forecloses the possibility of a radical break with the past by setting into motion a cycle of mourning that ultimately amounts to a recycling of "set forms." Such incessant repetition allows no space for the eruption of the non-idolatrous deviation that Milton envisions. Milton's ideal celebration of divinity "may orb itself into a thousand vagancies of glory and delight, and with a kind of eccentrical equation be, as it were, an invariable planet of joy and felicity."[69] In the midst of these "vagancies," God's will is no longer enclosed in the "confined" space of idolatrous forms, but rather emerges out of the rupture of these forms; it is realized in the infinite differential between what are deemed to be false arbitrary representations of God and his truly unrepresentable nature. For Milton, the "eccentrical" is, paradoxically, a manifestation of the "invariable." The more the inherited rhythms of tradition are disrupted by throwing set forms radically out of joint, the more the will of God becomes imminent in human understanding and experience, a sign of the promised reconciliation of the human and the divine. It is important to add that this experience of reconciliation, for Milton, appears significantly individualized, a matter of the individual's "affections" of the "heart" (*Eikonoklastes* [second edition], 146) in relation to God. Set forms of liturgy and the *Eikon Basilike* are negative to Milton insofar as they inhibit an individualistic approach to the divine. However, such an emphasis, given eloquent expression by Milton's singular literary genius, is in danger of losing sight of the social dimension of worship, the way in which these forms may remain meaningful for their capacity to continually engender forms of Christian community. Given his historical situation, Milton does grasp the intertwining of social, political, and religious forms, as his appeal to the trope of martyrdom demonstrates. The radical iconoclasm of his position (at least as articulated in *Eikonoklastes*), however, leaves little room for a productive tension between traditional liturgical order and more experimental rhythms of worship and forms of social organization.

The incorporation of the Pamela prayer in *Eikon Basilike* does represent precisely the kind of productive, experimental tension that enables the overall text to re-create a version of the *corpus mysticum*. The insufficiency of Milton's arguments ominously foreshadows a larger cultural failure to capture the martyrological imagination; England during the Interregnum never coalesces into the fully Reformed republic projected by Milton's sonnet on the Piemontese martyrs. Milton's critiques fall short insofar as they fail to acknowledge or adequately respond to the actual work performed by the *Arcadia* prayer and similar supplementary texts in reinforcing the martyrological context of the "King's Book" and enhancing its performative effect for readers.

Insofar as the Pamela prayer from the *Arcadia* is a later addition to the *Eikon Basilike,* it exemplifies the collaborative, open-ended structure of the book described in the previous section of this chapter. Its very addition to the king's book is a reminder of that work's broader appeal, which in subtle ways belies the more obvious stoic and hierarchical content of the appropriated text. Pamela's prayer provides a plausible script for the martyred king: it enunciates a vision of providential history that transcends the distress of immediate circumstances. In the context of the *Arcadia* itself, the prayer occurs as Pamela, a princess in distress, is engaged in a struggle of the will with her captor, the enemy queen Cecropia, who argues for a philosophy that emphasizes the rule of contingency, a position bordering on atheism from an early modern perspective. Pamela's stoic prayer is thus positioned within the narrative as categorically opposed to "politic" heresy.[70] With its appeal to the "all-seeing light and eternal life of all things, to whom nothing is either so great that it may resist or so small that it is contemned,"[71] the prayer is easily aligned with the interests of an absolutist monarchy seeking a divine analogy for its style of rule. Yet in its encompassing appeal to a wider divine and earthly economy—the "eternal life of all things"— the prayer also alludes to a less overtly hierarchical order, imagining a mystical sympathy binding together the world, including the human social order (perhaps derived from the stoic doctrine of *sympatheia*).

The rhetorical force of the prayer is illustrated in the context of Sidney's narrative by the fact that it strikes even the underdeveloped conscience of a seasoned politic adversary. When the depraved Cecropia overhears the imprisoned Pamela's prayer, she has a fleeting attack of conscience that adds a flicker of complexity to her otherwise relentlessly ambitious figure. As Cecropia encounters the scene of Pamela's prayer, the prayer itself combines with the spectacle of "so heavenly a creature (with such a fervent grace, as if devotion had borrowed her body to make of itself a most beautiful representation)" to charm her away from plotting, if only momentarily. The sensual signs of Pamela's devoted submission "all together had so strange a working power that even the hard-hearted wickedness of Cecropia, if it found not a love of that goodness, yet felt an abashment at that goodness . . . so that she was put from the bias of her fore-intended lesson."[72] Cecropia irresistibly affirms the sovereign power of Pamela's prayer insofar as it causes her to swerve away from her predetermined rhetorical tactics. Thus Pamela's prayer can be seen to depersonalize her virtue, making her "borrowed body" the container of a more abstract grace. Such a posture bears comparison to that of Foxe's martyrs, who similarly act as conduits of transpersonal grace in their sacramental performances of suffering. Even in its original context, the prayer reinforces a martyrological vision.

Removed from its place in the fictional romance and slightly Christianized in its finale, Pamela's prayer is retrofitted as an appendix to the *Eikon Basilike* and, in this capacity, recapitulates motifs from the Marshall frontispiece of the king's spiritual autobiography (figure 8). Pamela imagines a relation to God that echoes the most striking motif of the emblem of Charles the martyr; Pamela-Charles prays that "'Thou [God] wilt suffer some beam of thy majesty so to shine in my mind, that I . . . may still in my greatest Afflictions depend confidently on Thee.'"[73] The image of the "beam" internally connecting the mind of the suffering one to the grace of God reiterates in this context the "beams" passing in and out of Charles's head in the frontispiece (the beams that enact his passage from "Affliction" to apotheosis, *clarior e tenebris*, strengthened by darkness) to merge with a vision of heavenly sovereignty, *coeli specto*. Pamela's stoicism in distress gives a devotional voice to the Charles of the frontispiece. The actual difference in the sources for these texts furthers the eternalizing trope; the message of sovereign divinity under duress remains the same throughout its articulations across various genres. The prayer goes beyond simply reiterating the frontispiece, moreover. Insofar as it models the reader's personal devotions, it invites the reader to imitate and internalize a key element of the emblematic image, enhancing even further the affective force of both text and image. As it is resituated in the context of *Eikon Basilike,* the Pamela prayer neatly epitomizes both the ideology of the royal mystical body and the collaborative, performative means of incorporating subject-readers into this version of the mystical body.

As Pamela's prayer becomes Charles's prayer, it illuminates how the royal martyrology as a whole is able to reanimate the ideal of the mystical body, not simply as the personal property of the king, but more significantly, as a collective effort on the part of a large number of his subjects. This revival of a form of the mystical body overcomes the division that had consumed it in the years of political squabbling and civil war, the problem described by Kantorowicz at the beginning of this chapter. The integration of the Pamela prayer into the text of the *Eikon Basilike* shows the mechanism through which the mystical body migrates from the Parliament (where it appeared to reside in the opening anecdote from *The King's Two Bodies*) back to the monarch. This mechanism works by rechanneling the liturgical, participatory aspects of the *corpus mysticum,* which linger within the martyrological formula inherited from Foxe. While the Pamela prayer is originally part of a work of fiction, it takes on a second, liturgical life as it is attached to a text that purports to offer a documentary account of a martyr's life, a text which mimics the claims to historical authenticity of *Actes and Monuments.* The prayer transcends its status as a fiction when it is repurposed as an invitation for readers to participate more deeply in imagining the martyr's life, incorporating it into their devotional habits. Milton's exposé of the fictional origins of the Pamela prayer is ultimately insufficient because it fails to acknowledge the force of the second, "mystical" life of the fiction. In its insistence on dismantling and disenchanting the liturgical impulse as a mere slavery to set forms, Milton's argument misses the deeper dynamic aspect of the martyrological legacy of Foxe.

The political and religious upheaval of the mid-seventeenth century culminates in a total transformation of the social and sacramental *corpus
mysticum* tradition in England. Both of its Reformation-era iterations
(liturgical and martyrological) dissolve into new concepts of social order,
which anticipate the concept of the modern, secular state. This development can be briefly traced by aligning the late work of Milton with the
new political philosophy of his apparent ideological antagonist, Thomas
Hobbes.

The political and theological status of both liturgy and martyrdom
is dramatically interrogated in Milton's late drama *Samson Agonistes,*
which represents a response to the revival of the liturgical mystical body
in the restored Anglican Church and the lingering image of royal martyrdom that had laid the ground for the political Restoration of Charles II.
Milton's Samson represents a counter-martyr to Charles I insofar as
he is a divinely inspired actor who destroys liturgy with his own ironically crypto-liturgical act. Samson's ambiguous iconoclastic act may
also be read as a corollary to the production of the Hobbesian state of
nature, despite Milton's more obvious political differences with Hobbes.[1]
Hobbes ultimately surpasses Milton's radicalism, however, as he establishes a paradigm for conceptualizing social order that overwrites the
sacramental tradition of the mystical body, enabling the emergence of a
modern notion of "Society."[2]

As he recasts Samson's story, Milton imaginatively destroys the liturgical form of the post-Commonwealth mystical body, opening up a
potentially messianic space in which new communal and spiritual forms
might freely take shape. I claim, however, that the conceptual space that
Milton's Samson clears is ultimately occupied by the immanence of the
Hobbesian state of nature. In his *Leviathan,* Hobbes conspicuously
replaces the sacramental tradition of the mystical body with a materialistic account of the pre-political social world as a sphere of equality
of a violently negative valence. Although *Leviathan* clearly references
the tradition of conceiving of social order as a collectively constituted
living body, it radically alters the logic through which this social body
is composed as well as the quality of that composition. The imaginative implementation of Hobbes's scheme calls for precisely the kind of

creative destruction of performative rituals of social order undertaken by Milton's *Samson*. From the longer perspective of the tradition of the mystical body traced by this study, Samson's destruction of the Temple appears conceptually continuous with Hobbes's larger project to replace the communitarian medieval tradition of the mystical body with a materialistic simulacrum.

As *Samson Agonistes* drives toward its anti-liturgical apocalypse, the drama subtly aligns its Old Testament tragic hero with the more current figure of the seventeenth-century Protestant martyr. Samson is the savior of his community, but he enters the scene famously isolated and blind, cut off from meaningful fellowship. He represents the pure individual as the establishing condition of possibility for national liberation. He also potentially alludes to Milton's revolutionary comrades, persecuted by the government of the restored monarchy. Martyrological accounts of the recent executions of the regicides—which include frequent recapitulations of Foxe's narrative formulae—have been shown to have deeply influenced elements of Milton's tragedy. The specific term "multitude" arises in a passage which critics have read as a reproach of the treatment of the regicides. This passage is situated in the Chorus's bitter reflection on the unhappy fate of God's elect (most immediately Samson), summoned "to some great work" yet degraded by ill-fortune:

> Oft leav'st them to the hostile sword
> Of Heathen and profane, thir carcases
> To dogs and fowls a prey, or else captiv'd:
> Or to th'unjust tribunals, under change of times,
> And condemnation of th'ingrateful multitude.
> (*Samson Agonistes*, 680–96)

Merritt Hughes suggests an allusion to "the insult to the bodies of Cromwell, Irenton, and Bradshaw" in these lines, as does Laura Knoppers.[3] The "carcases" of the regicides (martyrs for the "Good Old Cause" that Milton wholeheartedly supported) heighten, by association, the abased state of Samson himself. These "carcases" do summon forth a collective body, but it is figured in entirely negative terms. "Th'ingrateful multitude" is as a kind of negative mystical body, a mutable horde united only in the act of ritualistic "condemnation."

Knoppers develops the political affinity between Samson's position and that of the regicides further as she argues that Samson's final speech before destroying the Philistines' temple is reminiscent of the martyrological scaffold speeches of the regicides recently executed in Restoration

England which were published and distributed by those, like Milton, who remained sympathetic to the cause of the Commonwealth.[4] According to Knoppers, Samson echoes the regicide-martyrs' effort to subvert the meaning of their own demise:

> "Hitherto Lords, what your commands impos'd
> I have perform'd, as reason was, obeying,
> Not without wonder or delight beheld.
> Now of my own accord such other trial
> I mean to show you of my strength, yet greater;
> As with amaze shall strike all who behold." (1640–45)

Knoppers comments: "Like the regicides, Samson's speech and behavior on the scaffold—or stage—overturns the intended meaning of the display, this time literally."[5] Knoppers assumes, in a Foucauldian vein, that martyrology is essentially a "discourse" of "power." However, as this study has shown, discourses inspired by Foxe's martyrology were also a resource for reimagining the communitarian mystical body. As we have seen throughout this study, Protestant accounts of martyrological performance frequently convey aspirations for social unity through quasi-liturgical acts and gestures, encrypting a social and spiritual dynamic that cannot be fully assimilated to pure power politics.

Greater attention to Samson's ambivalent posture immediately before his "scaffold speech" reveals an ironic counter-liturgical dimension consistent with the tradition of Foxe's martyrology. Before speaking, Samson with "eyes fast fixt . . . stood, as one who pray'd, / Or some great matter in his mind revolv'd" (1636–37). The Messenger's account renders Samson's position characteristically unstable: the audience is asked to judge whether Samson occupies a devotional or purely intellectual position. The undecidability of Samson's pose also works as an emblem of resistance to the restored liturgy of the Church of England, as David Gay has argued. Noting, as many scholars have, that Milton omits the prayer given at this moment in scripture (Judges 16:28–30), Gay claims that this omission underscores "the public context of Samson's prayer." By omitting the prayer, the drama associates Samson with those Restoration dissenters (like Milton himself) who rejected the revived Book of Common Prayer as a means of "inculcating a collective political memory." As he assumes an inscrutable posture like prayer immediately before destroying a space dedicated to ritual celebration, Samson becomes "emblematic of a lone individual claiming the space of speech and prayer in a hostile public assembly."[6] Prayers are nonetheless indisputably essential elements of any liturgy, so we may understand Samson as enacting in his public yet silent prayer a form of counter-liturgy with the potential to summon forth a purified, more individualistically realized form of mystical body among those of his extended audience with the capacity to interpret the implications of his gesture. This expectation is fully consistent with the tradition of Foxe's martyrs as elaborated in previous chapters of this study. Viewed in this light, *Samson Agonistes* could be considered a dissenting martyrological alternative to the Book of Common Prayer, with Samson modeling a resistant devotional posture for a community of readers who hold themselves apart from the authorized mystical body of the restored Church of England.[7]

The larger context in which Samson's prayer and subsequent sacrificial act occur also heightens the sense that Milton evokes at this moment a paradoxical anti-liturgical liturgical drama. Samson explicitly destroys a form of collective liturgical celebration, the festival of Dagon, which, as Joanna Picciotto observes, is held in an "idolatrous structure that is both a theater and a temple housing a Laudian blend of 'Sacrifice' and 'sports.' As many readers have noted, Milton could not have chosen a more legible symbol of Restoration festive culture or its persecuting church: it is Charles's theatrical reign that Milton's drama . . . symbolically levels or 'evens.' "[8] In terms of both setting and action, then, Milton merges Samson's Old Testament narrative with current political and religious concerns and stages a confrontation between martyrological and liturgical modes of ordering the mystical body in which neither emerges in unqualified triumph.

The liturgical dimension of Milton's drama is so suggestive that critics have, on occasion, interpreted the work as a more straightforward (albeit Protestantized) form of liturgical drama. T. S. K. Scott-Craig claims that while Milton naturally "objected to traditional liturgical worship," *Samson Agonistes* can be read as a "typological" representation of the "spiritual agony of Christ": "*Samson Agonistes* is really Christus Agonistes." Craig further argues that Milton's "dissonances" and the "broken images of his drama" are "really liturgical in character; priest has become poet writ large . . . Poetry is Milton's substitute for liturgy; the celebration of the agony of Samson is a surrogate for the unbloody sacrifice of the Mass. It is a lustration of fear."[9] In the current context, Craig's analysis holds great interest, but it is important to recognize that the iconoclastic spirit of Milton's drama runs deeper than a simple logic of substitution. Milton's drama seeks to shatter the logic of typology itself, at least insofar as it is implicated in any set liturgical form. Although a typological dynamic may be discerned in the larger context of *Samson*'s original publication in the same 1671 volume as *Paradise Regained,* the text of Milton's Old Testament drama so resists conventional liturgical forms that it is as possible to read Samson as an Antichrist enacting an anti-liturgy, as much as a typological anticipation of Christ.

If *Samson Agonistes* can be understood as a Reformed liturgical drama in any way, it must only be in the most ironic sense, as it culminates in destroying the very shape and space of liturgy from within its idolatrous heart (the Temple of Dagon doubling the restored Church of England). As Samson's ambiguous prayer illustrates, Milton's drama is liturgical in a profoundly negative sense, insofar as it functions as a liturgy to end all liturgy, or at least, to invite its audience to imagine the end of liturgy. The fact that Milton's drama has more recently been suspected of terribly antisocial—perhaps even "terroristic"—tendencies (as some post–9/11 analysis of the drama has explored)[10] might actually be understood as a symptom of its self-negating liturgical structure, which strives to undo a form of social coherence that still remained central for a significant mainstream of seventeenth-century culture. Most pertinent in the present context is the drama's effort to abolish the social ideal of the mystical body insofar as it is intertwined with liturgical celebration. As Julia Lupton has observed, Samson seeks to "destroy the structure of publicity itself . . . Samson destroys the civic conditions of Gaza itself, both its material support and space for collective assembly, recreation and ritual that it had sheltered." Lupton defines Samson's action as a "massacre" in the sense that it is "not just a slaughter, but a desecration," occurring as it does "within a sacred space that is itself destroyed."[11] This destruction is redoubled by the counter-liturgical rhythm of the last section of the drama, which reinforces the literal act of destruction with a more rhetorical form of iconoclasm. In destroying the Temple of Dagon, and with it, the persons and structures of political sovereignty, which are utterly identified with its liturgical order, Samson also potentially reforms the mystical body of his own people by re-creating himself as material for a martyrological "monument." At the same time, though, he releases the Philistine "multitude" into a negative equality that Hobbes will, in turn, re-create as the "state of nature."

A negative counter-liturgical aura envelops Samson's final episode at the Temple of Dagon even before Samson's deed is fully known. The first inkling of the anti-liturgical nature of Samson's destruction arrives as distantly conveyed acclamations are transformed into "hideous noise" when the collective "shout" of the celebrants dissolves into the agony of Samson's destruction of the temple:

MANOA: —O what noise!
    Mercy of Heav'n! what hideous noise was that?
    Horribly loud, unlike the former shout.
CHORUS: Noise call you it or universal groan
    As if the whole inhabitation perish'd?
    Blood, death, and deathful deeds are in that noise,
    Ruin, destruction at the utmost point. (1508–14)

The repetitively referenced "noise" is a sign of disorder and "death." It contains within itself "ruin." This "noise" is the sound of a community disaggregating, dispersing from a ruined social and religious order. Milton associates this "noise" of social and liturgical disintegration with a Pauline eschatological motif as the chorus redescribes the "noise" as a "universal groan," a phrase which unmistakably echoes Paul's description of the eschatological yearning of the entire universe for the return of the Messiah: "For wee know that every creature groneth with us also, and travaileth in paine together unto this present. And not onely *the creature,* but we also which have the first fruites of the Spirit, even we doe sigh in our selves, waiting for the adoption, *even* the redemption of our body" (Rom. 8:22–23).[12] Milton assimilates the "hideous noise" engendered by Samson's revenge to the eschatological expectation that binds together the messianic community and the created universe in Paul's text. Samson, from this perspective, becomes a rough midwife whose destructive work forms part of a larger providential birth for the community who must be liberated from idolatrous "sport" to gain eternal life. Immediately before this passage Paul contrasts "the afflictions of this present time" with the "glory, which shall be shewed unto us" (Rom. 8:18). "The "universal groan" signifies this incipient yet still abstract "glory," while the false "glory" of Dagon's liturgy had merely obscured it. Samson's anti-liturgy is inflected with an eschatological significance formerly attributed to the sacraments and acclamations of traditional Christian liturgy. This eschatological horizon only emerges, however, at the moment that liturgical forms (in this case, the repeated acclamation) dissolve into a "universal groan." This dissolution surpasses simple travesty and becomes a performative act of iconoclasm insofar as it makes the eschatological dimension of liturgy manifest only through its utter destruction.

The ceremonial framing of the Messenger's account of Samson's destruction of the temple further invites the reader to understand Samson's act as a liturgical destruction of liturgy itself. Samson's audience consists of Philistine worshippers arranged hierarchically according to estate in an image of social order evocative of medieval and early modern conceits of the bodies mystical and politic. The hierarchical arrangement also enhances the quasi-liturgical sense of the scene:

> MESSENGER: Occasions drew me early to this City,
>   And as the gates I enter'd with Sunrise,
>   The morning Trumpets Festival proclaim'd
>   Through each high street: little I had dispatch't
>   When all abroad was rumour'd that this day
>   *Samson* should be brought forth to show the people
>   Proof of his mighty strength in feats and games;
>   I sorrow'd at his captive state, but minded
>   Not to be absent at that spectacle.
>   The building was a spacious Theater
>   Half round on two main Pillars vaulted high,
>   With seats where all the Lords and each degree
>   Of sort, might sit in order to behold,
>   The other side was op'n, where the throng
>   On banks and scaffolds under Sky might stand;
>   I among these aloof obscurely stood.
>   The Feast and noon grew high and Sacrifice
>   Had fill'd thir hearts with mirth, high cheer, and wine,
>   When to thir sports they turn'd. Immediately
>   Was Samson as a public servant brought,
>   In thir state Livery clad. (1596–1615)

The Messenger describes the scene of Samson's act in theatrical terms as a "show" or "spectacle" of "Sacrifice" and "wine" staged in a "Theatre." These theatrical motifs clearly allude to the commonplace Protestant view of the Mass (or its liturgical equivalent, to the Milton of the 1670s, the Communion service from the Book of Common Prayer) as a piece of theater or a play, a stage artifice.

The stagy quality of the celebration in the Temple is reinforced by its distinct mapping of a hierarchical political order, which the Messenger reproduces in detail. The description of the Temple evokes both the performance conditions of the early modern theater and the restored Church of England. The liturgical character of the space of the Temple is intimately intertwined with the ranks of political hierarchy:

> The building was a spacious Theater
> Half round on two main Pillars vaulted high,
> With seats where all the Lords and each degree

> Of sort, might sit in order to behold,
> The other side was op'n, where the throng
> On banks and scaffolds under Sky might stand.

While the "Lords" and any of "degree" are incorporated into the architecture of the Temple which is designed to seat them, the "throng" or multitude are exiled from the shelter of the political order. In this polemical setting, the "throng" standing "under" the "Sky" are already situated in a state of nature. This position implies that they are already excluded from any authentic place in the hierarchically ordered mystical body of the commonwealth; by this positioning, the drama hints that Samson's destruction only actualizes and radicalizes an already existent situation. Such a view would be consistent with Milton's endless suspicion of a liturgically legitimated social order.

Samson's final act exacerbates the situation of the multitude in a disorienting act of liberation:

> MESSENGER: . . . those two massy Pillars
> With horrible convulsion to and fro,
> He tugg'd, he shook, till down thy came, and drew
> The whole roof after them with burst of thunder
> Upon the heads of all who sate beneath,
> Lords, Ladies, Captains, Counsellors, or Priests,
> Thir choice nobility and flower, not only
> Of this but each *Philistian* City round
> Met from all parts to solemnize this Feast.
> *Samson* with these immixt, inevitably
> Pulld down the same destruction on himself;
> The vulgar only scap'd who stood without. (1648–59)

It is the fate of the "vulgar" who "only scap'd," the ambivalent masses remaining "without" in ambiguous disarray, deprived of an order of acclamation, that imaginatively evokes the Hobbesian state of nature, as I shall develop in what follows. As in the Messenger's first speech, this description elaborates in detail the high political order that Samson destroys ("Lords, Ladies, Captains, Counsellors, or Priests"). The social order is reconstructed at the moment Samson deconstructs it, literally, by pulling down the pillars. Samson's subsequent fate, "with these immixt," suggests a certain ambivalence about the act, but also curiously heightens its political and even liturgical power insofar as Samson is "immixt" with those of high political and religious significance. Samson's corpse is notably "immixt" with those of "Priests," suggesting he might be understood as the high priest of his own sacrifice. Samson performs a "spectacle" to end all "spectacle," in an apocalyptic liturgy that annihilates liturgy itself as a political and social economy.

The "multitude," the "vulgar," the "common rout," the rabble to which the poem obsessively returns throughout, may end imaginatively in a Hobbesian nature, as will be shown, but Milton's poem does not present this as their inevitable fate. More precisely, it may be the fate of the Philistines, but not the Israelites, who appear to have another option for re-forming into a mystical body at the end. Samson's iconoclastic outburst is immediately contained within the frame of the martyrological narrative, as Manoa's "Monument" illustrates:

> Let us go find the body where it lies
> Soak't in his enemies 'blood, and from the stream
> With lavers pure and cleansing herbs wash off
> The clotted gore. I with what speed the while
> (*Gaza* is not in plight to say us nay)
> Will send for all my kindred, all my friends
> To fetch him hence and solemnly attend
> With silent obsequy and funeral train
> Home to his Father's house: there will I build him
> A Monument, and plant it round with shade
> Of Laurel ever green, and branching Palm,
> With all his Trophies hung, and Acts enroll'd
> In copious Legend, or sweet Lyric Song.
> Thither shall all the valiant youth resort,
> And from his memory inflame thir breasts
> To matchless valour, and adventures high:
> The Virgins also shall on feastful days
> Visit his Tomb with flowers, only bewailing
> His lot unfortunate in nuptial choice,
> From whence captivity and loss of eyes. (1724–44)

According to Manoa, Samson will be disambiguated from the "clotted gore" of his enemies, and his "Acts enroll'd" in a stately "Monument." Milton's clear allusions to Foxe's famous Protestant martyrology assimilate Samson to the ranks of martyrs. Samson's true "Monument" seems to be textual—the text of Milton's poem. Given the ambivalence of his act, its uncertain inspiration, its paradoxically liturgical destruction of idolatrous liturgy, the reader may not be sure at this moment whether

Manoa's solution is celebrated or subtly critiqued. As Daniel Shore has recently observed, "Manoa's monument amounts to a new object of worship in place of the Philistine idols destroyed with the theater. Again the symptoms of idolatrous 'infection' present themselves: iconoclastic destruction gives rise to uncritical devotion to objects, succeeded in turn by new acts of matchless valor."[13] The possibility that Milton's drama may implicitly rebuke Manoa's desire to engage in monumental memory-making might be reinforced by the proximity of this moment to book 11 of *Paradise Lost,* where the fallen Adam's desire to remain in Eden to build "Altars" (323) and "monuments" (326) to his lost affinity with God is rebuffed by the Archangel Michael: "Surmise not . . . his presence to these narrow bounds confined" (340–41). *Samson Agonistes,* however, presents no such divine countermand to Manoa's projected memorial. Shore ultimately argues that we must remain conscious of the possibility that Milton's "representation of iconoclasm" functions as "both an analysis of and an attempt to avoid iconoclasm's failure."[14] To this, I would add that we need also to consider the possibility that the "analytic" side of the equation can always break down, as indeed Shore himself demonstrates in other Miltonic texts.[15] While many things can function as "idols" in Milton's belief system, not all "idols" may be considered equally pernicious.

Manoa's project to memorialize Samson may appear ambivalent given Milton's myriad vehement denunciations of idolatry, yet we cannot dismiss the possibility that Milton's poem endorses the replacement of the more pernicious idolatry of the Dagon liturgy with the still-imperfect yet ennobling idolatry of the "Monument" to Samson. This is so particularly if we take seriously the political context of the poem and its allusive references to the martyred regicides, who—as Knoppers shows—were memorialized in their own Foxean textual monuments. If Milton's poem is read as affirming Samson's martyrological "Monument," then we may understand the poem as seeking to contain the radical potential of Samson's act of erasure within a martyrological genre that holds the promise of a re-formed and Reformed mystical body. The Israelites, the elect people, have the hope to attain, precisely through Samson's creative destruction and its memorial celebration, a new form of mystical body, although transposed into a heroic key as a source of patriotic inspiration for "the valiant youth."

From a perspective that emphasizes Samson's capacity to incarnate or inspire a new form of mystical body, it is intriguing to reconsider Julia Lupton's suggestion that Samson enters the poem as a being who curiously appears at the same time singular and collective. While on one hand, Samson's giant stature is evocative of "Leviathan," his "restless thoughts ... like a deadly swarm" (*Samson Agonistes,* 19) add another dimension: "The insectile disposition of creeping and swarming ... counter the sublime singularity of Leviathan with the multitudinous character of infinite ecrudescence, evoking the fetid fecundity of the unformed populace that represents the resistant precondition of state-imposed power. Behind the capture, harnessing, and disabling of Samson looms the larger spectre of the multitude itself, hobbled ... and put to work."[16] In Lupton's account, this doubled aspect of Samson foreshadows the way in which later on "Samson maintains a link with the Philistine multitude even while destroying their public space and massacring their public representatives."[17] In such an account, Samson himself nearly foreshadows the famous frontispiece of Hobbes's *Leviathan,* in which the sovereign body is composed of a collective mass of individual beings. If Samson does have this collective dimension in Milton's text, however, it ultimately appears attributable to his status as a martyr, a locus of both mourning and celebration for his fellow countrymen who recollect a mystical body in his memory. Hobbes's monstrous Leviathan, by contrast, collects singular beings into a unified body by the immanent force of the sovereign contract. The Leviathan is constructed in decidedly unsacramental terms, in the tension Hobbes poses between the violent individualism of the state of nature and the cohesive bond of the contractual convention. Nonetheless, Hobbes's Leviathan visually tropes the tradition of the mystical body, just as Samson poetically tropes this same tradition, which illuminates a line of continuity between residual and emergent social ideas.

In replacing the sacramental residue of the martyrologically oriented community with new artificial conventions, Hobbes forges a new concept of social order that goes beyond the still-traditional aspects of the political radicalism of Milton's *Samson Agonistes.* The "vulgar" Philistines who "'scape" Samson's ruin of the temple are not destined to be recaptured in Manoa's envisioned martyrological "Monument" as a focus of a purified national mystical body, but they may be fated to wander into the Hobbesian state of nature and be regathered under the social contract that forms the condition of possibility for the giant sovereign body in Hobbes's frontispiece. Released from the bonds of the liturgically constituted mystical body, the dispersed Philistines might be imagined as the raw material for the new dispensation of the secular state, which reoccupies the space of the *corpus mysticum* as the immanent sphere of society. While Hobbes's reconstructed social order presupposes something like Samson's destructive anti-liturgical liturgy, his *Leviathan* offers an even more drastic answer than Milton's to the problem of the sacramental mystical body as a social form of life, whether conceived in liturgical or martyrological terms.

Unlike Milton, Hobbes does *not* want to perpetuate martyrology as a locus of national identity or unity, as the affective charge of the passions would prove too volatile and the appeal to a transcendent authority implied by the martyr as witness too unstable. Instead, Hobbes attempts to re-create the mystical body through the artifice of a civil liturgy understood in absolutely materialistic terms. The transcendence implied by the martyrological performance is precisely what Hobbes seeks to foreclose by disclosing a newly defined sphere of radical immanence.[18] Hobbes's effort at redefinition is evident in the preface to *Leviathan,* where the old organological trope of the body politic is purged of its mystical connotations as it is recast in purely mechanistic and materialist terms. This mechanistic impulse is conveyed by Hobbes's obsessive repetition of "Art" and Artificiall" in his initial account of the constitution of the Leviathan: "*Art* goes yet further, imitating that Rationall and most excellent worke of Nature, *Man.* For by Art is created that great LEVIATHAN called a COMMON-WEALTH, or STATE, (in latine CIVITAS) which is but an Artificiall Man ... and in which, the *Sovereignty* is an Artificiall *Soul,* as giving life and motion to the whole body."[19] Even the sovereign "*Soul*" is rendered as an automatic mechanism, divorced from any authentic transcendence. Hobbes enumerates the parts of this "Artificiall" body in a way that underscores their artifice, producing an almost parodic variation on Paul's account of the mystical body of the Christian community ("For as the bodie is one, and hath many members, and all the members of the bodie, which is one, yet are but one body: even so is Christ. For by one Spirit are wee all baptized into one body, whether we be Jewes, or Grecians, whether we be bond, or free, and have bene all made to drink into one Spirit. For the body also is not one member, but many" [1 Cor. 13:12–14]). For Hobbes, the "many members" of a body remain, but the "Spirit" that unifies them has been replaced by "Art." While reference to divinity is not totally eliminated, it is accessed only in terms of an immanent analogy: "Lastly, the *Pacts* and *Covenants,* by which the parts of this Body Politique were at first made, set together, and united, resemble that *Fiat,* or the *Let us make man,* pronounced by God in the Creation."[20] The creative force of the celebrated Hobbesian contract is at the outset portrayed as imitating God's freely willed creative action. Unlike the traditional notion of the liturgy or the martyrological performance, however, the contract is kept firmly in the realm of the "Artificiall"—it may imitate God's creation, but it does not claim to participate directly in or provide direct access to the more transcendent aspects of divinity.

Later on, in chapter 13, the absolute immanence of the contract is reinforced insofar as it appears as a form of order developed under the duress of the negative equality in the state of nature—the necessary solution to the perpetual war of all against all. Hobbes casts the natural state as one of equality in the following terms:

> Nature hath made men so equall, in the faculties of body, and mind; as that though there bee found one man sometimes manifestly stronger in body, or of quicker mind then another; yet when all is reckoned together, the difference between man and man is not so considerable . . . For as to the strength of body, the weakest has strength enough to kill the strongest, either by secret machination, or by confederacy with others, that are in the same danger with himselfe.[21]

In this passage, Hobbes might well be describing the state of the "ingrateful multitude" of Philistines in Milton's drama, once they have been released from the liturgical spectacle of the Temple of Dagon. In positing "Nature" in these terms Hobbes concocts a powerful fiction of an originally atomized condition, perpetually fractured by self-interested anarchic violence. Hobbes himself acknowledges the fictional quality of his construction: "It may peradventure be thought, there was never such a time, nor condition of warre as this; and I believe it was never generally so, over all the world: but there are many places, where they live so now."[22] This fiction of nature gains a special purchase by reference to the relatively unknown "America"—the blank spaces of the map provide a contemporary warrant for Hobbes's sociological thought experiment. Hobbes's fiction of nature in this way overwrites an older tradition (inspired by texts such as 1 Corinthians) in which social unity was founded in an implicit, imagined spiritual (if not political or economic) equality that was enacted in sacramental rituals of communion. In the tradition that Hobbes seeks to foreclose, the performative rites of the liturgy were imagined to conjoin immanent social life with a transcendent mystical fellowship. The social coherence bequeathed by the liturgical tradition had already been challenged by the institution of sacramentalized martyrdom, the preferred mode for performatively enacting the mystical body among the radical Protestants of Milton's cohort. However, to Hobbes, all forms of sacramental social order had proven too volatile after decades of Reformation and resistance. While the notion of a mystical body had once conveyed social coherence, it now represented social division more than anything else.

To reconstruct a semblance of social order according to a new mystical protocol would be to Hobbes too dangerous, given the spiritual enthusiasms that had emerged in the recent collapse of church and state, which was itself brought on by fundamental disputes about religious ritual. So Hobbes dissolves the aspiration for spiritual equality implied in the tradition of the *corpus mysticum* into his new narrative of conflict in nature. This conflict reestablishes the social unity formerly achieved in mystical terms in materialistic, artificial terms, as collective agreement with a political convention: "This is more than Consent, or Concord; it is a reall Unitie of them all, in one and the same Person, made by Covenant of every man with every man."[23] The convention of the social contract does resemble the original divine fiat, as Hobbes suggests in his new definition of the Commonwealth: "the Multitude so united in one Person, is called a COMMON-WEALTH, in latine CIVITAS. This is the Generation of that great LEVIATHAN, or rather (to speake more reverently) of that *Mortall God*, to which we owe under the *Immortall God*, our peace and defence."[24] However, in his insistence on the "mortality" of the Leviathan, Hobbes firmly keeps the realm of human political convention separate from a divinity understood as absolutely transcendent. As the prior fiction of the negative equality of the state of nature implies, the possible analogy between divine and human covenants is not the primary rationale for the efficacy of the contract as an institutor of social unity. The immanent formality of the contractual agreement replaces the more fluid interplay between immanence and transcendence that had characterized the traditional concept of the mystical body.

In *We Have Never Been Modern,* Bruno Latour assesses the scope of Hobbes's achievement as the inventor of modern sociology and political science:

> Hobbes invents the naked calculating citizen, whose rights are limited to possessing and to being represented by the artificial construction of the Sovereign. He also creates the language according to which Power equals Knowledge, an equation that is at the root of the entire modern Realpolitik. Furthermore, he offers a set of terms for analyzing human interests which, along with Machiavelli's, remains the basic vocabulary for all of sociology today.[25]

Hobbes conspicuously constructs this sociological vocabulary out of the frayed material of the medieval social ideal of the *corpus mysticum,* with

Milton's Samson as an ironic and perhaps unwitting accomplice. Hobbes offers a materialistic travesty of the mystical body in his new vision of the commonwealth. It is only after an extensive reckoning with the depth and complexity of the prior history of the *corpus mysticum* that we can appreciate fully the boldness of Hobbes's venture. This study has sought to make legible again the sacramental communitarian social tradition that preceded Hobbes's invention, as a possible prelude to imagining the possibility of post-Hobbesian social worlds.

NOTES

Introduction

1. Beyond the literary sphere, the conventions of the English language itself embed these tensions to this day, as witnessed by the fate of the word "church" in my argument. As I wrote the manuscript of this book, I consistently capitalized "Church" whenever it was associated with the concept of the mystical body as an ideal unified and universal collective, a practice which is also consistent with myriad premodern sources and their modern historical and theological expositions. This choice always causes consternation to copy editors, however, as it is no longer recognized as valid by the *Chicago Manual of Style:* "church" in any general sense (understood now as an "institution" rather than a "body") must be lowercased; only proper names of denominations ("the Roman Catholic Church" or "the Church of England") warrant capitalization. (*Chicago Manual of Style Online,* 16th ed. [Chicago: University of Chicago Press, 2010], http://www.chicagomanualofstyle.org/). My final text follows the current convention of lowercasing "church," but the story that it tells illuminates the complex history and discourse of the *corpus mysticum* that this convention, with its enforced distinction between general institution and proper (often politically marked) name, suppresses.

2. Ernst Kantorowicz, *The King's Two Bodies: A Study in Mediaeval Political Theology* (Princeton, N.J.: Princeton University Press, 1957).

3. The following edition will be cited throughout this volume: Henri Cardinal de Lubac, *Corpus Mysticum: L'Eucharistie et l'église au Moyen-Age,* 2nd ed. (Paris: Aubier, 1949). Translated into English as *Corpus Mysticum: The Eucharist and the Church in the Middle Ages,* trans. Gemma Simmonds, with Richard Price and Christopher Stephens, ed. Laurence Paul Hemming and Susan Frank Parsons (Notre Dame, Ind.: University of Notre Dame Press, 2007).

4. William Haller, *The Elect Nation: The Meaning and Relevance of Foxe's "Book of Martyrs"* (New York: Harper and Row, 1963). Relevant criticism addressing Haller's thesis is noted in chapter 2.

5. Stephen Greenblatt, *Hamlet in Purgatory* (Princeton, N.J.: Princeton University Press, 2001), 253–54. Also relevant to this discussion is Greenblatt's famous essay on *King Lear,* "Shakespeare and the Exorcists," in *Shakespeare and the Question of Theory,* ed. Patricia Parker and Geoffrey Hartman (London: Routledge, 1985), 163–87.

6. See, for example, Sarah Beckwith, *Signifying God: Social Relation and Symbolic Act in the York Corpus Christi Plays* (Chicago: University of Chicago Press, 2001). Beckwith's most recent work focuses on the legacy of sacramental drama in Shakespeare's late romances; see *Shakespeare and the Grammar of Forgiveness* (Ithaca, N.Y.: Cornell University Press, 2011).

7. Again, see Beckwith, *Shakespeare and the Grammar of Forgiveness.* A recent article by Thomas Fulton on *Measure for Measure* offers a pertinent citation of Beckwith's view: "Sarah Beckwith suggests that Shakespeare's medievalism is ultimately 'radical,' even though it is 'almost invariably seen by modern readers as nostalgic, conservative, or both,' " quoted in "Shakespeare's *Everyman: Measure for Measure* and English Fundamentalism," *Journal of Early Modern and Medieval Studies* 40, no. 1 (2010): 119–20.

8. Eric Santner's recent work offers one version of what such an analysis would look like, however. See Santner, *The Royal Remains: The People's Two Bodies and the Endgames of Sovereignty* (Chicago: University of Chicago Press, 2011).

9. Within Catholic theology, William Cavanaugh has gone the furthest in extending a concept of the Eucharistic *corpus mysticum,* derived from de Lubac, to diagnose modern and postmodern pathologies, which appear as parodies or travesties of the original ideal of a Eucharistic body of Christ. See his *Torture and Eucharist: Theology, Politics, and the Body of Christ* (Oxford: Blackwell, 1998) and *Theopolitical Imagination: Discovering the Liturgy as a Political Act in an Age of Global Consumerism* (Edinburgh: T. and T. Clark, 2002).

10. Giorgio Agamben, *The Kingdom and the Glory: For a Theological Genealogy of Economy and Government,* trans. Lorenzo Chiesa with Matteo Mandarini (Palo Alto, Calif.: Stanford University Press, 2011).

11. Ibid., 181.

12. Ibid., 254–59.

13. Ibid., 248.

14. Ibid., 194.

15. For the crucial passages, see Agamben, *Kingdom and Glory,* 245–49.

16. I refer, of course, to a series of discourses initiated in Jean-Luc Nancy's *The Inoperative Community,* trans. Peter Conner, Lisa Garbus, Michael Holland, and Simona Sawhney (Minneapolis: University of Minnesota Press, 1991); and Maurice Blanchot's *The Unavowable Community,* trans. Pierre Joris (Barrytown, N.Y.: Station Hill, 1988); and continued in Agamben's own *The Coming Community,* trans. Michael Hardt (Minneapolis: University of Minnesota Press, 1993).

17. John Milbank, *Theology and Social Theory: Beyond Secular Reason,* 2nd ed. (Oxford: Blackwell, 2006), 13.

18. Milbank does address Agamben's concept of *homo sacer* in an analysis of the "political theology" of the scriptural passion narratives in *Being Reconciled: Ontology and Pardon* (London: Routledge, 2003), 90–104. Agamben, to my knowledge, has not, so far, engaged with Milbank's work in a similar way.

19. See Milbank's extended engagements with de Lubac in *Being Reconciled* and *Theology and Social Theory,* as well as his brief study *The Suspended Middle: Henri de Lubac and the Debate Concerning the Supernatural* (Grand Rapids, Mich.: Eerdmans, 2005). Catherine Pickstock also provides an extended "Radical Orthodox" treatment of de Lubac's work on the mystical body in *After Writing: On the Liturgical Consummation of Philosophy* (Oxford: Blackwell, 1998).

20. Milbank, *Theology and Social Theory,* 9.

Chapter One

1. Kantorowicz, *The King's Two Bodies: A Study in Mediaeval Political Theology.* Page numbers are hereafter cited in the text.

2. *Representations* 106 (Spring 2009). The articles concerned with Kantorowicz's legacy include Stephen Greenblatt, "Introduction: Fifty Years of *The King's Two Bodies,*" 63–66; Richard Halpern, "The King's Two Buckets: Kantorowicz, *Richard II,* and Fiscal *Trauerspiel,*" 67–76; Victoria Kahn, "Political Theology and Fiction in *The King's Two Bodies,*" 77–101; and Lorna Hutson, "Imagining Justice: Kantorowicz and Shakespeare," 118–42.

3. See Agamben's comments on Schmitt and Kantorowicz in *Homo Sacer: Sovereign Power and Bare Life,* trans. Daniel Heller-Roazen (Palo Alto, Calif.: Stanford University Press, 1998), 91–94.

4. For example, Kahn contrasts Kantorowicz's project with Schmitt's by way of the role of fictionalizing activity in their accounts of political theology: "Unlike Schmitt's 'Catholic political form,' however, Kantorowicz's political form requires a self-conscious act of mythmaking, invoking the deliberate appropriation and manipulation of signs and symbols" ("Political Theology and Fiction," 88). Hutson makes a similar point: "Renaissance literary critics focusing on Kantorowicz's use of the word 'mystical' seem not to have noticed how nearly synonymous it is with 'fictional' in the centuries-long intellectual developments that Kantorowicz traces: Aquinas's '*corpus mysticum*' or '*persona mystica*' hardly differed, wrote Kantorowicz, from the *persona ficta* of the jurists. Kantorowicz argues that designations of sacredness are markers of fictiousness and abstraction" ("Imagining Justice," 124–25). Kahn and Hutson are largely accurate in their portrayal of the thrust of Kantorowicz's argument; in this context, however, I want to emphasize that in transmuting theology into fiction, Kantorowicz is also partially misrepresenting sources that offer a different theological path toward both critiquing Schmitt and conceptualizing the "mystical." The Aquinas example, in particular, is one to which I will turn in greater detail later in the argument.

5. De Lubac, *Corpus Mysticum: The Eucharist and the Church in the Middle Ages.* In *The King's Two Bodies,* Kantorowicz consistently cites the second French edition of this work: *Corpus Mysticum: L'Eucharistie et l'église au Moyen Age,* 1949. I will provide page citations for both the 1949 French and English translations in the text throughout this chapter. Page numbers are hereafter cited in the text.

6. Both M. B. Pranger, "Politics and Finitude: The Temporal Status of Augustine's *Civitas Permixta,*" in *Political Theologies: Public Fictions in a Post-Secular World,* ed. Hent de Vries and Lawrence Sullivan (New York: Fordham University Press, 2006), 113–21; and Regina Schwartz, *Sacramental Poetics: At the Dawn of Secularism* (Palo Alto, Calif.: Stanford University Press, 2008), replicate Kantorowicz's use of de Lubac in their own arguments, without assessing the extent to which Kantorowicz is accurately representing de Lubac's claims.

7. Kantorowicz, *King's Two Bodies,* xviii. This passage of the "Preface" has been read as a veiled reference to Schmitt by Kahn, "Political Theology and

Fiction," 79–80; Halpern, "King's Two Buckets," 67–68, and Agamben, *Homo Sacer*, 91–92.

8. In this section, I draw upon the following accounts for background on de Lubac's life, career, and theology: Hans Urs von Balthasar, *The Theology of Henri de Lubac: An Overview*, trans. Joseph Fessio and Michael Waldstein (San Francisco: Ignatius, 1991); John Milbank, *The Suspended Middle: Henri de Lubac and the Debate Concerning the Supernatural*; Michel de Certeau, *The Mystic Fable*, vol. 1: *The Sixteenth and Seventeenth Centuries*, trans. Michael B. Smith (Chicago: University of Chicago Press, 1992); and Lawrence Paul Hemming, "Henri de Lubac: Reading *Corpus Mysticum*," *New Blackfriars* 90, no. 1029 (2009): 519–34.

9. Milbank, *Suspended Middle*, 3.

10. Ibid.

11. Milbank, *Suspended Middle*, 6–14, 33–47; and von Balthasar, *Theology of Henri de Lubac*, 12–19, 63–73, address this controversy and its resolution in greater detail.

12. Hans Boersma, "Sacramental Ontology: Nature and the Supernatural in the Ecclesiology of Henri de Lubac," *New Blackfriars* 88, no. 1015 (2007): 249. See also Boersma's book *Nouvelle Théologie and Sacramental Ontology: A Return to Mystery* (Oxford: Oxford University Press, 2009).

13. Certeau, *Mystic Fable*, 82–85. For the "caesura," see de Lubac, *Corpus Mysticum*, 281–82; trans., 250.

14. Certeau, *Mystic Fable*, 82–85.

15. Ibid., 84.

16. Ibid., 85.

17. See Hemming's critique in "Henri de Lubac," 524–27.

18. As previously noted, de Lubac is a major inspiration for a largely Anglo-Catholic group of scholars who identify under the label "Radical Orthodoxy" and pursue a project of merging postmodern critiques of secular modernity with a reinterpretation of early church traditions. *Corpus Mysticum*, in particular, appears prominently in several works; see John Milbank, *Being Reconciled: Ontology and Pardon*, 122–26, as well as *Suspended Middle*; and Catherine Pickstock, *After Writing: On the Liturgical Consummation of Philosophy*, 121–67. Milbank in particular has more recently entered the wider ongoing interdisciplinary discourse of political theology; see especially the edited collection *Theology and the Political: The New Debate*, ed. Creston Davis, John Milbank, and Slavoj Žižek (Durham, N.C.: Duke University Press, 2005).

19. Carl Schmitt, *Roman Catholicism and Political Form*, trans. G. L. Ulmen (Westport, Conn.: Greenwood, 1996). Hereafter cited in the text.

20. See the translator's "Introduction" to Schmitt's *Roman Catholicism* for more details on the relationship between Schmitt's tract and Weber's arguments, ix–xxxvi.

21. For Sohm's influence on Weber's concept of "charismatic authority," see David Norman Smith, "Faith, Reason, and Charisma: Rudolf Sohm, Max Weber and the Theology of Grace," *Sociological Inquiry* 68, no. 1 (1998): 32–60. Smith argues that Weber actually radically transforms the notion of

charisma that he derives from Sohm, ending up with propositions that deeply contradict Sohm's own formulations. Peter Haley similarly argues that Weber subjects Sohm's ideas about charisma to a "psychological reduction." See Haley, "Rudolf Sohm on Charisma," *Journal of Religion* 60, no. 2 (1980): 185–97. However, Wolfgang Fietkau suggests that in Schmitt's view, Weber had indeed replicated some of Sohm's claims about charisma and spiritual authority too closely. See Fietkau's sketch of Schmitt's response to Sohm and Weber in "Loss of Experience and Experience of Loss: Remarks on the Problem of the Lost Revolution in the Work of Benjamin and His Fellow Combatants," *New German Critique* 39 (1986): 169–78.

22. Quoted in Smith, "Faith, Reason, and Charisma," 44. Smith cites a 1904 English translation of vol. 1 of Sohm's *Kirchenrecht,* first published in German in 1892.

23. See Smith's distinction between Weber and Sohm on the issue of "office charisma" in "Faith, Reason, and Charisma," 48–51.

24. This point should throw into question the notion that Schmitt presents an authentically "Catholic" vision of representation and authority. Victoria Kahn cites Schmitt's claim that the Catholic Church "represents Christ himself, in person" as symptomatic of a political-theological tendency that will eventually lead Schmitt to embrace Nazi ideology: "Here we see that political theology doesn't simply name the process of secularization for Schmitt; it also refers to a specifically Catholic paradigm, which Schmitt proposes as the solution to the modern political crisis of liberal states. It seems likely that it was precisely this at once 'personalist' and 'institutionalist' notion of sovereignty that inclined Schmitt to support Hitler and the Nazi party in the 1930s, after the failure of the Weimar state" ("Political Theology and Fiction," 83). Kahn moves somewhat too quickly to imply that Schmitt represents the slippery slope that leads from Catholicism to Nazism. It is important to recognize that Schmitt's "personalist" interpretation of the "institution" of Catholicism is inspired, at least in part, by a critical response to the Protestants Sohm and Weber, and that, in making these arguments, Schmitt is effacing other possible interpretations of Catholic tradition.

25. Schmitt, "Visibility of the Church," in *Roman Catholicism,* 52.

26. Ibid.

27. Ibid., 53.

28. Schmitt, *Political Theology: Four Chapters on the Concept of Sovereignty,* trans. George Schwab (Chicago: University of Chicago Press, 2005), 36.

29. Halpern, "The King's Two Buckets," 71.

30. Both Kantorowicz and de Lubac acknowledge the influence of a modern revival of the idea of the *corpus mysticum* in the papal encyclical of 1943, *Mystici Corporis,* which affirms the validity of the phrase for describing the communal life of the modern Catholic Church. See Kantorowicz, *King's Two Bodies,* 194n4; and *Corpus Mysticum,* 133; trans., 117. For the text of this encyclical, see http://www.papalencyclicals.net/Pius12/P12MYSTI.HTM. De Lubac discusses the relationship between his account of the *corpus mysticum*

and *Mystici Corporis* at greater length in a later work, *The Splendor of the Church*, trans. Michael Mason (San Francisco: Ignatius, 1999), esp. chap. 3, 84–125.

31. The sentence cited here is *Summa theologica* III.q.48, a.2, also cited by de Lubac, *Corpus Mysticum*, 127n60; trans., 112n60.

32. De Lubac, *Corpus Mysticum*, 128; trans., 113: "Nevertheless, we also find [in the Third Part of the *Summa*]: '*the true body of Christ represents the mystical body,*' which takes us back to the origins of the phrase as it is used by Master Simon and the *Treatise of Madrid.*"

33. Kantorowicz, *King's Two Bodies*, 202n25, gives Sohm's German: "Aus dem Körper Christi hat sich die Kirche in eine Körperschaft Christi verwandelt," in Sohm, *Das altkatholische Kirchenrecht und das Dekret Gratians* (Munich: Duncker und Humblot, 1918), 582.

34. Sohm, *Das altkatholische Kirchenrecht*, 582.

35. For a useful précis of Sohm's project in *Das altkatholische Kirchenrecht* and the controversy surrounding it among twentieth-century scholars of canon law, see Bruce Brasington, "Avoiding the 'Tyranny of a Construct': Structural Considerations Concerning Twelfth Century Canon Law," in *Das Eigene und das Ganze: Zum individuellen im mittelalterlichen Religiosentum*, ed. G. Melville and M. Schürer, Vita Regularis 16 (Münster, Ger.: LIT Verlag, 2002), 419–38.

36. For de Lubac's defense of the visibility of the church, see *Splendor of the Church*, 88. For Sohm's possible influence on the view of the eleventh and twelfth centuries in the work of Yves Congar, a close affiliate of de Lubac's, see Boersma, *Nouvelle Théologie*, 231n225. See also Congar's own essay, "R. Sohm nous interroge encore," *Revue des Sciences philosophiques et théologiques* 57 (1973): 263–94, particularly Congar's critique of Sohm's rejection of the visible church, 280. It is unlikely, however, that de Lubac himself was familiar with Sohm's work at the time of writing *Corpus Mysticum*, as he had insufficient German-language ability (*Corpus Mysticum*, "Editor's Preface," x).

37. Kantorowicz, *Kaiser Friedrich der Zweite* (Berlin, 1927).

38. The pertinent footnote refers the reader back to the earlier note 16, which cites de Lubac on the *corpus figuratum* as the equivalent of the *corpus mysticum*.

39. De Lubac, *Splendor of the Church*, 132.

40. But see also David George Hale, *The Body Politic: A Political Metaphor* (The Hague: Mouton, 1971), a study that also rehearses the Kantorowicz and de Lubac material on the *corpus mysticum*, tracing it into Renaissance literature. Hale also pays more explicit attention to the pressure of the Reformation on this figure. More recently, Jonathan Gil Harris's study of the pervasive and shifting metaphor of the *corpus politicum* in sixteenth- and seventeenth-century England establishes the frequency with which the political entity in the process of becoming the "English nation" was identified as an organic body with unstable boundaries. It is not surprising that one of the primary culprits destabilizing the English *corpus politicum* in the

political and literary discourses that Harris examines is the invasive Catholic agent. However, a peculiar instability afflicts the characterization of the Catholic threat as an outside invader. For example, when one polemical allegory of the body politic attacks specifically the "enuious tongue of false and lying Papists," Harris finds that "'infirmity' is equated with 'enemy,' a rhetorical move which cannot help but create uncertainty as to whether the disease does originate inside the body . . . the enemy within—or the enemy without?" (*Foreign Bodies and the Body Politic: Discourses of Social Pathology in Early Modern England* [Cambridge, Eng.: Cambridge University Press, 1998], 42–43). The uncertain origin of the Catholic "enemy" in such discourses is not only the effect of changing concepts of embodiment and disease; it is also a reflection of the precarious relation of Catholicism (and the medieval Catholic legacy of the mystical body) to a burgeoning English Protestant identity.

41. The convergence between de Lubac and Kantorowicz forms part of the intellectual background for the historian John Bossy's influential efforts to understand the sacramental structures of late medieval and Reformation Christianity as social phenomena. While neither de Lubac nor Kantorowicz are intent on an analysis of the turmoil of the Reformation at any length, Bossy, as a historian of the sixteenth century, is concerned with precisely this break and what it makes visible about correlations between the social and the sacred (or the "holy") in the period immediately before and after the Reformation. Bossy's work of the 1970s and 1980s seeks to complicate the modern historian's habit of projecting a contemporary notion of secular society into an age that could not have comprehended it. Bossy cites both de Lubac and Kantorowicz in his classic article, "The Mass as a Social Institution," *Past and Present* 100 (1983): 29–61. They are particularly important for Bossy's discussion of the "transfer" of "the socially integrative powers of the host away from the mass as such and into the feasts of Corpus Christi, and by way of that feast to rituals of monarchy and secular community" (59; de Lubac and Kantorowicz are cited "for the theory" in n85). In later arguments for a recalibrated concept of the "social" in the work of early modern historians (a "social" not to be treated as something over and against "religion" but intimately bound up with it), Bossy proposes more serious attention to the Eucharist as "the supreme symbol and embodiment of Christian society" in the period in question: in this connection he cites "Henri de Lubac on the doctrine of the Body of Christ" along with other historians of "times and situations somewhat earlier" as "distinguished examples of how to go about this central topic" ("Unrethinking the Sixteenth Century Wars of Religion" in *Belief in History: Innovative Approaches to European and American Religion,* ed. Thomas Kselman [Notre Dame, Ind.: University of Notre Dame Press, 1989], 280). In *Christianity in the West, 1400–1700* (Oxford: Oxford University Press, 1985), Bossy explores sacramental life as a fundamental principle of social order in the premodern European world; its rituals (foremost the Eucharist in the Mass) instantiate social cohesion as an extension of Christian peace and charity in the profane world insofar as they extend the sacrificial model of reconciliation between God and man to effect

reconciliation between man and man. While Bossy acknowledges that such ideals were often imperfectly actualized, particularly when the late medieval church strayed from the situation of the early church in its implementation of social imperatives, he argues that they nonetheless significantly underlay the coherence of medieval Christian society. While Bossy's work is aligned with that of other important historians of the Reformation, such as Natalie Zemon Davis, it should be noted that some of his claims have provoked ongoing debate. Miri Rubin's study, *Corpus Christi: The Eucharist in Late Medieval Culture* (Cambridge, Eng.: Cambridge University Press, 1991), expresses some skepticism toward enthusiastically communitarian interpretations of the late medieval Eucharist, a view she associates with Bossy (see 4, and 76–77 especially). Rubin offers a helpful cautionary note when she argues that Eucharistic celebration, including the processions and feasts associated with it, could express tensions and contradictions within the social world as well as unity. However, it should also be noted that Bossy often acknowledges the possibility and actuality of such tensions in his own accounts. Most importantly, the larger hypothesis that these sacramental events were intrinsically social seems corroborated even when they are shown to be occasions of antagonism as much as amity.

42. Kantorowicz cites S. B. Chrimes, *English Constitutional Ideas in the Fifteenth Century* (Cambridge, 1936), 68–69, as the source of this anecdote.

43. For example, Bossy picks up on this detail from Kantorowicz as a data point in his article on the Mass but he places a somewhat different emphasis on its significance. For Bossy, the anecdote illustrates the extent to which pre-Reformation Eucharistic ritual is inextricably bound up with the ways the society imagines itself as a community: this "piece of political theology . . . likened a meeting of parliament to a mass considered as a sacrifice, in that it served, among other things to integrate the otherwise disparate purposes of kings, lords, and commons" ("Mass as a Social Institution," 35). To Bossy, the image of the Parliament as a Mass reveals the reciprocity between the liturgical and the socio-political worlds. The metaphorics of the Mass is not simply "mysticizing" but reflective of a larger dynamic order; the Mass was a "social institution" that functioned on at least two different levels: "as a sacrifice it tended . . . to represent its social universe as a concatenation of distinct parts, while as a sacrament it represented and embodied unity and wholeness" (34–35).

44. See Bossy's reference to "the anti-Lollard parliament of 1401" ("Mass as a Social Institution," 35). For the anti-heresy legislation passed by Parliament in 1401, see *Documents Illustrative of English Church History*, ed. Henry Gee and William John Hardy (London: Macmillan, 1896), 133–37.

45. On the influence of *City of God* on medieval political thought, see Gerhart B. Ladner, "Aspects of Medieval Thought on Church and State," *Review of Politics* 9, no. 4 (1947): 403–22; and R. W. Dyson, "Introduction," *The City of God Against the Pagans* (Cambridge, Eng.: Cambridge University Press, 1998): "Augustine forms the turning-point from which the historian can date the beginning of the medieval Christianisation of political thought" (xxix).

46. The importance of Augustine for de Lubac's research on the earliest notions of the *corpus mysticum* cannot be overestimated. In some sense, de Lubac's entire argument can be understood as an effort to learn how to read Augustine again in a way lost as a result of "rationalism" and "dialectic." See especially de Lubac's extended commentary on Augustine, *Corpus Mysticum* (trans., 230–36), and also Lubac's later remark, "This is the habitual perspective of Augustine, who always sees the ecclesial body as an extension of the Eucharist" (trans., 257).

47. Chrimes, *English Constitutional Ideas in the Fifteenth Century,* 68–69.

48. Augustine quotes Romans 12:3 here.

49. Saint Augustine, *The City of God Against the Pagans* (X.6), trans. and ed. R. W. Dyson (Cambridge, Eng.: Cambridge University Press, 1998), 400.

50. De Lubac, *Corpus Mysticum,* trans., 17. William Cavanaugh glosses this passage from *City of God* in terms reminiscent of de Lubac's analysis: "sacrifice is simply a *becoming whole,* with God and with one another. Sacrifice is an action of the whole Body, which is simultaneously Christ, the community, and the bread and wine that we offer" ("Eucharistic Sacrifice and the Social Imagination in Early Modern Europe," *Journal of Medieval and Early Modern Studies* 31, no. 3 [Fall 2001]: 601).

51. Eamon Duffy's *The Stripping of the Altars* (New Haven, Conn.: Yale University Press, 1992) illustrates with careful historical documentation how such ideals remained powerful up until the political inception of the Reformation: early sixteenth-century Eucharistic prayers convey "the sense that the Host was the source simultaneously of individual and of corporate renewal and unity" (92). Duffy acknowledges counter-examples and contradictions of this ideal scheme in the late Middle Ages—power politics and class tensions inflected Eucharistic rituals and related feasts such as Corpus Christi long before Henry VIII conceived of the break with Rome. However, in Duffy's interpretation, even such tensions and contradictions are testaments to the imaginative force of the Mass in the era: "the Eucharist could only be used to endorse existing community power structures because the language of Eucharistic belief and devotion was saturated with communitarian and corporate imagery" (92).

52. The phrase is Catherine Pickstock's. Pickstock argues in terms complementary to the present argument that the medieval world cohered around charity as a socially binding and reconciling force, radiating outward from a primary expression in the Mass into social organizations of guilds, lay fraternities, and institutions of godparenthood and marriage (*After Writing: On the Liturgical Consummation of Philosophy* (Oxford: Blackwell, 1998). Without going so far as to affirm fully Pickstock's somewhat idealistic view of the liturgical social order of the high Middle Ages, her phrase "ecstatic collectivity" ("Within the social realm . . . peace, like charity, was characterized as a state of being attained through repeated affirmations of ecstatic collectivity" [146]) seems apt for describing the constitution of the pre-Reformation *corpus mysticum* sketched here, even as we must acknowledge that this "ontological condition" of charity—and its expression in the liturgy of the Mass—likely

was never perfectly realized and certainly was particularly under pressure in the late fourteenth and fifteenth centuries due to emerging political, economic, and cultural factors. See also Bossy, *Christianity in the West* and "The Mass as a Social Institution," who presents a more measured view of the situation, while offering historical evidence that supports some of Pickstock's assertions.

53. See Otto von Gierke's classic *Political Theories of the Middle Ages,* trans. F. W. Maitland, 2nd ed. (Cambridge, Eng.: Cambridge University Press, 1913), also a source heavily relied upon by Kantorowicz. Gierke characterizes the medieval view of temporal and spiritual powers as distinct "co-ordinate Powers . . . *Sacerdotium* and *Imperium* were two independent spheres instituted by God Himself" (16) encompassed by "Christendom . . . as a single universal Community" (10). "Mankind is one 'mystical body' " in this view, which might, alternatingly yet equally, be understood as "the Universal Church (*ecclesia universalis*)" or "the Commonwealth of the Human Race (*respublica generis humani*)" (10). Such a view may seem contradictory from a modern perspective formed by the secular "separation of church and state," but its paradox expresses an outlook consonant with the religio-social history traced so far. It is this delicate synthetic system that is irrevocably rent by the Reformation, as Gierke himself notes (19). See also Pickstock: "In the Middle Ages, the monarchs were not *absolute* monarchs and were themselves included within the liturgical congregation" (*After Writing,* 173).

54. Duffy's *Stripping of the Altars* remains the most meticulous account of the vitality of late medieval religion and the halting progress of the Reformation of churches and liturgy at the parish level throughout the Tudor dynasty. Bossy's *History of Christianity in the West* is also illuminating on the general situation on the eve of the Reformation.

55. The later arc of Kantorowicz's chapter 5 moves from a sacramentally constituted *corpus mysticum* overtaken by the political order to a political *corpus mysticum* constituted through imitations of Christian martyrdom performed in defense of the state (section 3, "*Pro Patria Mori*"). For Kantorowicz, it is the growing personal sanctity of the ruler that enables this transference to occur. Interestingly, he focuses on the development of the pre-Reformation Gallican church-state complex to exemplify this trend: in the rhetoric of the early 1300s in France, the idea developed that "death on the battlefield for the political *corpus mysticum* headed by a king who was a saint and therefore a champion of justice, became officially 'martyrdom.' It equaled the self-sacrifice of canonized martyrs for the *corpus mysticum* of the Church, the head of which was Christ" (*King's Two Bodies,* 256). See also Kantorowicz, *King's Two Bodies,* 234–35. For the idea that we can understand the French Gallican church as a prototype for the political takeover of the English church in the sixteenth century, see John Neville Figgis, *The Divine Right of Kings* (New York: Harper and Row, 1965), who develops a comparison between "Anglican" and Gallican positions (110–12). For more recent elaborations on this theme, see William Cavanaugh, *The Myth of Religious Violence* (Oxford: Oxford University Press, 2011).

Chapter Two

1. Geraldine V. Thompson, "Foxe's *Book of Martyrs:* A Literary Study" (dissertation, University of Oregon, 1974), 185. Thompson's larger thesis, that "the Eucharist is the focus of a vast debate extending throughout the *Book of Martyrs* and constitutes a structural principle of it" (6), anticipates some of the arguments in the current chapter, although it has remained marginal to most recent Foxe criticism. It is my intention to develop more fully the implications suggested by Thompson's thesis. In an entirely separate inquiry, Janel Mueller arrives at a similar intuition about the centrality of Eucharistic theology to Foxe, although her argument, as Alice Dailey and Susannah Monta have observed, is somewhat naive about the extent of the break between Protestantism and medieval religion; see "Pain, Persecution, and the Construction of Selfhood in Foxe's *Acts and Monuments,*" in *Religion and Culture in Renaissance England,* ed. Claire McEachern and Debora Shuger (Cambridge, Eng.: Cambridge University Press, 1997), 161–87. Mueller seems unaware of Thompson's dissertation. I discuss critiques of Mueller's arguments in a further note later.

2. This is the title for Haller's book used in Great Britain. The book was published in the United States under a different title: *The Elect Nation: The Meaning and Relevance of Foxe's "Book of Martyrs"* (New York: Harper and Row, 1963). All citations refer to this American edition.

3. In his chapter on Foxe in *Forms of Nationhood: The Elizabethan Writing of England* (Chicago: University of Chicago Press, 1992), Richard Helgerson also attempts to split the difference between these two schools of thought, albeit in a different manner than the one proposed here.

4. Warren Wooden, *John Foxe* (Boston: Twayne, 1983), 21.

5. Ibid.

6. See Frances Yates, *Astrea: The Imperial Theme in the Sixteenth Century* (London: Routledge and Kegan Paul, 1975); and Thomas Freeman, "Providence and Prescription: The Account of Elizabeth in Foxe's 'Book of Martyrs,'" in *The Myth of Elizabeth* (London: Palgrave Macmillan, 2002), 27–55, on this theme.

7. Wooden, *John Foxe,* 30, although see also Freeman, "Providence and Prescription," on the changing, increasingly critical view of Elizabeth in later editions of *Actes and Monuments.*

8. See Duffy, *Stripping of the Altars,* on the extensive efforts of Mary Tudor's regime to restore the rituals and accoutrements of pre-Reformation religion in England.

9. Wooden, *John Foxe,* 10.

10. See Freeman, "Providence and Prescription," for the details and mixed success of these orders.

11. Alice Dailey has shown that a dependence on medieval martyrologies such as the *Golden Legend* is mixed in with Foxe's efforts at documentary history. When Janel Mueller dwells on the "transubstantive" language inscribed in many of Foxe's martyrdoms, Dailey rightly notes that such "transubstantive images" need not be considered merely "compensations for [the martyrs']

rejection of a Catholic ontology of presence" (Mueller, "Pain, Persecution," 171), but actually illustrate the extent to which Foxe must work within established medieval traditions of martyrdom to make his martyrologies legible to an early modern audience (Alice Dailey, "Typology and History in Foxe's *Acts and Monuments,*" *Prose Studies* 25, no. 3 [2002], 5). Susannah Monta makes a similar point in *Martyrdom and Literature in Early Modern England* (Cambridge, Eng.: Cambridge University Press, 2005), 76n13. Building on these previous critical insights, my argument insists that Foxe borrows and indeed depends upon not only medieval martyr narrative traditions but also a Eucharistic tradition that was vitally "corporate and communitarian," in Eamon Duffy's phrase.

12. Separate essays by Margaret Ashton and Elizabeth Ingram and John King relate this image to *Actes and Monuments,* although neither delves into an extended treatment. See Ashton and Ingram, "The Iconography of *Acts and Monuments,*" 66–142, and John King, "Fiction and Fact in Foxe's *Book of Martyrs,*" 12–35, in *Foxe and the English Reformation,* ed. David Loades (Aldershot, Eng.: Scolar Press [Ashgate], 1997). The provenance of *The Lambe Speaketh* is also the topic of several brief articles published in the *Journal of the Warburg and Courtauld Institutes,* cited later.

13. Aston and Ingram also link *The Lambe Speaketh* of 1555 to Timothy Bright's 1589 *Abridgement* of Foxe's *Book of Martyrs* ("Iconography of *Acts and Monuments,*" 78–79).

14. See King ("Fact and Fiction," 30n27) and Aston and Ingram ("Iconography of *Acts and Monuments,*" 79n23). On the broadsheet version, see also Rowena J. Smith, "*The Lambe Speaketh* . . .: An English Protestant Satire," *Journal of the Warburg and Courtauld Institutes* 61 (1998): 261–67.

15. See Malcolm Jones, "*The Lambe Speaketh:* An Addendum," *Journal of the Warburg and Courtauld Institutes* 63 (2000): 287–94. Jones conjectures that the original plate must have been engraved in Germany with a Latin text for the Turner volume (evidently the earliest extant version), and subsequently "re-engraved in English for the popular English market (indeed it is far too well executed to be an English engraving of the 1550s!)" (287–90).

16. See Smith, "*The Lambe Speaketh,*" 261; 264. For the text of the Marian Heresy Bill, see Gee and Hardy, *Documents Illustrative of English Church History,* 384.

17. On Bishop Gardiner's career as a Protestant bogeyman, see Michael Riordan and Alec Ryrie, "Stephen Gardiner and the Making of a Protestant Villain," *Sixteenth Century Journal* 34, no. 4 (2003): 1039–63.

18. Smith, "*The Lambe Speaketh,*" 261.

19. Ibid., 264.

20. Smith suggests the iconographic association with the crucifixion, but not the further analogue to the elevation of the host in the Mass ("*The Lambe Speaketh,*" 261).

21. According to Smith, the scriptural intertext here is Hebrews 10:10–18, which emphasizes the singularity of Christ's sacrifice and the need for "no more offering for sin" as a result of it ("*The Lambe Speaketh,*" 262).

22. For more extensive coverage of these debates, see William Cavanaugh, "Eucharistic Sacrifice and the Social Imagination in Early Modern Europe;" and Francis Clark, *Eucharistic Sacrifice and the Reformation* (London: Darton, Longman and Todd, 1960).

23. On the genre of the medieval host desecration narrative, see Miri Rubin, *Gentile Tales: The Narrative Assault on Late Medieval Jews* (Philadelphia: University of Pennsylvania Press, 2004).

24. John Foxe, *Actes and Monuments* (1583), 1509. All quotations of *Actes and Monuments* are taken from John Foxe, *The Unabridged Actes and Monuments Online* or *TAMO* (Sheffield: HRI Online Publications). Available from http//www.johnfoxe.org. All citations refer to the 1583 edition unless otherwise noted; the page numbers (hereafter cited in the text) follow the original Foxe numeration throughout. I have also consulted the following editions at the Folger Shakespeare Library in Washington, D.C.: Foxe, *Actes and Monuments of matters most speciall and memorable, happenyng in the Church, with an vniuersall history of the same,* 2 vols. (London, 1583); Foxe, *The First Volume of the Ecclesiasticall history contaynyng the Actes and Monumentes of thynges passed in euery kynges tyme in this Realme, especially in the Church of England principally to be noted* and *The Second Volume of the Ecclesiasticall history, conteynyng the Actes and Monumentes of Martyrs* (London, 1570); and Foxe, *Actes and Monuments of these latter and perillous dayes, touching matters of the Church* (London, 1563). While I have emended some of Foxe's abbreviations, I have largely followed the spelling and conventions of the original printed texts.

25. Aston and Ingram note that Bright's title page shares with Foxe's original the "double theme" of the "true and false, persecuted and persecuting Churches" ("Iconography of *Acts and Monuments,*" 76), but they do not analyze how specific Eucharistic and sacrificial imagery is foregrounded in Bright's title page in any great detail, beyond noting its link to the 1555 engraving.

26. See Jesse Lander's discussion in "Foxe's *Book of Martyrs:* Printing and Popularizing the *Acts and Monuments*" in *Religion and Culture in Renaissance England,* ed. McEachern and Shuger, 69–92. Lander argues that Haller's controversial thesis that Foxe's work is responsible for the emergence of an exceptionalist sense of English national identity can be defended in terms of "reader responses" such as Bright's, even if Foxe himself expresses a more universalist, ecumenical agenda. Glyn Parry makes a similar argument in "Elect Church or Elect Nation? The Reception of the *Acts and Monuments*" in *John Foxe: An Historical Perspective,* ed. David Loades (Aldershot, Eng.: Ashgate, 1999), 180. Patrick Collinson's observations are also of interest in this context: "John Foxe and National Consciousness," in *John Foxe and His World,* ed. Christopher Highley and John N. King (Aldershot, Eng.: Ashgate, 2002), 10–59. For a relevant overview of the tendency of critical accounts of Foxe's work to "inevitably reproduce the basic structure of Protestant propaganda," see Ryan Netzley, "The End of Reading: The Practice and Possibility of Reading Foxe's *Actes and Monuments,*" *ELH* 73, no. 1 (2006): 187.

27. Lander, "Foxe's *Book of Martyrs,*" 87.

28. Lander reproduces this "Note" in his article ("Foxe's *Book of Martyrs*," 84).

29. Haller, *Elect Nation*, 245.

30. On this visual logic, see Helgerson, *Forms of Nationhood*, 256; and Monta, *Martyrdom and Literature*, 55–57. Thomas Betteridge proposes a reading of Foxe's title page which privileges the left of the image as the "known, the self-evident, the given" while the right is the "place of the problematic, provisional, and the new" ("Truth and History in *Acts and Monuments*," in *John Foxe and His World*, ed. Highley and King, 149).

31. Aston and Ingram, "Iconography of *Acts and Monuments*," 74.

32. See Betteridge for the claim that the vertical axis represents the scale from "ideal" to "real" ("Truth and History," 149).

33. Aston and Ingram identify the middle section of the title page as "a sacramental passage from this world to the next" ("Iconography of *Acts and Monuments*," 74).

34. Betteridge ("Truth and History," 149–50) and Aston and Ingram ("Iconography of *Acts and Monuments*," 74–76) highlight how Foxe's title page illustration is indebted to the prior work of artists of the German Reformation, such as Georg Pencz, who first developed the "two churches" motif.

35. As Betteridge suggests in his reading of the title page: "Read as a single text—and not artificially broken down into word and image—it articulates an understanding of history in which the 'truth' is static and unchanging. Real movement or change is all located on the 'false' right-hand side of the text. History, in terms of this text, is the enactment over time of the conflict between movement and stasis, debate and worship, persecution and persecuted. In these terms the binary opposition between the visible and invisible that Foxe constructs as the basic dynamic of his historiography needs to be understood in Augustinian terms as a conflict between 'truth'/presence versus falsehood/lack of presence. It is not that 'truth' is invisible but that its meaning, its presence or completeness, is deferred until the end of time or history" ("Truth and History," 151).

36. Betteridge notes how the "boundaries between the three images of 'false' religion are porous and failing" ("Truth and History," 150).

37. See Ruth Luborsky, "The Illustrations: Their Pattern and Plan," in *John Foxe: An Historical Perspective*, ed. Loades, 76–84, for a comprehensive catalogue; as well as Aston and Ingram, "Iconography of *Acts and Monuments*."

38. Susannah Monta summarizes the argument of Foxe's title page in these terms: "The title page argues that the sacrifice of the martyr's flesh replaces the Mass's central miracle because their mortification of the flesh powerfully reveals the 'trewe and lyvely faithe' for which the martyrs suffer" (*Martyrdom and Literature*, 57). In this claim, Monta's reading of the title page image comes close to my own. However, I seek to emphasize more strongly than Monta the communal aspect of the scene, guided by my attention to the tradition of the *corpus mysticum*. Also, instead of "replacement," I would prefer to think of the dynamic depicted as one of *transference*. What Foxe's title page acknowledges, perhaps in spite of itself, is the communally binding force of the Eucharistic celebration—a force that it seeks to reorient around the community of martyrs.

39. For such arguments, see Elizabeth Eisenstein, *The Printing Revolution in Early Modern Europe* (Cambridge, Eng.: Cambridge University Press, 1983); and Helgerson, *Forms of Nationhood*, 264. As is well known, Foxe himself also makes this association in *Actes and Monuments* in his discussion of the printing press; see, for example, Foxe's excursus on the "inuention and benefite of printing" in Book Six of the 1583 edition of *Actes and Monuments* (731–32).

40. The point about the admixture of medieval and modern in Foxe's text at large is made by several critics already cited, notably Dailey ("Typology and History"); Monta (*Martyrdom and Literature*), and Wooden (*John Foxe*). My argument builds on those claims in its focus on Foxe's continuing visible connection to the *corpus mysticum* tradition.

41. Eisenstein emphasizes this point in *Printing Revolution*, 170–71.

42. On the social aspects of the Corpus Christi celebration, the classic account is Mervyn James, "Ritual, Drama, and Social Body in the Late Medieval Town," *Past and Present* 98 (1983): 3–29. Miri Rubin also provides an extensive account of the celebration that is sometimes at odds with James's more idealistic claims—for her discussion of the processions in particular, see *Corpus Christi*, 243–71.

43. Monta emphasizes how Foxe (like the Counter-Reformation martyrologies of subsequent Catholic apologists) seeks to form interpretive communities of faith by shaping readers' responses to competing claims of martyrdom (*Martyrdom and Literature*, 35–49). From this perspective, the early modern martyrology (whether Catholic or Protestant) is a clear outgrowth of the burgeoning print culture of the sixteenth century—a tradition refashioned according to new technological capabilities that produce new literacies and devotional habits.

44. Netzley, "The End of Reading," 207. Netzley cites Evelyn Tribble's analysis as a rare example of a critical reckoning with the Book Ten preface: Evelyn Tribble, "The Peopled Page: Polemic, Confutation, and Foxe's *Book of Martyrs*," in *The Iconic Page in Manuscript, Print, and Digital Culture*, ed. George Bornstein and Theresa Tinkle (Ann Arbor: University of Michigan Press, 1998), 109–22.

45. Netzley, "The End of Reading," 207.

46. Natalie Zemon Davis describes similar texts circulating in France during the Wars of Religion as emerging on the same continuum with acts of iconoclastic violence in "The Rites of Violence: Religious Riot in Sixteenth-Century France," *Past and Present* 59 (1973): 51–91. These Protestant texts carry on a similar work of desecration, understood as a kind of ritual purification, enacted on "priests' manuals, missals, and breviaries" which the Reformed polemicists subject to "gross and comic satire" (Davis, "Rites of Violence," 76, esp. n82). Davis describes such textual performances not only as forms of violence but also as ultimately comprehensible in terms of the goals, "values, and self-definition of a community" (90) that seeks to purify itself of forms of worship considered polluting or idolatrous. Davis proposes a view from which we can consider Foxe's anti-missal as itself a counter-ritual, a performance that

declares a new form of sacred society in a pre-secular era in which political, social, and religious life cannot be firmly distinguished.

47. On such critiques, see Bossy: "Critics like Becon objected that the mass represented the Christian community neither in its parts nor as a whole, since the entire action, both sacrificial and (normally) sacramental, was monopolized by the priest, took place where the congregation could neither see nor hear what was being done, and was performed in a language it did not understand" ("Mass as a Social Institution," 35). Furthermore: "They differed in their judgment of what were symbolically appropriate elements because they differed in their conception of what was entailed in creating unity and peace" ("Mass as a Social Institution," 49–50). As we will see, Foxe echoes many of Becon's complaints.

48. On Cranmer's liturgical project, see Dom Gregory Dix, *The Shape of the Liturgy* (London: Dacre, 1945) for a broad overview; and Janel Mueller ("Pain, Persecution," 178–79) for links between Cranmer's liturgy and Foxe's martyrology.

49. See Bossy: "For the devout as for the average soul, the elevation of the Host at the end of the Middle Ages was a moment of transcendental experience" (*Christianity in the West,* 68). See also complementary accounts by Miri Rubin, *Corpus Christi;* Lee Palmer Wandel, *The Eucharist in the Reformation: Incarnation and Liturgy* (Cambridge, Eng.: Cambridge University Press, 2006); and Eamon Duffy on "sacring," *Stripping of the Altars.*

50. On debates over "communion in both kinds," see Bossy (*Christianity in the West,* 70); and Wandel (*Eucharist in the Reformation,* 79; 216; 223).

51. See Cavanaugh's article on Luther's resistance to the "sacrificial" elements of the Eucharistic liturgy ("Eucharistic Sacrifice and the Social Imagination in Early Modern Europe," 586–99); and also see Bossy, "Mass as a Social Institution," on Reformist critiques.

52. Qtd. in Mueller, "Pain, Persecution," 178.

53. Ibid.

54. See Dailey ("Typology and History," 5) and Monta (*Martyrdom and Literature,* 76n13) for this critique of Mueller's article.

55. Sarah Beckwith, *Signifying God: Social Relation and Symbolic Act in the York Corpus Christi Plays,* esp. chaps. 2, 4, and 7.

56. Ibid., 135.

57. Ibid., 24.

58. Eamon Duffy, "Lay Appropriation of the Sacraments in the Later Middle Ages," *New Blackfriars* 77 (1996): 64.

59. Mueller more extensively links and compares Foxe and Cranmer's projects in "Pain, Persecution," 178. On the gap between the Reformers' aspirations "to restore the eucharist to its place at the centre of social unity" in their revisions of the liturgy and the results, see Bossy: "They created no sacred symbol as powerful as the host. A sense of fatality, of results achieved which were the opposite of those intended, hangs over their efforts: as if the current of social and cultural evolution which was carrying them forward was at the same time pushing them aside into shallow waters" ("Mass as a Social

Institution," 59–60). While Bossy may be correct about the long-term trend, Foxe seems to achieve some Reformation success by replacing the host with an amplified version of the traditional Christian martyr. Mark Breitenberg argues that Foxe adapts a transubstantive logic to sixteenth-century print culture: "Just as the dominant strategy of Protestantism in general is to return to the Word, the Protestant martyr is transformed from his own corporeality into the *logos* made immortal by texts such as the *Acts and Monuments*" ("The Flesh Made Word: Foxe's *Acts and Monuments*," *Renaissance and Reformation* 15 [1989]: 404). It is also worth noting that, at a later point in the English Reformation, in the crisis of the early 1640s, petitioners who sought to defend Cranmer's liturgy from those godly Parliamentarian critics who ultimately disestablished it during the Interregnum used Cranmer's status as one of Foxe's martyrs to defend the integrity of his liturgical work. See Judith Maltby, *Prayer Book and People in Elizabethan and Early Stuart England* (Cambridge, Eng.: Cambridge University Press, 1998): "The status of Cranmer as a martyr—and the kudos that imparted to both the office he occupied and the liturgy he composed—is a recurring theme through these diverse petitions. The Kentish petitioners . . . spoke of 'the solemn Liturgy of the Church of England, celebrious of holy Bishops and Martyrs, who composed it' " (115). That Foxe's martyrology developed a dynamic, mutually reinforcing relationship with the official English liturgy over time underscores my claim that the martyrology itself incorporates significant liturgical elements. On the 1640s crisis, see chapter 5.

60. Susannah Monta comments on this passage: "In this version, the entire multitude exclaims at the wonder as if it were like the transcendent conjunction of heaven and earth (what Catholic theologians claimed happened in the Mass); the marvel is seemingly universally acclaimed" (*Martyrdom and Literature*, 59).

61. Monta emphasizes Foxe's effective narrowing of the interpretive community in the 1583 version of Haukes's martyrdom (*Martyrdom and Literature*, 60).

62. Monta notes that the effect of the exclamation in the woodcut, which imitates both Christ and the proto-martyr Stephen, is "to place this marvelous death in Christian tradition" (*Martyrdom and Literature*, 60).

63. But see Monta, who observes that Foxe suppresses evidence that some of those present later recanted: this "suppression illuminates Foxe's efforts to present a Protestant community unified in their understandings of Protestant martyrs' sacrifices, despite evidence that some sympathizers were far from steadfast" (*Martyrdom and Literature*, 40).

64. On this continuity between the Mass and the community feast, see Bossy, *Christianity in the West,* 70–72, and "The Mass as a Social Institution," 53–54.

65. John Marbecke is also included in the original group persecuted, although he escaped burning through a royal pardon. In the 1583 edition Foxe adds extensive material on this episode (including a fold-out woodcut illustrating the main events), partially to correct errors in earlier editions of *Actes and Monuments* (such as an inconsistency about whether or not Marbecke

actually was martyred at this time). See *Actes and Monuments* (1583 edition), 1210–23 for the full account, including Foxe's address to critics of his accuracy.

66. Malcolm Jones cites this line from Person in his contextual study of the 1555 engraving ("*The Lambe Speaketh:* An Addendum," 192).

67. On the evolution of medieval and post-Reformation marriage customs, see Bossy, *Christianity in the West,* 19–26; and chapter 4.

68. Breitenberg, "The Flesh Made Word," 384–85.

69. David Loades traces this struggle over the legacy of Foxe from the conflicts within the English church in the 1580s through the crisis of the 1630s and 1640s, when Puritan-inflected editions of *Actes and Monuments* made a clear and direct "equation of the Arminian authorities with the Roman church" and Foxe turned from a supporter of royal supremacy in the English church "into an ally of the Puritan opposition" ("Afterword: John Foxe in the Twenty-First Century," in *John Foxe and His World,* ed. Highley and King, 283–84).

70. Damian Nussbaum, "Whitgift's *Book of Martyrs:* Archbishop Whitgift, Timothy Bright, and the Elizabethan Struggle over John Foxe's Legacy," in *John Foxe: An Historical Perspective,* ed. Loades, 144.

Chapter Three

1. See criticism on Shakespeare's use of Foxe in his history plays, especially *Henry IV* (for example, Gary Hamilton, "Mocking Oldcastle: Notes Toward Exploring a Possible Catholic Presence in Shakespeare's *Henriad,*" in *Shakespeare and the Culture of Christianity in Early Modern England* [New York: Fordham University Press, 2003]), *King John,* and *Henry VIII* (see especially Susannah Monta's claim that the last counts as a counter-Foxean play in *Martyrdom and Literature in Early Modern England,* 158–93).

2. Jonathan Bate, the editor of the Arden edition of *Titus Andronicus,* makes the influential claim that the play's repeated use of the term "martyr" inevitably evokes "Foxe's virulently Protestant martyrology *Acts and Monuments*" and a chain of associations to contemporary anxieties about maintaining Protestant rule in England. See *Titus Andronicus,* ed. Jonathan Bate (London: Routledge, 1995), 20–21. In a somewhat different vein, Darryl Palmer develops a contrast between the "coherent and triumphant" martyrological violence of Foxe and the "inescapable obscurity" of violence in *Titus:* both the play and the martyrology constitute "histories of violence," insofar as they both explore connections between reading, writing, and violence, although Palmer finds that the "lucidity" of the faith of Foxe's martyrs is countered by the "opacity" of the devastation in Shakespeare's play. See Darryl Palmer, "Histories of Violence and the Writer's Hand: Foxe's *Actes and Monuments* and Shakespeare's *Titus Andronicus,*" in *Reading and Writing in Shakespeare,* ed. David M. Bergeron (University of Delaware Press, 1996), 93. For Cynthia Marshall, writing in a psychoanalytic register, *Titus* clearly draws upon a vein of erotic violence also mined by Foxe's *Book of Martyrs;* both texts reflect the "congruency" between "early modern pornography" and "the imagery of martyrdom." See

Marshall, *The Shattering of the Self: Violence, Subjectivity and Early Modern Texts* (Baltimore: Johns Hopkins University Press, 2002), 114. More recently, Nicholas Moschovakis has discerned an implicit critique of martyrdom in the play (although he does not address potential affiliations between *Titus* and Foxe at any length): "the play's martyrological resonances are directed against the ideological dynamic that made deadly violence a linchpin of ecclesiastical and moral authority in post-Reformation culture, for those who endured it and those who inflicted it" ("'Irreligious Piety' and Christian History: Persecution as Pagan Anachronism in *Titus Andronicus*," *Shakespeare Quarterly* 53, no. 4 [2002]: 470). Moschovakis argues for an "irenic" Shakespeare, who stages spectacles that mock contemporary celebrations of martyrdom to (indirectly) advocate for religious tolerance. While this argument contains some fine observations about the complex character of religious anachronism in the play, the larger claim that the play's religious travesties are the product of a "tolerant" Shakespeare is insufficiently substantiated by the text.

3. But see Jonathan Bate on "Lucius" as the first Christian monarch in Britain in Foxe; Bate speculatively connects Foxe's Lucius to Shakespeare's Lucius as the supposed redeemer in the play (*Titus Andronicus,* Arden edition, 20–21). Bate emphasizes a "Reformation context" in the play, although his conclusions are quite different in many ways from what will be argued in the current chapter.

4. Although Palmer and Marshall approach the potential links between Shakespeare's tragedy and Foxe's martyrology from different theoretical and methodological perspectives, they both emphasize how Shakespeare's play unfolds the violence that Foxe describes in vivid theatrical tableaus that disclose more complex dimensions of the martyrological situation.

5. All quotations from the play follow the Arden Shakespeare *Titus Andronicus,* ed. Jonathan Bate, unless otherwise noted.

6. Gillian Kendall notes how "the image of the body politic" establishes a literal correlation between the fragmented political state of Rome and the dismembered bodies of the Andronici: "the combined image of the body politic and the body personal makes Rome, on the one hand, a Frankenstein monster, and Titus, on the other, a headless trunk. Titus may be superficially in control of his rhetoric, but rhetoric has an uncanny and disturbing life of its own" ("'Lend Me Thy Hand': Metaphor and Mayhem in *Titus Andronicus*," *Shakespeare Quarterly* 40, no. 3 [1989]: 300). Katherine Rowe similarly focuses on how the recurrent figure of the severed hand in the play also wreaks havoc on the hand as a frequent early modern metaphor for political agency: "The severed hands of *Titus Andronicus* display both the adequacies and insufficiencies of the metaphor of the body as a means of constituting political community" ("Dismembering and Forgetting in *Titus Andronicus*," *Shakespeare Quarterly* 45, no. 3 [1994]: 280). Like Kendall, Rowe finds in the tragedy a surrealistic world in which politically charged body metaphors disarticulate themselves when they materialize as the literally dismembered bodies on the stage. For further commentary on motifs of bodily disintegration in the play, see Mary Laughlin Fawcett, "Arms/Words/Tears: Language and the Body in

Titus Andronicus," *English Literary History* 50 (1983): 261–77; and Louise Noble, who explores how the troubled figure of the body politic in the play is inflected with references to early modern medical practice: "'And Make Two Pasties of Your Shameful Heads': Medical Cannibalism and Healing the Body Politic in *Titus Andronicus,*" *English Literary History* 70 (2003): 677–708. For a more general overview of the body politic metaphor in conjunction with developments in medicine and political rhetoric in early modern England, see Jonathan Gil Harris, *Foreign Bodies and the Body Politic.*

7. Thomas Anderson, *Performing Early Modern Trauma from Shakespeare to Milton* (Aldershot, Eng.: Ashgate, 2006).

8. Ibid., 32.

9. Thomas Rist has recently suggested that *Titus,* like many other early modern revenge tragedies, is preoccupied with the traditional rituals of commemoration that had recently been disrupted by the forces of religious reform: *Revenge Tragedy and the Drama of Commemoration in Reforming England* (Aldershot, Eng.: Ashgate, 2008). Along similar lines, Helga Duncan explores the elusive religious subtext of *Titus Andronicus* in terms of the play's interest in "the constitution of and challenges to sacred space": "'Sumptuously Re-Edified': The Reformation of Sacred Space in *Titus Andronicus,*" *Comparative Drama* 43, no. 4 (2009): 426. According to Duncan, "The playwright, by staging the tragic profanation of ancient holy sites and the grotesque counter-reformations it produces, offers a bleak portrait of spatial and spiritual *displace*ment in a culture on the cusp of profound religious change" (426). Both of these arguments offer compelling testimony to the play's engagement with Reformation religious crisis; in the current argument, I seek to contextualize the play within a religious conception that encompasses and indeed makes possible both funeral practices and the consecration of sacred spaces. The apparent derangement of each of these traditions in the play is symptomatic of the larger disintegration of the *corpus mysticum* that the tragedy registers.

10. Anderson's emphasis on the issue of signification as primary in episodes of Eucharistic debate in Foxe echoes Richard Helgerson's account of these debates, which also foregrounds the contested relation of sign and signifier (Helgerson, *Forms of Nationhood,* 266).

11. This argument will involve elaborating in a different direction on Cynthia Marshall's claim that *Titus* recycles the "motifs of bodily fragmentation familiar from images of saints and martyrs" to impose "a "type of temporary shattering of viewers" (*Shattering of the Self,* 137). Although Marshall's Lacanian emphasis on the psychosexual implications of the play's representations of dismemberment is in many ways distant from the frame of analysis proposed here (particularly in its insistence that the play "secularizes" such motifs), her suggestion that the tragedy forces its audience into a conceptual impasse with its competing, contradictory invitations to identify with victims and also with their victimizers, conflicting and unresolved "sadistic and masochistic" drives, remains relevant to an assessment of the connections between Foxe and *Titus.* It is not only the plight of Lavinia (the locus of Marshall's

reading, and so many others) that forces the audience into such a fragmented state; many other remainders and echoes of the sacramental universe strewn throughout the play also evoke this effect. Lavinia is the one that most obviously continues to resonate with a contemporary audience.

12. For instance, Bate glosses Titus's command to Lavinia in this scene, "Receive the blood" (5.2.197), as a "dark parody of the language of the holy eucharist?" (n263), a reading Moschovakis also develops ("'Irreligious Piety,'" 472), while Miola disputes ("'An Alien People Clutching Their Gods?'" Shakespeare's Ancient Religions," *Shakespeare Survey* 54 [2001]: 31–45.). See the final section of this chapter for further analysis of this crucial scene.

13. In addition to critics already cited, scholars who have addressed the issue of religious anachronism in the play include Dorothea Kehler, "*Titus Andronicus:* From Limbo to Bliss," *Shakespeare Jahrbuch* 128 (1992): 125–31; and Robert Miola, "'An Alien People Clutching Their Gods'?"

14. *Titus Andronicus,* ed. Bate, 19–20. Bate cites Samuel Kliger's book, *The Goths in England* (Cambridge, Mass., 1972), 33–34. See also Kliger's article "The Gothic Revival and the German '*Translatio,*'" *Modern Philology* 45, no. 2 (1947): 73–103.

15. Lukas Erne, "'Popish Tricks' and a 'Ruinous Monastery': *Titus Andronicus* and the Question of Shakespeare's Catholicism," in *The Limits of Textuality,* ed. Lukas Erne and Guillemette Bolens (Tübingen, Ger.: Gunter, 2000), 136–55, esp. 149. Erne's observation is also taken up by Thomas Rist (*Revenge Tragedy,* 60n127). For biographical speculation about Shakespeare's religious background, perhaps the most comprehensive recent account is Richard Wilson, *Secret Shakespeare: Studies in Theatre, Religion and Resistance* (Manchester, Eng.: Manchester University Press, 2004). See also Stephen Greenblatt, *Will in the World* (New York: Norton, 2004), for an account of Shakespeare's possible Catholic connections aimed at a general audience.

16. Erne, "'Popish Tricks," 149.

17. Nicholas Moschovakis nicely terms the play's resistance to readings that insist on straightforward religious allegory, "cryptological vertigo" ("'Irreligious Piety,'" 472).

18. Edward Ravenscroft, *Titus Andronicus, or The Rape of Lavinia* (London, 1687).

19. For a more complete account of Ravenscroft's political agenda, see Matthew Wikander, "The Spitted Infant: Scenic Emblem and Exclusionist Politics in Restoration Adaptations of Shakespeare," *Shakespeare Quarterly* 37, no. 3 (1986): 340–58.

20. Moschovakis, "'Irreligious Piety,'" 468.

21. Moschovakis links the sacrifice of Alarbus to the context of sixteenth-century religious polemics insofar as the language describing the ritual casts it as a travesty of Eucharistic sacrifice that mimics frequent Protestant attacks on the literalism of the Catholic Mass ("'Irreligious Piety,'" 464–65). Thomas Rist comments on the ways this sacrifice resembles a funeral Mass (*Revenge Tragedy,* 48). Anna Swärdh finds Titus and his family being defined from an anti-Catholic point of view in this scene: *Rape and Religion in English Renaissance*

Literature: A Topical Study of Four Texts by Shakespeare, Drayton & Middleton, Studia Anglistica Upsaliensia 124 (Uppsala University, 2003), 81.

22. Charles Taylor refers to the medieval concept of "sin" as akin to a "failed immune system" in the medieval church and emphasizes an earlier notion of church rituals as defensive of a collective, communal body as much as individual bodies: *A Secular Age* (Cambridge, Mass.: Harvard University Press, 2007), 39; 42. See also Regina Schwartz, *Sacramental Poetics,* esp. chaps. 1–2, for another recent effort to link early modern English literature to the breakdown of sacramental theology in the Reformation.

23. Palmer, "Histories of Violence and the Writer's Hand," 100–101.

24. On the *Aeneid* connection, see *Titus Andronicus,* ed. Bate, 18; and Heather James, who connects the surname Pius to Titus's classical predecessor Aeneas as an example of the play's overall subversion of the Roman elements of "Tudor ideology": *Shakespeare's Troy: Drama, Politics and the Translation of Empire* (Cambridge, Eng.: Cambridge University Press, 1997), esp. 51. John Klause relates "Pius" to the name of the pope (Pius V) who excommunicated Elizabeth in 1570: "Politics, Heresy and Martyrdom in Shakespeare's Sonnet 124 and *Titus Andronicus,*" in *Shakespeare's Sonnets: Critical Essays,* ed. James Schiffer (New York: Garland 1999), 234. On the connection to Pope Pius V as well as Aeneas, see also Lisa Hopkins, *The Cultural Uses of the Caesars on the English Renaissance Stage* (Aldershot, Eng.: Ashgate, 2008), 17, who cites Erne and Swärdh (among others) in support of this link.

25. For the problems presented by this passage, see *Titus Andronicus,* ed. Bate, 99–100; the lines are present only in the first quarto printing and omitted in the second quarto.

26. Duncan, "Sumptuously Re-Edified," 435.

27. William Slights argues that Titus becomes a "*pharmakos*" later in the tragedy: "The Sacrificial Crisis in *Titus Andronicus,*" *University of Toronto Quarterly* 49, no. 1 (1979): 22. However, the first *pharmakos* (a figure of both poison and cure via expiating sacrifice) appears to be Alarbus, as Noble has also argued ("And Make Two Pasties," 693).

28. Philip Schwyzer notes some parodic purgatorial overtones in this episode, *Archaeologies of English Renaissance Literature* (Oxford: Oxford University Press, 2007), 126.

29. See Georges Bataille, "Hegel, Death and Sacrifice," trans. Jonathan Strauss in *The Bataille Reader,* ed. Fred Botting and Scott Wilson (Oxford: Blackwell, 1997), 278–95 for the theory of "general" and "restricted" economies of sacrifice embedded in the Hegelian-Kojevian dialectic of master and slave. See further Derrida's early analysis of Bataille's critique of Hegel: "From a Restricted to a General Economy: A Hegelianism Without Reserve," trans. Alan Bass, in *Writing and Difference* (Chicago: University of Chicago Press, 1978), 251–77. In a Girardian idiom, William Slights analyzes the "perverse sacramentalism" of violence at the outset of the play as the hallmark of inefficacious rituals that try and fail to contain sacred violence ("Sacrificial Crisis," 22).

30. On the Abraham-Titus connection, see Moschovakis ("'Irreligious Piety,' " 468).

31. See *Titus Andronicus*, ed. Bate, 13–15, on parallels with *Coriolanus*, particularly with regard to the exile plot.

32. Robert Miola, "*Titus Andronicus*: Rome and the Family," in *Titus Andronicus: Critical Essays*, ed. Philip Kolin (New York: Garland, 1995), 199.

33. On Richard Verstegan's *Theatrum* as a Catholic response to Foxe, see Christopher Highley, "Richard Verstegan's Book of Martyrs," in *John Foxe and His World*, ed. Highley and King, 183–97. See also Susannah Monta's account of both Catholic and Protestant martyrologies of the era in *Martyrdom and Literature in Early Modern England*, esp. 35–78.

34. Jonathan Gil Harris, *Untimely Matter in the Time of Shakespeare* (Philadelphia: University of Pennsylvania Press, 2008), 135.

35. See the entry for "ruinous" in the *Oxford English Dictionary*, esp. 2 and 3. "Ruinous" as the state of "being brought into ruin or decay" is illustrated by a quotation from *Timon of Athens* ("Is yon'd despis'd and ruinous man my Lord?" [4.3.465]), while "ruinous" in the active sense of "bringing or tending to bring to ruin; disastrous, destructive, pernicious" appears in *King Lear* ("Machinations, howllownesse, treacherie, and all ruinous disorders follow us disquietly to our Graves" [1.2.123]). *Oxford English Dictionary Online*, 2nd ed., 1989, http://www.oed.com/.

36. Schwyzer, *Archaeologies*, 100. Hopkins also associates the Goth with "sightseeing" (*Cultural Uses of the Caesars*, 33).

37. Miola associates Aaron's Protestant discourse and demand for an "oath" at this moment with the trauma of the series of oaths imposed on the Catholic population of England by successive Tudor and Stuart rulers, the first of which (the Act of Succession) was most memorably opposed by Sir Thomas More on the grounds of "conscience," another term of abuse in Aaron's diatribe: "Aaron's anachronistic derision evokes a potent cultural paradigm which destabilizes and subverts: the villainous Moor acts the role of Tudor magistrate; he casts the victorious pagan Roman as defeated Roman Catholic" ("'An Alien People Clutching Their Gods?'" 34).

38. The sense of Aaron as degenerate Protestant radical is heightened a bit later in one of the more memorable moments in his extensive list of criminal activities:

> Oft have I digged up dead men from their graves
> And set them upright at their dear friends' door,
> Even when their sorrow almost was forgot,
> And on their skins, as on the bark of trees,
> Have with my knife carved in Roman letters,
> 'Let not your sorrow die though I am dead.' (5.1.135–40)

Thomas Rist notes that Aaron's stance as a "violator of remembrance" associates him with a Reformed tradition counterpoised in the play by Titus, who emphasizes the "*value* of remembrance" in a way "consonant with traditional and Catholic funeral, but *not* with the reduced remembrances persistently proposed by Reformers" (*Revenge Tragedy*, 53–54). Indeed, as Schwyzer notes, the desecration of tombs and skeletal remains was a noted habit of enthusi-astic Reformers for whom "dishonouring the bodies of the dead was also a way of striking a blow by proxy at the body of the Catholic Church" (*Archae-ologies*, 110). The same author also provocatively connects Shakespeare's famous epitaph on the Stratford tomb ("Blessed be the man that spares these stones / And cursed be he that moves these bones") precisely to the poten-tial anxieties generated by frequent Reformist attacks on the dead (114–20). The prank that Aaron describes exhumes the dead at the point where "sorrow was almost forgot," only to mock the renewed grief. Aaron grotesquely literal-izes, by bringing the actual decaying body to the doorstep of the mourner, the ritualized forms of remembrance common to traditional pre-Reformation reli-gion (complete with "Roman letters"). His grim joke recapitulates a pattern throughout the play of recycling the detritus of religious tradition in displaced forms.

39. Clare Asquith, *Shadowplay: The Hidden Beliefs and Coded Politics of William Shakespeare* (New York: PublicAffairs, 2005), 92.

40. See *Titus Andronicus*, ed. Bate, 87, on the influence of Marlowe's *The Jew of Malta* on the structure of *Titus* and the character of Aaron in particular.

41. In attempting to hush the baby, according to the report of the Goth, Aaron dwells on the infant's displacement from a proper imperial inheritance: "Villain thou mightest been an emperor / But where the bull and the cow are both milk-white, / They never do beget a coal-black calf" (5.1.30–32). To an audience trained in the protocols of reading "race" in the early modern text, Aaron's preoccupation with the child's color seems paramount in these lines, which underscore the problem of Aaron's color and identity as a "moor." For an account of early modern notions of race and miscegenation in the play, see, for example, Francesca T. Royster, "White-Limed Walls: Whiteness and Gothic Extremism in Shakespeare's *Titus Andronicus*," *Shakespeare Quarterly* 51, no. 4 (2000): 432–55. However, the infant's skin color is intertwined with questions of inheritance that are not unrelated to the ruined monastery that surrounds this family tableau. The "coal-black" color that Aaron has passed along to his son appears here as a threat to the child's future well-being. As Alison Shell has recently shown, in early modern sacrilege narratives associ-ated with the fate of dissolved monasteries, ruined religious property passed along through family lines may also operate as a kind of cursed inheritance, visiting destitution on future generations: *Oral Culture and Catholicism in Early Modern England* (Cambridge, Eng.: Cambridge University Press, 2007), 27. Emphasizing this strand does not imply that questions of religion super-sede those of race (or gender) in the play; indeed, this spiritual trauma cannot approach legibility without the marked materiality of the gendered or racial-ized body. Nonetheless, the theological and political crises that these bodies encode can cause them to deviate from more modern expectations concerning gender and race.

42. Julia Reinhard Lupton, "The Jew of Malta," in *The Cambridge Com-panion to Christopher Marlowe*, ed. Patrick Cheney (Cambridge, Eng.: Cam-bridge University Press, 2006), 154–55.

43. In the Arden *Titus,* Bate, ed., faithfully reproduces the "ruines" of the early modern text, 191, while *The Riverside Shakespeare,* 2nd ed. (New York: Houghton Mifflin, 1997), emends to "urns," 1099.

44. For more on Southwell's possible influence on Shakespeare, in particular the closely related *Rape of Lucrece,* see F. W. Brownlow, *Robert Southwell* (New York: Twayne, 1996). Alison Shell has offered a dissent to this view, but see also her *Catholicism, Controversy, and the English Literary Imagination, 1558–1660* (Cambridge, Eng.: Cambridge University Press, 1999) for Southwell's generally strong influence on the poetics of tears in late-sixteenth-century English verse (56–104).

45. Anne Sweeney situates Southwell's work in relation to the sacramental deprivation of the late Elizabethan Catholic community in *Robert Southwell: Snow in Arcadia: Redrawing the English Lyric Landscape, 1586–95* (Manchester, Eng.,: Manchester University Press, 2006): "Southwell's English Catholic readers supplied the extra context of Magdalen's tears from their own experience: they knew that she was also crying for the loss of Christ's body from the Roman Catholic Mass" (141). Gary Kuchar similarly argues that "Southwell's representation of Magdalene addresses and seeks to mitigate the recusant experience of religious/social paralysis" in "Gender and Recusant Melancholia in Robert Southwell's *Mary Magdalene's Funeral Tears,*" in *Catholic Culture in Early Modern England,* ed. Ronald Corthell, Frances E. Dolan, Christopher Highley, and Arthur F. Marotti (Notre Dame, Ind.: Notre Dame University Press, 2007), 136.

46. Swärdh, *Rape and Religion,* 117. In a separate reading, John Klause argues for some not-entirely-persuasive verbal echoes of Robert Southwell's more political prose works in *Titus Andronicus,* particularly in the fate of the hapless clown of act 4, sent by Titus to deliver an ill-fated "supplication" to the corrupt emperor. The clown in Klause's account becomes a tragicomic double for the Jesuit martyr-poet, who was imprisoned and tortured by the Elizabethan government shortly before the first performances of the play ("Politics, Heresy and Martyrdom," esp. 225–26). While Klause's identifications of echoes of Southwell's prose in *Titus* can seem strained, Swärdh's arguments for the influence of Southwell's devotional poetry, particularly in the play's imagery of tears, tend to be more persuasive.

47. Geoffrey Chaucer, *The Canterbury Tales,* "General Prologue," 1–8, in *The Riverside Chaucer,* ed. Larry D. Benson (Boston: Houghton Mifflin, 1987).

48. But see Joel Fineman, who associates these lines in Chaucer with the figure of rape, another provocative connection in the immediate context of *Titus;* see the long footnote appended to Fineman's important essay, "Shakespeare's *Will:* The Temporality of Rape" in *The Subjectivity Effect in Western Literary Tradition* (Cambridge, Mass.: MIT Press, 1991), 217.

49. Numerous analogous passages of extravagant parental grief occur in prior sixteenth-century revenge tragedies; one could compare, for example, Hieronimo's laments in Thomas Kyd's *Spanish Tragedy,* ed. J. R. Mulrayne (London: A. and C. Black, 2007). However, Kyd remains closer to the idiom of Senecan tragedy, his classical precursor, while Shakespeare turns to Chaucer to

evoke a more specifically English and medieval literary context in the midst of Titus's complaint.

50. A. G. Harmon argues that Shakespeare introduces clear parallels between the struggle between Richard and Bolingbroke and the earlier conflict between Becket and Henry II in his *Richard II*. Harmon explores the strong association between Stratford and the cult of Becket the martyr that lingered past the Reformation into Shakespeare's childhood: "Shakespeare's Carved Saints," *Studies in English Literature* 45, no. 2 (2005): 315–31.

51. On the destruction of Becket's shrine, see Duffy, *Stripping of the Altars,* 412; and Schwyzer, *Archaeologies,* 110.

52. See Miola's discussion of "martyrdom" in *Titus* in "'An Alien People Clutching Their Gods?,'" 33–36.

53. Asquith provocatively associates Lavinia's mutilation with the trauma of iconoclastic violence (*Shadowplay,* 92–93). For images of iconoclastic deface-ment, see Shell, *Catholicism, Controversy, and the English Literary Imagina-tion;* and Duffy, *Stripping of the Altars.*

54. For example, Asquith reads this scene as "a forlorn attempt to perpetu-ate the old forbidden Mass" (*Shadowplay,* 95).

55. On this aspect of Southwell's prose poem, see Kuchar, "Gender and Recusant Melancholia," 136; and Sweeney, *Robert Southwell,* 141.

56. Richard Wilson associates the position of the Andronici with that of the great Catholic aristocratic families of the late sixteenth century, subject to Protestantizing "Goths" (*Secret Shakespeare,* 22).

57. Slights associates the fly with the figure of sacrifice: "the fly-killing epi-sode of III.ii takes on a new significance in light of the loss of distinctions occasioned by the sacrificial crisis" ("Sacrificial Crisis," 26).

58. Miola, "'An Alien People Clutching Their Gods?,'" 36. Miola does not deny the potential for religious anachronism in the scene, however; he instead prefers to read the banquet as a "final parodic expression of the reliquary imagination" (36).

59. Hopkins, *Cultural Uses of the Caesars* (18). Hopkins extends here Erne's comments on the relevance to the play of the "mutilation" of the church as the body of Christ. Other critics who have made Eucharistic connections to Titus's cannibalistic banquet plot include Bate and Moschovakis, as well as Asquith, who also finds a "black parody of the Mass" in Titus's actions (*Shadowplay,* 89). In keeping with her emphasis on Reformation controversies concerning burial and sacred space, Duncan focuses on how Titus's plan represents a sort of "counterreformation" that turns Tamora herself into a parodic sacred burial site ("Sumptuously Re-Edified," 446). Rist claims that the Eucharistic echoes in the scene are not necessarily anti-Catholic because the intent of Titus's revenge is to emphasize the value of traditional funeral remembrance by denying it to Tamora's sons, who are "buried" in their mother's belly (*Revenge Tragedy,* 53).

60. On Shakespeare's adaptation of *Thyestes* and his blending of Senecan and Ovidian source material in the final banquet scene of *Titus Andronicus,* see Robert Miola, *Shakespeare and Classical Tragedy: The Influence of Seneca* (Oxford: Oxford University Press, 1992), 23–32.

61. John Kerrigan briefly analyzes the Christianizing of the Latin original of *Thyestes* in Jasper Heywood's 1560 translation in *Revenge Tragedy: From Aeschylus to Armageddon* (Oxford: Oxford University Press, 1996), 110–13. Seneca's original play presents a stoic view of the universe: natural order disoriented and convulsed by human crime, but also characterized by an absence of divine anger. The "casual fatalism" of Senecan stoicism (seemingly paradoxically) associates revenge with excess rather than simple equivalence. Heywood, by contrast, adds a prayer: "submits horrible actions to divine wrath." To Kerrigan, this shift exemplifies the tension between classical stoic thinking about anger and revenge and more providential Christian views. However, Kerrigan fails to linger on the Reformation difference within the English Christian experience that precisely the life of the Catholic exile Heywood exemplifies. See also Miola's discussion of Heywood's addendum (*Shakespeare and Classical Tragedy*, 31).

62. *Jasper Heywood and His Translations of Seneca's Troas, Thyestes and Hercules Furens,* ed. H. de Vocht (Louvain: A. Uystpruyst, 1913), 180.

63. Kerrigan, *Revenge Tragedy,* 112.

64. See the etymology of "witness, n.," in *Oxford English Dictionary Online,* Oxford University Press, http://www.oed.com/.

65. See *Titus Andronicus,* ed. Bate, 20; and Moschovakis, "Irreligious Piety," 472.

66. See "office, n.," in *Oxford English Dictionary Online,* Oxford University Press, http://www.oed.com/.

67. In Louise Noble's reading, Titus's recipe and preparation represents a parody of early modern pharmacology; Chiron and Demetrius "form the polluting corpse drugs of Titus's corrective ... the crucial ingredients of early modern pharmacology are deployed for the health of Rome" ("And Make Two Pasties," 699). Noble does not address the potential Eucharistic overtones in this scene, however, which can be taken to cast a harsher light on the proposed remedy, insofar as Titus is shown perverting the performance of traditional religion in the course of concocting his revenge drug—Rome may be superficially healed, but it is cut off from the ultimate spiritual remedy of salvation.

68. Bate (ed.) in the Arden *Titus* provides the reference (263, note to 5.3.203).

69. *Ovid's Metamorphoses Translated by Arthur Golding,* ed. Madeleine Forey (New York: Penguin, 2002), 357.

70. Sheri McCord emphasizes the communal implications of this banquet in her dissertation, "To Heal and Harm: Seventeenth-Century Literature, Medicine and the Body" (Saint Louis University, 2010).

71. Thomas Rist offers a pertinent view of Marcus's lines and the closing of the play, although his focus is more overtly on the play's obsession with memorials of the dead that may invoke the pre-Reformation church, and his reading of this final allusion (which also cites Erne's article, referenced earlier in this chapter) is somewhat more optimistic: "The consciously educational close seeks to transform the whole bloodletting and mutilation of the drama into a Christian redemption story, the broken limbs reunited in one body inevitably echoing ... the redemptive broken body celebrated in the Roman

Eucharist. This lesson extrapolated by Lucius, in which the drama becomes an emblem of Christianity, may ring hollowly today; however it reminds us that sacrifice—even sacrifice as terrible as that of Alarbus or Lavinia—is part of a traditional Christian 'mystery' in which vendetta, sacrifice, and therefore mourning are central" (*Revenge Tragedy*, 60–61). While I agree that "traditional Christian 'mystery'" forms the backdrop for the ending of the play, it does not seem to me that things are quite so straightforward: the Christian subtext is only intermittently visible here and throughout the play, suggesting a less-than-stable redemptive ending. Moreover, reaching such apparent redemption has required (and continues to require, up until virtually the last lines of the play) repeated acts, which travesty, often in gruesome ways, traditional sacramental rituals, another factor that undercuts confidence that the *corpus mysticum* of Rome will ever achieve a renewed coherence.

72. De Lubac provides many examples of this traditional allegory in *Corpus Mysticum:* "The ecclesial body is composed of members who are united and utterly purified . . . like the grains of pure wheat or the drops of grape juice from which the bread and wine are made" (*Corpus Mysticum*, trans. 169).

73. Duncan also notes this continuity, as well as the parallelism between Aaron and Tamora's punishments, although her focus falls more on how the play imagines (and violates) sacred spaces: like Titus, who "invalidates the culture of spatial sacredness" by turning Tamora herself into a tomb for her sons, Lucius "continues his father's practices; his actions further compromise the sacredness of the grave when he consigns Aaron to a hole in the ground . . . he begins with the funeral parody with which his father ended." She also notes how Aaron's fated self-consumption recapitulates Tamora's consumption of her own flesh in the form of her children ("Sumptuously Re-Edified," 446).

74. Noble reads Aaron's position at the end of the play as that of the scapegoat, or *pharmakos*, "the surrogate victim . . . for the furor of revenge that troubles the play . . . Aaron, the polluting cannibal threat, will slowly leach the residual violence of Rome's therapy into the Roman soil: providing a double-edged *pharmakon*—remedy or poison, purifier or pollutant—for a Roman state sustained by revenge" ("And Make Two Pasties," 701). Slights similarly reads Aaron as "substitutive victim" ("Sacrificial Crisis," 30), although he sees Titus himself as the ultimate *pharmakos:* "As the initiator of the sacrificial crisis, Titus can best function as *pharmakos*, the personified societal poison that . . . was its own antidote" (28). Both readings emphasize the ambivalence of the ritualism of the final sequence in the play, although without addressing the potential Christian subtext.

75. See, in particular, Rist, *Revenge Tragedy*, 54–55.

Chapter Four

1. Certeau, *The Mystic Fable*, 83.

2. Ibid., 84.

3. Unless otherwise noted, all quotations from *Measure for Measure* are taken from the New Folger Library Edition, ed. Barbara Mowat and Paul Werstine (New York: Washington Square, 1997).

4. Bossy, *Christianity in the West,* 4. On Bossy's relevance to readings of *Measure for Measure,* see Peter Lake with Michael Questier, *The Antichrist's Lewd Hat: Protestants, Papists and Players in Post-Reformation England* (New Haven, Conn.: Yale University Press, 2002): "Both [Shakespeare and Bossy] seem frankly nostalgic about a moral world that preceded both the reformation and counter-reformation; a world of which Bossy's is the most compelling modern evocation" (628n4). Lake focuses mostly on Bossy's discussion of the shift in focus in moral discussions from the pre-Reformation period's emphasis on the Seven Deadly Sins to the post-Reformation fixation on the Ten Commandments; my argument complements this analysis with a focus on how other elements of pre-Reformation tradition in Bossy's account (such as Anselm's doctrine of satisfaction and sacramental marriage) collide with their post-Reformation analogues particularly in the midst of the play's obsessive economic language.

5. I would like to thank John Parker for clarifying Luther's position in comments on a section of this chapter circulated at the Shakespeare Association of America 2012 seminar, "Rethinking Shakespeare's Secularity."

6. Bossy, *Christianity in the West,* 93.

7. On the fiscal theology of Isabella's speech, see Mowat and Werstine's note on this scene, Folger Library Edition of *Measure for Measure,* 215–16.

8. The quoted text is from the Geneva Bible translation: *The Bible that is, the Holy Scriptures conteined in the Olde and Newe Testament / translated according to the Ebrew and Greeke, and conferred with the best translations in diuers languages; with most profitable annotations vpon all the hard places, and other things of great importance,* Imprinted at London: By the deputies of Christopher Barker . . . , 1599 [i.e., Amsterdam: J. F. Stam, ca. 1639]. *Early English Books Online,* http://eebo.chadwyck.com.

9. The phrase "King James Version" is first associated with Shakespeare's play in Richard Levin's article "The King James Version of *Measure for Measure,*" *Clio* 3, no. 2 (1974): 129–63. Significant and sophisticated developments of the "King James" thesis include Jonathan Goldberg, *James I and the Politics of Literature* (Stanford, Calif.: Stanford University Press, 1989); Andrew Barnaby and Joan Wry, "Authorized Versions: *Measure for Measure* and the Politics of Biblical Translation," *Renaissance Quarterly* 51 (1998): 1225–29; and Debora Shuger, *Political Theologies in Shakespeare's England: The Sacred and the State in "Measure for Measure"* (New York: Palgrave, 2001).

10. In addition to Nigel Smith, critics who have addressed economic language and issues in the play at length include Marc Shell, *The End of Kinship: "Measure for Measure," Incest, and the Ideal of Universal Siblinghood* (Stanford, Calif.: Stanford University Press, 1988); and Stephen Deng, *Coinage and State Formation in Early Modern England* (New York: Palgrave Macmillan, 2011).

11. Concluding a study of the "two economies" of the play, Nigel Smith writes that *Measure for Measure* "seeks to attain a version of civic and domestic identity in which the separate economies, the modes of organisation of

production and exchange, are integrated. That monetary imagery is used to represent this seems to point to a parallel between that moment in time when money as an autonomous force was emerging from the notion that it should be controlled by a moral law, and the power of sexual or religious desire to burgeon forth within a monetary economy": "The Two Economies of *Measure for Measure,*" *English* 36 no. 186 (1987): 228.

12. It should be noted, of course, that Marx himself brilliantly analyzes the conflation of materialism and mysticism in the form of the commodity fetish in *Capital: A Critique of Political Economy,* vol. 1, trans. Ben Fowkes (New York: Penguin, 1976), 163–77. For a recent reappraisal (within early modern studies) of Marx's account of the commodity fetish and its debt to Luther, see John Parker, "What a Piece of Work Is Man: Shakespearean Drama as Marxian Fetish, the Fetish as Sacramental Sublime," *Journal of Medieval and Early Modern Studies* 34, no. 3 (2004): 643–72. My argument here aligns in some ways with this subtler account of Marx's thought.

13. See Agamben, *Kingdom and Glory,* chap. 3 (17–52).

14. The phrase is taken from Kantorowicz, *The King's Two Bodies,* 202.

15. Jean Bodin, *République,* book 1, chap. 10, *On Sovereignty,* trans. Julian H. Franklin (Cambridge, Eng.: Cambridge University Press, 1992), 78.

16. Bodin, *République,* 45.

17. Saint Augustine, *The City of God Against the Pagans* (V.18), 222.

18. For further anecdotes on the identification between the ruler and his fiscal resources in early modern rituals of sovereignty, see Sergio Bertelli, *The King's Body: Sacred Rituals of Power in Medieval and Early Modern Europe,* trans. R. Burr Litchfield (University Park: University of Pennsylvania Press, 2001).

19. Bodin, *République,* 80.

20. For further material on the theological grounds for this view of marriage, see Bossy, *Christianity in the West,* 21–22; and Sarah Beckwith, *Shakespeare and the Grammar of Forgiveness,* 69–73.

21. See Bossy on the Tridentine developments (*Christianity in the West,* 22–26); and, in relation to *Measure for Measure* specifically, see Margaret Scott, "'Our City's Institutions: Some Further Reflections on Marriage Contracts in *Measure for Measure,*" *ELH* 49, no. 4 (1982): 790–804. Scott gives many details on the new marriage order imposed by Trent, but lacks a strong sense of the possible continuity of older concepts of sacramental marriage, both in England and on the Continent. As Bossy shows, the demand for more rigorous regulation of marriage was as much a characteristic of the Reformation as the Counter-Reformation, a point not fully accounted for in Scott's analysis. The specific case of England was particularly complex: "The Church of England, which retained the existing *law* of marriage until Parliament enacted an equivalent of the Tridentine system in 1753, had from the start [of the Reformation] adopted a *ritual* of marriage which bore a family resemblance to the new Roman rite in that it enhanced the role of the priest or minister and abolished the location at the church door" (Bossy, *Christianity in the West,* 25).

22. Julia Reinhard Lupton, *Citizen-Saints: Shakespeare and Political Theology* (Chicago: University of Chicago Press, 2005), 146.

23. Quoted in Mowat and Werstine, Folger Library Edition of *Measure for Measure*, 8. See also Matthew 5:14–16.

24. C. E. Challis, *The Tudor Coinage* (New York: Manchester University Press, 1978), 213.

25. See "touch, v." 8 a-b for use as a technical term in coinage, the application of the touchstone (Shakespeare's *Timon of Athens* is cited in the figurative sense: "They have all bin touch'd, and found Base-Mettle" [3.3]) and 2 b for the latter, monarchical sense. For "touched gold," see specifically "touched, ppl. a.": "the touch-piece given by the sovereign when he touched for the 'king's evil', supposed to retain a healing virtue," *Oxford English Dictionary*, 2nd ed., 1989, http://dictionary.oed.com/. See also J. W. Lever's note on this passage in the Arden Edition of *Measure for Measure* (London: Methuen, 1965), 5–6.

26. Shell, *End of Kinship*, 29.

27. See Lever's note, Arden Edition of *Measure for Measure*, 6.

28. See Smith, "Two Economies," 201; and Shell, *End of Kinship*, 30.

29. Shell, *End of Kinship*, 30.

30. Sarah Beckwith also discusses the relevance of the king's two bodies concept in connection with *Measure for Measure* in somewhat different terms in *Shakespeare and the Grammar of Forgiveness*, 73–81.

31. The idea that Angelo represents a "Puritan" type is a commonplace in the critical literature; Peter Lake's analysis in *The Antichrist's Lewd Hat* is probably the most thorough treatment of this angle to date (chap. 15, "*Measure for Measure*, Anti-Puritanism and 'Order' in Early Stuart England," 621–700).

32. On these equivocations, see *Measure for Measure*, New Variorum Edition, ed. Mark Eccles (New York: Modern Language Association of America, 1980). Lake comments on the economic puns in this scene in similar terms (*Antichrist's Lewd Hat*, 646).

33. Rubin, *Corpus Christi*, 39.

34. Marc Shell, *Art and Money* (Chicago: University of Chicago Press, 1995), 15.

35. Peter Lake draws on John Bossy's account in *Christianity in the West* (116–24) to argue that *Measure* dwells upon and critiques the shift to a Ten Commandments-based morality, although, curiously, he does not specifically address Lucio's actual citation of the commandments in 1.2 (*Antichrist's Lewd Hat*, 628).

36. See Mowat and Werstine, Folger Library Edition of *Measure for Measure*, for this gloss, 213.

37. Ibid.

38. Lake, *Antichrist's Lewd Hat*, 672–73.

39. See Robert Watson, "False Immortality in *Measure for Measure*: Comic Means, Tragic Ends," in *Critical Essays on Shakespeare's Measure for Measure*, ed. Richard P. Wheeler (New York: G. K. Hall, 1999), 95–119. Watson claims: "From the very start [Isabella's] dedication as a spiritual Bride of

Christ is subverted, even parodied by her conversion into a procreative bride for the body politic" (109).

40. See, for example, Lake's discussion of the "irony" of the Angelo and Claudio juxtaposition in the play (*Antichrist's Lewd Hat,* 641–42).

41. Bodin, *République,* 58.

42. On the religious versus legal validity of the Duke's claim, see Lever's commentary, Arden Edition of *Measure for Measure* (liv–lv; 100).

43. Michael Friedman claims that the marriage proposal is intended as recompense for the Duke's demand that Isabella slander herself at the beginning of act 5, "'O Let Him Marry Her!': Matrimony and Recompense in *Measure for Measure,*" *Shakespeare Quarterly* 46, no. 4 (1995): 454–64. However, Friedman does not address the reasons why the Duke must stage this particular crisis.

44. In *Citizen-Saints,* Julia Lupton discusses the tension between lateral and vertical models of sovereignty in the Duke's two proposals and in *Measure*'s civic allegory at large (152–53).

45. Lupton, *Citizen-Saints,* 152.

46. I am indebted to Nichole Miller for this observation.

47. On the influence of such antiquarian discourses, which often imply recusancy or nostalgia for a Catholic past, in Shakespeare's work, see Eamon Duffy, "'Bare Ruined Choirs,'" in *Region, Religion and Patronage: Lancastrian Shakespeare,* ed. Richard Dutton, Alison Findlay, and Richard Wilson (Manchester, Eng.: Manchester University Press, 2003), 40–57. James Ellison also links Angelo's declaration to the iconoclastic trauma of Reformation England: Angelo "aligns the sexual enjoyment of the Catholic novice Isabella by a Puritan with the wholesale destruction of church fabric and buildings during the early years of the Reformation ('raze the sanctuary'), an event which many moderate Protestants of Shakespeare's time were starting to regret": "*Measure for Measure* and the Executions of Catholics in 1604," *English Literary Renaissance* 33, no. 1 (2003): 75.

48. Shell connects the Duke's marriage proposal to Isabella to the "dissolution of the monasteries" as a "symbol of the Reformation" (*End of Kinship,* 167–68). Nichole Miller first drew my attention to this parallel.

49. Shell claims that "Angelo's comparison between minting and begetting, or counterfeiting and bastardizing, is crucial to the political economy of Vienna, where both monetary and sexual commerce involve the 'figure' of authority" (*End of Kinship,* 98). This analysis is in accord with elements of the argument in this chapter, but ultimately, in my view, it fails to acknowledge the actual pathology of Angelo's claim in the context of the wider play. The contrast between this passage and alternative models of fiscal theology suggested by Isabella, the Duke, and even, to some extent, Lucio demonstrates that Angelo's rhetoric is not as normative as Shell seems to suggest.

50. See Lake's discussion of this line (*Antichrist's Lewd Hat,* 661).

51. Anna Kamaralli discusses Isabella's repetitious rhetorical strategy in "Writing About Motive: Isabella, the Duke and Moral Authority," *Shakespeare Survey* 58 (2005): 51.

52. See, for example, Carolyn E. Brown, "Erotic Religious Flagellation and Shakespeare's *Measure for Measure,*" *English Literary Renaissance* 16, no. 1 (1986): 139–65.

53. Kamaralli provides a good overview of the critical debate concerning these lines, touching on both the "sexual repression" hypothesis and those critics who emphasize links to virgin martyr traditions ("Writing About Motive," 50–53). She particularly challenges Lisa Jardine's claim, in *Still Harping on Daughters: Women and Drama in the Age of Shakespeare* (New York: Columbia University Press, 1989), 190–92, that Isabella's aspiration to saintliness is undermined by her evident sexual neurosis. Alison Findlay connects Isabella's desire for martyrdom to the experience of early modern Catholic recusant women and to an erotic ideal within medieval martyr traditions: *A Feminist Perspective on Renaissance Drama* (London: Blackwell, 1999), 37–38.

54. It is also true, however, that Isabella evokes a form of spiritual abjection that was already eroticized in medieval Catholicism as well as in Reformation polemics. On the "pornographic repetitiousness" of the virgin martyr tradition in the *Golden Legend,* see Marina Warner, *Alone of All Her Sex: The Myth and Cult of the Virgin Mary* (New York: Vintage, 1983), 70–72. On the sexualization of Catholic clerics in English anti-Catholic propaganda, see Arthur Marotti, *Religious Ideology and Cultural Fantasy: Catholic and Anti-Catholic Discourses in Early Modern England* (Notre Dame, Ind.: University of Notre Dame Press, 2005), esp. chap. 2.

55. For a medieval literary precedent, see Chaucer's "Prioress's Tale" in *The Canterbury Tales* where the body of the martyred clergeon is described in similarly "lapidary" terms:

> O grete God, that parfournest thy laude
> By mouth of innocentz, lo, heere thy myght!
> This gemme of chastite, this emeraude,
> And eek of martirdom the ruby bright,
> Ther he with throte ykorven lay upright,
> He *Alma redemptoris* gan to synge
> So loude that al the place gan to rynge. (607–13)

56. Julia Reinhard Lupton, *Afterlives of the Saints: Hagiography, Typology and Renaissance Literature* (Stanford, Calif.: Stanford University Press, 1996), 117.

Chapter Five

1. Janel Mueller, "Embodying Glory: The Apocalyptic Strain in Milton's *Of Reformation,*" in *Politics, Poetics, and Hermeneutics in Milton's Prose,* ed. David Lowenstein and James G. Turner (Cambridge, Eng.: Cambridge University Press, 1990), 25.

2. Ibid., 35.

3. Ibid., 23–24.

4. Ibid., 24.

5. Joanna Picciotto, "The Public Person and the Play of Fact," *Representations* 105 (2009): 85–132.

6. Ibid., 87.

7. Ibid., 98.

8. Ibid., 101.

9. For a recent account of the perceived proliferation of heretics in the Interregnum, see David Loewenstein, "Heresy and Treason," in *Cultural Reformations,* ed. Brian Cummings and James Simpson (Oxford: Oxford University Press, 2010), 264–86. See also Bossy, *Christianity in the West,* on the "extraordinary multiplication of English religious expressions" in the Interregnum (110–14).

10. John Morrill, *The Nature of the English Revolution* (London: Longman, 1993), 174–75.

11. Morrill argues that the resistant force of a significant majority of traditionally inclined English worshippers has been underestimated in accounts of the period. He claims, based on a wide review of parish records from the 1640s, that "the greatest challenge to the respectable Puritanism of the Parliamentarian majority came from the passive strength of Anglican survivalism" (*Nature of the English Revolution,* 150). The full chapter presents compelling evidence for the continued popularity and use of the Book of Common Prayer and associated holiday celebrations even after their official prohibition ("The Church in England, 1642–1649," in *Nature of the English Revolution,* 148–75). Building on Morrill's earlier work, Judith Maltby offers a more extensive account of continued loyalty to the liturgy of the Book of Common Prayer on the eve of the Civil War in her important study, *Prayer Book and People in Elizabethan and Stuart England.* Maltby prefaces her review of petitions in favor of the Book of Common Prayer in the early 1640s with an observation that accords with the argument presented here: "[The petitions] reveal critical consumers, attached to what had become in 1641 the 'old religion', but as with the laity traumatized by the Reformation which Eamon Duffy has so vividly described, able to provide theological reasons to defend the Christian tradition they were about to lose" (*Prayer Book and People,* 88). My overall argument, particularly in this final chapter, which emphasizes the significant social dimension of the liturgy in the *corpus mysticum* tradition, might be understood to complement Morrill and Maltby's historical analyses and reinforce their conclusions about the significance of liturgy in seventeenth-century England.

12. Mark Rankin, "Rereading Henry VIII in Foxe's *Acts and Monuments,*" *Reformation* 12 (2007): 93.

13. Rankin notes that the 1563 edition of *Actes and Monuments* literally does describe Henry as clothed "like a lambe," a detail omitted in later editions, a sign, according to Rankin, of an increasingly critical treatment of the king's role ("Rereading Henry VIII," 95).

14. I refer to the sense of "flesh" developed in Eric Santner's recent extension of Kantorowicz's thesis in *The Royal Remains: The People's Two Bodies and the Endgames of Sovereignty.*

15. This argument affirms the continuity between Foxe's work and the Protestant revolutionaries of the seventeenth century, most famously suggested by Haller in *Elect Nation*. That Haller's "nation" is understood as a "mystical communion of chosen spirits" (245) is an idea that must be accounted for as the transference of medieval sacramental tradition into Protestant martyrological narrative.

16. On Foxe's increasingly critical view of Elizabeth, see Freeman, "Providence and Prescription: The Account of Elizabeth in Foxe's 'Book of Martyrs.'"

17. Rankin notes the difference between the 1563 and 1570 versions ("Rereading Henry VIII," 96). The revision is maintained into the 1583 edition.

18. See Mueller, "Embodying Glory," 14–25; and John R. Knott, "Suffering for Truths Sake: Milton and Martyrdom," in *Politics, Poetics and Hermeneutics in Milton's Prose*, 153–70.

19. John Cook, *King Charls his Case, or An appeal to all rational men, concerning his tryal at the High Court of Iustice* (London, 1649), 40. *Early English Books Online*, http://eebo.chadwyck.com.

20. On Laud's punitive measures against Puritan polemicists such as William Prynne, which deeply affected Milton's political perspective and use of metaphors of the "body politic," see Mueller, "Embodying Glory," 26–28.

21. Quoted in William Lamont, "The Great Fear," *London Review of Books* 5, no. 13 (July 21, 1983): 19–20.

22. For the classic account of these circumstances, see Caroline Hibbard, *Charles I and the Popish Plot* (Chapel Hill: University of North Carolina Press, 1983).

23. Sharon Achinstein, "Texts in Conflict: The Press and the Civil War," in *The Cambridge Companion to the Writing of the English Revolution*, ed. N. H. Keeble (Cambridge, Eng.: Cambridge University Press, 2001), 60.

24. Ibid., 59.

25. See Knott, "'Suffering for Truths Sake,'" 163–66.

26. Elizabeth Sauer, "Tolerationism, the Irish Crisis, and Milton's 'On the Late Massacre in Piemont,'" *Milton Studies* 44 (2005): 40–61.

27. John Milton, *Complete Poems and Major Prose,* ed. Merritt Y. Hughes (Upper Saddle River, N.J.: Prentice Hall, 1957), 167–68.

28. See Knott, "'Suffering for Truths Sake,'" 165; Sauer, "Tolerationism," 53.

29. Sauer, "Tolerationism," 41.

30. Sauer, "Tolerationism," 43, citing Haller's work on Foxe, *Elect Nation*.

31. Sauer, "Tolerationism," 56.

32. "The Reason of Church Government," in Milton, *Complete Poems and Major Prose,* ed. Hughes, 664.

33. On Athens, Erechtheus, and the complicated implications of civic myths of autochthony for Athenian women, see Nicole Loraux, *The Children of Athens: Athenian Ideas About Citizenship and the Division Between the Sexes,* trans. Caroline Levine (Princeton, N.J.: Princeton University Press, 1993), 37–71.

34. For comparisons between Athenian and Theban myths of autochtho-nous origin, see Marcel Detienne, "The Art of Founding Autochthony: Thebes, Athens, and Old-Stock French," trans. Elizabeth Jones, *Arion* 9, no. 1 (2001): 46–55; and Marcel Detienne, "Being Born Impure in the City of Cadmus and Oedipus," trans. S. Preisig and F. Preisig, *Arion* 10, no. 3 (2003): 35–47.

35. This account is indebted to Marcel Detienne's analysis in "Being Born Impure in the City of Cadmus and Oedipus."

36. When Carl Schmitt writes—in reference to the "marvelous union of the patriarchal and the matriarchal" contained in the idea of the "pope as father" and the "Church" as "the Mother of Believers and the Bride of Christ"—"Has there ever been a revolt against the mother?" (*Roman Catholicism and Political Form,* 8), he clearly was not thinking of Milton!

37. For the reference to the Roman church as the "old *red Dragon*" oppos-ing the "unresistable might of Weakness" of "the *Martyrs*" in Milton's *Of Reformation,* see Knott, "'Suffering for Truths Sake,'" 167; and Mueller, "Embodying Glory," 17.

38. John Milton, *Eikonoklastes, in Answer to a Book Intitl'd "Eikon Basi-like,"* 2nd ed. (London, 1650), 153. *Early English Books Online,* http://eebo.chadwyck.com/. All citations from *Eikonoklastes* will refer to this edition, unless otherwise noted. Page numbers are hereafter cited in the text.

39. Patrick Collinson provides an overview of the tradition of historical debate about the extent to which the English Civil War can be considered a "war of religion" (*The Birthpangs of Protestant England: Religious and Cul-tural Change in the Sixteenth and Seventeenth Centuries* (Houndmills, Eng.: Macmillan, 1988), 132–36. He cites John Morrill's claim that "'the English Civil War was not the first European revolution: it was the last of the Wars of Religion'" (qtd. in Collinson, *Birthpangs,* 133). Collinson himself favors an emphasis on the struggle's religious character, although as a historian of Puri-tanism he locates the source of religious tension in the separatist and moral-izing tendencies of strict Calvinist Protestantism. In a culture prone to speak in terms of binary oppositions, there was "no halfway house between truth and error" (148). As a consequence of this extremism, "crypto-papists or anyone whose religious views were in any respect suspect, were liable to be assimi-lated to the papists" (148). It is, in part, the imaginative mechanism of such an "assimilation" that concerns the present argument, as well as its tendency toward excess, a perception of the Catholic threat "blown up out of all pro-portion" (148). More recently, Ethan Shagan, "Introduction: English Catholic History in Context," in *Catholics and the Protestant Nation: Religious Politics and Identity in Early Modern England* (Manchester, Eng.: Manchester Uni-versity Press, 2005) locates the difficulty of defining the difference between proper Protestants and Catholics at the heart of the national conflict of the 1640s: "In Charles I's reign, moderate puritans could be accused by radical separatists of 'popery,' while those same moderate puritans could be accused by Arminians and Roman Catholics of radical separatism; can we not see the Civil War itself as a political struggle through which such ambiguities were disputed?" (15).

40. This growing disjunction is noted by Robin Clifton, "The Popular Fear of Catholics During the English Revolution," *Past and Present* 52 (1971): 23–55. Clifton observes that while popular Protestant sentiment in the reigns of Elizabeth and James fixated on their vulnerability to assassination and identified "Catholicism with regicide," by the eve of the Civil Wars, there had been a definitive shift away from this thinking with regard to Charles: "As a victim, he was replaced by the Protestant population itself, a transition expressing public awareness that for the first time since the Reformation England had a ruler whose views on Catholicism seemed to differ markedly from those of the majority of his subjects" (54). This shift in attitudes paved the way for actual Protestant subjects to supplant imagined Catholic operatives as agents of regicide.

41. On the "media storm of the early 1640's," see David Cressy, *England on Edge: Crisis and Revolution 1640–1642* (Oxford: Oxford University Press, 2006), 281–346.

42. For debate about the authorship of *Eikon Basilike* in the seventeenth century and an overview of the current understanding of the provenance of the work, see the "Introduction" to *Eikon Basilike with Selections from Eikonoklastes,* ed. Jim Daems and Holly Faith Nelson (Peterborough, Ont.: Broadview Editions, 2006), 16–21. All subsequent citations of *Eikon Basilike* will refer to this edition, unless otherwise noted. Page numbers are hereafter cited in the text.

43. See Richard Helgerson, "Milton Reads the King's Book: Print, Performance, and the Making of a Bourgeois Idol," *Criticism* 29, no. 1 (1987): 7–9. See also Daems and Nelson, "Introduction," 39.

44. Helgerson, "Milton Reads the King's Book," 9.

45. Daems and Nelson, "Introduction," 24.

46. Ibid., 25.

47. Lois Potter, *Secret Rites and Secret Writing: Royalist Literature 1641–1660* (Cambridge, Eng.: Cambridge University Press, 1989), 175.

48. Elizabeth Skerpan-Wheeler, "*Eikon Basilike* and the Rhetoric of Self-Representation," in *The Royal Image: Representations of Charles I,* ed. Thomas N. Corns (Cambridge, Eng.: Cambridge University Press, 1999), 132.

49. In a suggestive article, Elizabeth Spiller suggests that the affinity between romance and royalism in *Eikon Basilike* stems from a shared concern with "resurrection" or the construction of a "textual afterlife," a trait that partially emerges from the incompleteness of the romance narrative pattern constructed by Sidney: "The use of the Pamela prayer signals that we are not simply in a narrative of death, but also in one of redemption. The prayer appendix becomes a continuation that imaginatively narrates an interval—like that in *The Winter's Tale*—between what seems like a last moment and its metamorphosis into a new beginning. With this addition, the *Eikon Basilike* offers hope for resurrection, if not of the king whose execution in some sense produced this text, then of the monarchy he represents" (238). Elizabeth Spiller, "Speaking for the Dead: King Charles, Anna Weamys, and the Commemorations of Sir Philip Sidney's *Arcadia,*" *Criticism* 42, no. 2 (2000): 229–51.

50. Skerpan-Wheeler, "*Eikon Basilike* and the Rhetoric of Self-Representation," 122–40.

51. Ibid., 123.

52. Ibid., 130.

53. Ibid. One commonly cited measure of the relative rhetorical success of Milton's *Eikonoklastes* versus *Eikon Basilike* is the number of editions produced in the period: on sale on the day of the king's execution, *Eikon Basilike* ran through thirty-five editions in England in a single year (1649) (Daems and Nelson, "Introduction," 14), while Milton's *Eikonoklastes* had two total editions between 1649 and 1650 (43).

54. Isabel Rivers, "Prayer-Book Devotion: The Literature of the Proscribed Episcopal Church," in *The Cambridge Companion to Writing of the English Revolution*, ed. Keeble, 205.

55. As Maltby notes, a fusion of liturgy and martyrology was evident even before the regicide, in the early 1640s, as petitioners in favor of the prayer book defended it in part as the sanctified work of the martyred Archbishop Cranmer; see *Prayer Book and People*, 115–16. The *Eikon Basilike*'s presentation of the martyr Charles as defender of the Book of Common Prayer thus capitalizes on an already established linkage between these two genres. See also the discussion of Cranmer and Foxe, chapter 2.

56. The arguments articulated by the persona of Charles in *Eikon Basilike* are interestingly anticipated by the popular petitions to Parliament in defense of the English liturgy of the Book of Common Prayer in the early 1640s, as documented by Maltby, *Prayer Book and People*, 83–129. Maltby argues that corporate worship as a "social" phenomenon (precisely in the sense Bossy associates with the Mass) was also attributed to the English liturgy by a significant part of the English population, who were distressed by the growing disarray of the established church in the early 1640s (118–19). At this earlier stage, however, the king was not addressed or significantly affiliated with the effort to save the Prayer Book, although most such petitioners did ultimately become supporters of the Royalist cause (127–29). From Maltby's perspective, the defense of the Book of Common Prayer appears to have been a popular, "bottom-up" (88) religious cause that emerged to counter strident Reformist attacks, which eventually morphed into the political position of Royalism. In *Eikon Basilike*, when "the King" writes to defend the English liturgy, he borrows arguments that were first formulated by his subjects in the intense polemical climate of the early 1640s, when his own credibility and authority were at their lowest ebb.

57. On the genesis of *Eikonoklastes* as a politically "authorized" response to *Eikon Basilike* likely requested by the Council of State, see Daems and Nelson, "Introduction," 29–34.

58. On the Cornish Prayer Book Rebellion in the early 1550s, see Sarah Beckwith, *Signifying God*, 138, and Maltby, *Prayer Book and People*, 6.

59. Marshall Grossman, *The Story of All Things: Writing the Self in English Renaissance Narrative Poetry* (Durham, N.C.: Duke University Press, 1998), 242.

60. Ibid. For further observations on Milton's rhetorical violence in this pamphlet, see Ernst Gilman, *Iconoclasm and Poetry in the English Reformation: Down Went Dagon* (Chicago: University of Chicago Press, 1986), who portrays Milton's understanding of idolatry as akin to an organic disease: "When this disease grips the body politic, as Milton believed it had with the publication of *Eikon Basilike* in 1649, iconoclasm becomes the necessary instrument of public health" (154). For an overview of Milton's wide-ranging conception of idolatry, including the way "idolatry" (the Catholic variety) marks the limits of Milton's arguments for religious toleration, see Barbara Lewalski, "Milton and Idolatry," *SEL: Studies in English Literature, 1500–1900* 43, no. 1 (2003): 213–32.

61. Lana Cable, *Carnal Rhetoric: Milton's Iconoclasm and the Poetics of Desire* (Durham, N.C.: Duke University Press, 1995), 149.

62. For a more thorough analysis of Milton's argument as aesthetic critique, see Steven Zwicker, *Lines of Authority* (Ithaca, N.Y.: Cornell University Press, 1993), 37–59.

63. See *Eikon Basilike,* 205n1 for details on this edition.

64. Grossman, *The Story of All Things,* 241.

65. Milton, *Complete Poems and Major Prose,* ed. Hughes, 794n46.

66. For the etymology and examples of early modern usage, see the *Oxford English Dictionary,* "Reversion.¹," 2nd ed., 1989, http://www.oed.com/.

67. See "ort, n." *Oxford English Dictionary:* "A fragment of food left over from a meal; fodder left by cattle; a refuse scrap; leavings. . . . Also fig.: a fragment, esp. of wisdom, wit, knowledge, etc." (draft revision, September 2004), http://www.oed.com/.

68. Milton, *Complete Poems and Major Prose,* ed. Hughes, 642.

69. Ibid.

70. "Politic" in the sense defined by Amelia Zurcher in *Seventeenth Century English Romance: Allegory, Ethics and Politics* (New York: Palgrave, 2007) as an influence on Sidney's political perspective: "By 'politic ideology' historians refer to what seemed in the later half of the sixteenth century a newly destabilizing confluence of skepticism, Tacitism, and reason of state theory" (5).

71. Sir Philip Sidney, *Arcadia,* book 3, 336. All citations of the *Arcadia* refer to *The Countess of Pembroke's Arcadia (The New Arcadia),* ed. Victor Skretkowicz (Oxford: Clarendon, 1987).

72. Sidney, *Arcadia,* 336.

73. *Eikon Basilike,* 205; Sidney, *Arcadia,* 335–36.

Epilogue

1. Christopher Warren and Victoria Kahn both offer thoughtful reconsiderations of the potential larger conceptual sympathies between Milton and Hobbes, despite their vastly different overt political allegiances. Although the argument that I develop here moves in a different direction, their approach has influenced my understanding of the relationship between these two writers. See Warren, "When Self-Preservation Bids: Approaching Milton, Hobbes and Dissent," *English Literary Renaissance* (2007): 118–50; and Kahn, "Political Theology

and Reason of State in *Samson Agonistes*," *South Atlantic Quarterly* 95, no. 4 (1996): 1064–97 and *Wayward Contracts: The Crisis of Political Obligation in England, 1640–1674* (Princeton, N.J.: Princeton University Press, 2004).

2. On the rise of "Society" after 1700, see Bossy, *Christianity in the West:* "In the fifteenth century, 'society' meant a state of companionship, fellowship or mutually recognized relation with one or more of one's fellow men. Like 'religion' in the humanist sense, it was a term of art, not a word of everyday life . . . By 1700 or shortly after, it had already come to mean mainly an objective collectivity, exterior to its members and delimited from other such collectivities. Above them, as above the numerous examples of religion, planed the larger abstraction of Society, an entity from which most of human contact had been evacuated" (170–71).

3. Milton, *Complete Poems and Major Prose,* ed. Hughes, 568n; Laura Knoppers, "'This So Horrid Spectacle': *Samson Agonistes* and the Execution of the Regicides," *English Literary Renaissance* 20, no. 3 (1990): 487–503.

4. Knoppers, "This So Horrid Spectacle," 490–91.

5. Ibid., 499.

6. David Gay, "Prayer, Temporality and Liberty in *Samson Agonistes,*" in *Milton on Rights and Liberties,* ed. Neil Forsyth and Christophe Tournu (Peter Lang, 2007), 358–59.

7. I am indebted to Kurt Schreyer for this suggestion.

8. Picciotto, "The Public Person and the Play of Fact," 110.

9. T. S. K. Scott-Craig, "Concerning Milton's Samson," *Renaissance Notes* 5, no. 3 (1952): 46–47.

10. See, for example, Feisal G. Mohamed, "Confronting Religious Violence: Milton's 'Samson Agonistes,'" *PMLA* 120, no. 2 (2005): 327–40. Mohamed writes in the wake of John Carey's controversial article, "A Work in Praise of Terrorism?" *Times Literary Supplement,* September 6, 2002: 15–16. See also responses to Mohamed by Joseph Wittreich and Peter Herman, "Milton and Religious Violence," *PMLA* 120, no. 5 (2005): 1641–44. See also Ryan Netzley, "Reading Events: The Value of Reading and the Possibilities of Political Action and Criticism in *Samson Agonistes,*" *Criticism* 48, no. 4 (2006): 509–33.

11. Lupton, *Citizen-Saints,* 197–98.

12. Scriptural quotations are taken from the Geneva Bible translation: *The Bible that is, the Holy Scriptures conteined in the Olde and Newe Testament, Early English Books Online,* http://eebo.chadwyck.com.

13. Daniel Shore, "Why Milton Is Not an Iconoclast," *PMLA* 127, no. 1 (2012): 33.

14. Ibid., 34.

15. See, for example, Shore's discussion of the "banality of intolerance" in Milton's discourse in *Of True Religion* ("Why Milton Is Not an Iconoclast," 31–32).

16. Lupton, *Citizen-Saints,* 189.

17. Ibid., 199. Joanna Picciotto develops a similar suggestion in a different way in her reading of Samson as a "public person" or an "Adamic

corporation." Against the common reading of drama's "radical internaliza-tion of the action," Picciotto claims "the anagnorisis is located in Samson's breast—in the 'rouzing motions' that propel him to the theater. But this is the breast of a public person, whose internal revolutions open out into public space . . . It is through this roused virtue that Samson's 'rouzing motions' roll outward into public space, leveling the ritual structure erected to contain it. Within this public space, one vision of the public confronts another: the popu-lated unity of Samson faces members of an ungathered multitude, 'in order rang'd,' separately assembled to consume a spectacle. They are annihilated, not by a spectacle, but by an interventionist vision that decomposes spectacle and divulges creation: a sovereign public" ("The Public Person and the Play of Fact," 112). As suggested in the previous chapter, Picciotto's assertions, while provocative and original, tend to locate the continuing possibility of mystical collectivity in purely intellectual forms and appear to give short shrift to the affective dimensions of sacramental forms of the mystical body, whether litur-gical or martyrological.

18. Bruno Latour's paraphrase of Shapin and Schaffer's *The Leviathan and the Air Pump* (Princeton, N.J.: Princeton University Press, 1985) in *We Have Never Been Modern* (Cambridge, Mass.: Harvard University Press, 1993) is apropos in this context: "The loyalty of the old medieval society—to God and King—is no longer possible if all people can petition God directly, or desig-nate their own King. Hobbes wanted to wipe the slate clean of all appeals to entities higher than human authority, He wanted to rediscover Catholic unity while at the same time closing off any access to divine transcendence" (19).

19. Thomas Hobbes, *Leviathan,* ed. C. B. Macpherson (New York: Penguin Classics, 1985), 81.

20. Ibid., 81–82.

21. Ibid., 183.

22. Ibid., 187.

23. Ibid., 227.

24. Ibid.

25. Latour, *We Have Never Been Modern,* 26.